Super Easy

Keto Diet

Book for Beginners

Over 60

2000+ Days Low Carb、Low Sugar & Delicious Keto Recipes Cookbook - Assist in Trimming Excess Fat | Includes 30 Day Meal Plans

Branimira Ivanec

Table of Contents

INTRODUCTION

Welcome to my cookbook, where the tantalizing world of flavors meets the transformative power of the ketogenic diet. In this cookbook, we invite you to embark on a culinary journey that redefines your approach to food, putting you in control of your health and well-being through the magic of low-carb, high-fat delights.

The ketogenic diet has taken the world by storm, offering a pathway to weight management, increased energy, and improved mental clarity. "Keto Kitchen Adventures" is more than just a collection of recipes; it's a celebration of creativity in the kitchen, a guide to crafting delicious meals that align with your keto lifestyle.

This book is not your typical cookbook; it's an exploration of taste, a discovery of new ingredients, and a celebration of the diversity that the keto diet can offer. We understand that embracing a low-carb lifestyle might feel daunting, and that's precisely why we've crafted a collection of recipes that make keto both accessible and delicious. Each dish is a testament to the idea that eating keto can be a culinary adventure rather than a restrictive journey.

What to Expect

1. Delicious Simplicity: Our recipes focus on using fresh, wholesome ingredients to create meals that are both delectable and uncomplicated. We believe that keto can be easy and enjoyable.

2. Balanced Nutrition: The cornerstone of keto success is finding the right balance between fats, proteins, and low-carb vegetables. Our recipes strike that balance, ensuring you get the nutrients you need while savoring every bite.

3. Flavorful Diversity: Say goodbye to monotony. From savory breakfasts to hearty dinners, and decadent desserts, "Keto Kitchen Adventures" offers a diverse range of recipes to suit every taste and occasion.

4. Mindful Eating: Alongside each recipe, you'll find tips on mindful eating and portion control. These insights are designed to empower you with the tools to make informed choices and build a sustainable, keto-conscious lifestyle.

Embark on a journey where the kitchen becomes your keto sanctuary, and every meal is an opportunity to nourish your body and delight your taste buds. "Keto Kitchen Adventures" is not just a cookbook; it's an invitation to embrace a delicious, low-carb, and high-fat way of living. We hope these recipes inspire you to savor the beauty of keto creativity and make each meal a moment of joy on your keto adventure.

Macronutrient Ratios

The macronutrient ratios of a ketogenic diet are characterized by a high intake of fats, a moderate intake of protein, and a low intake of carbohydrates. The primary purpose of these specific ratios is to shift the body into a state of ketosis, where it relies on fat for fuel instead of carbohydrates. The typical macronutrient breakdown for a standard ketogenic diet is as follows:

1. Fats:

Percentage of Daily Calories: Approximately 70-75%

Role: Fats are the primary energy source on a ketogenic diet. This includes both dietary fats and stored body fat.

Sources: Avocado, nuts, seeds, olive oil, coconut oil, butter, fatty cuts of meat, and full-fat dairy.

2. Proteins:

Percentage of Daily Calories: Around 20-25%

Role: Protein is essential for muscle maintenance and repair, but it is moderated to prevent excess protein from converting into glucose (a process called gluconeogenesis).

Sources: Meat, poultry, fish, eggs, tofu, dairy, and plant-based protein sources.

3. Carbohydrates:

Percentage of Daily Calories: Approximately 5-10%

Role: Carbohydrates are severely restricted to induce and maintain a state of ketosis, where the body produces ketones for energy in the absence of glucose.

Sources: Non-starchy vegetables (leafy greens, broccoli, cauliflower), berries in moderation, and limited nuts and seeds.

It's important to note that these percentages are general guidelines, and the actual macronutrient needs can vary based on individual factors such as age, gender, activity level, and specific health goals. Additionally, some individuals may follow variations of the ketogenic diet, such as the targeted ketogenic diet (TKD) or the cyclical ketogenic diet (CKD), which may involve adjusting macronutrient ratios based on physical activity and specific needs.

If you are considering adopting a ketogenic diet, it's advisable to consult with a healthcare professional or a registered dietitian to ensure that the diet aligns with your health goals and is tailored to your individual needs. Regular monitoring and adjustments may be necessary for optimal results and overall well-being.

Principles of the Ketogenic Lifestyle

The ketogenic lifestyle is founded on specific principles that guide individuals toward a low-carbohydrate, high-fat way of eating. Here are the key principles of the ketogenic lifestyle:

1. Low Carbohydrate Intake:

Principle: Restrict daily carbohydrate intake to induce and maintain a state of ketosis.

Implementation: Consume only a limited amount of carbohydrates, primarily from non-starchy vegetables, nuts, seeds, and low-carb fruits. Avoid or minimize high-carb foods like grains, sugars, and most processed foods.

2. Moderate Protein Intake:

Principle: Consume a moderate amount of protein to meet daily nutritional needs without stimulating excess gluconeogenesis (conversion of protein to glucose).

Implementation: Include protein sources such as meat, fish, eggs, and dairy in appropriate portions. Avoid excessive protein intake to maintain ketosis.

3. High Fat Intake:

Principle: Emphasize healthy fats as the primary source of energy, replacing the calories that would typically come from carbohydrates.

Implementation: Include sources like avocados, olive oil, coconut oil, butter, and fatty cuts of meat. Prioritize healthy fats while minimizing processed and trans fats.

4. Nutrient-Dense Whole Foods:

Principle: Prioritize nutrient-dense, whole foods to ensure the body receives essential vitamins and minerals.

Implementation: Focus on a variety of colorful vegetables, high-quality proteins, and fats. Minimize processed and refined foods, as they often lack essential nutrients.

5. Hydration and Electrolyte Balance:

Principle: Maintain proper hydration and electrolyte balance, which can be affected during the initial stages of ketosis.

Implementation: Ensure adequate water intake and consider including sodium, potassium, and magnesium-rich foods or supplements. Balance electrolytes to prevent symptoms like keto flu.

6. Individualization and Monitoring:

Principle: Recognize that the optimal macronutrient ratios may vary among individuals, and adjustments may be needed based on health goals and responses.

Implementation: Regularly monitor health markers, adjust macronutrient ratios as needed, and consult with healthcare professionals or registered dietitians for personalized guidance.

7. Meal Timing and Intermittent Fasting:

Principle: Explore meal timing strategies, such as intermittent fasting, to enhance fat burning and promote ketosis.

Implementation: Experiment with different fasting windows, such as 16/8 or 24-hour fasts, and find a schedule that aligns with individual preferences and lifestyle.

8. Mindful Eating and Hunger Awareness:

Principle: Practice mindful eating to become attuned to hunger and fullness cues.

Implementation: Listen to your body's signals and eat when hungry. Avoid unnecessary snacking and emotional eating. Recognize the difference between true hunger and cravings.

9. Whole Body Wellness:

Principle: View the ketogenic lifestyle as a holistic approach to well-being, addressing not only weight management but also overall health.

Implementation: Prioritize sleep, stress management, regular physical activity, and other lifestyle factors to support optimal health in conjunction with a ketogenic diet.

10. Continuous Learning and Adaptation:

Principle: Stay informed about the latest research, listen to your body's responses, and be open to adjustments.

Implementation: Keep up with reputable sources of information, be willing to modify your approach based on personal experiences, and consult with healthcare professionals for guidance.

Adopting the ketogenic lifestyle requires a commitment to these principles, along with a willingness to adapt and personalize the approach based on individual needs and responses. It's crucial to approach this way of eating with a focus on long-term sustainability and overall health. Consulting with healthcare professionals or registered dietitians can provide personalized guidance and support on your ketogenic journey.

Benefit of the Ketogenic Lifestyle

The ketogenic lifestyle, centered around the principles of the ketogenic diet, offers a range of potential benefits for individuals.

Here are some key advantages associated with adopting a ketogenic lifestyle:

1. Weight Loss:

Mechanism: Ketosis shifts the body from relying on carbohydrates to using stored fat for energy.

Benefits: Effective for weight loss, as the body burns fat, leading to reduced body fat percentage.

2. Blood Sugar Control:

Mechanism: Low-carb intake reduces blood sugar spikes and improves insulin sensitivity.

Benefits: Particularly beneficial for individuals with type 2 diabetes or those at risk of insulin resistance.

3. Increased Energy and Mental Clarity:

Mechanism: Ketones, produced during ketosis, provide a stable and efficient fuel source for the brain.

Benefits: Many individuals report enhanced cognitive function, sustained energy levels, and improved mental clarity.

4. Appetite Control:

Mechanism: A higher intake of fats and proteins promotes satiety and reduces overall appetite.

Benefits: Easier control of cravings and hunger, potentially leading to reduced caloric intake.

5. Improved Lipid Profile:

Mechanism: Favorable changes in cholesterol levels, including increased HDL ("good" cholesterol) and reduced triglycerides.

Benefits: Potential cardiovascular benefits, lowering the risk of heart disease.

6. Reduced Inflammation:

Mechanism: Ketogenic diets may have anti-inflammatory effects, partly due to the reduction in processed and inflammatory foods.

Benefits: Relief from inflammatory conditions and related symptoms.

7. Enhanced Physical Endurance:

Mechanism: Once adapted to using fat for fuel, individuals may experience improved endurance during physical activities.

Benefits: Athletes may find increased stamina and reduced reliance on frequent refueling.

8. Better Blood Pressure:

Mechanism: Lowering carbohydrate intake can contribute to lower blood pressure levels.

Benefits: Reduced risk of hypertension and improved overall cardiovascular health.

9. Epilepsy Management:

Mechanism: The ketogenic diet has been used for decades to help manage epilepsy, especially in children.

Benefits: Reduction in seizure frequency for some individuals with epilepsy.

10. Positive Metabolic Changes:

Mechanism: Ketosis may lead to changes in metabolic markers, including increased ketones and improved metabolic health.

Benefits: Improved metabolic flexibility and potential metabolic syndrome management.

11. Triglyceride Reduction:

Mechanism: Reduction in dietary sugars can lead to lower triglyceride levels.

Benefits: Lowered risk of cardiovascular issues associated with high triglyceride levels.

12. Hormonal Regulation:

Mechanism: Ketogenic diets may influence hormones related to hunger and metabolism.

Benefits: Potential improvement in hormonal balance, aiding in weight management.

13. Stable Energy Levels:

Mechanism: Steady energy release from fat metabolism can lead to reduced energy fluctuations.

Benefits: Consistent energy levels throughout the day.

14. Disease Prevention:

Mechanism: Ketogenic diets may contribute to reducing the risk of certain chronic diseases.

Benefits: Lowered risk of developing conditions such as type 2 diabetes and certain cancers.

15. Improved Skin Health:

Mechanism: Reduction in processed foods and sugar may benefit skin health.

Benefits: Potential improvement in conditions like acne or other skin issues.

It's important to note that individual responses to the ketogenic lifestyle can vary. Before making significant dietary changes, individuals should consult with healthcare professionals, especially those with existing health conditions, to ensure that the approach aligns with individual health goals and needs. Additionally, adopting a ketogenic lifestyle should be viewed as a long-term commitment for sustained benefits.

Chapter 1
Keto Kitchen Essentials

Chapter 1 Keto Kitchen Essentials

Pantry Staples

Building a keto-friendly pantry is essential for maintaining a ketogenic lifestyle. Here's a list of essential keto pantry items to have on hand:

Oils and Fats:

1. Coconut Oil: A versatile oil high in healthy saturated fats.
2. Olive Oil: A heart-healthy option for salads and cooking.
3. Avocado Oil: Great for high-heat cooking due to its high smoke point.
4. Butter (Grass-Fed): A rich source of saturated fats and great for cooking.

Low-Carb Flours:

5. Almond Flour: A versatile, low-carb alternative to regular flour.
6. Coconut Flour: Adds a subtle coconut flavor and texture to recipes.

Sweeteners:

7. Stevia: A natural, zero-calorie sweetener derived from the leaves of the Stevia plant.
8. Erythritol or Monk Fruit: Low-calorie sweeteners that do not spike blood sugar.

Proteins:

9. Canned Tuna or Salmon: High in omega-3 fatty acids and protein.
10. Canned Chicken: Convenient for quick meals and salads.
11. Canned Sardines: Rich in omega-3s and a great source of protein.

Nuts and Seeds:

12. Almonds, Walnuts, Pecans: Great for snacking or adding crunch to dishes.
13. Chia Seeds and Flaxseeds: High in fiber and omega-3 fatty acids.

Low-Carb Condiments and Sauces:

14. Mayonnaise (Sugar-Free): A keto-friendly base for sauces and dressings.
15. Mustard: Adds flavor without added sugars.
16. Hot Sauce: Low in carbs and can spice up various dishes.
17. Soy Sauce or Tamari (Gluten-Free): Adds savory flavor to

keto recipes.

Low-Carb Pasta and Rice Alternatives:

18. Shirataki Noodles: Low-carb, low-calorie noodles made from konjac yam.

19. Cauliflower Rice: A versatile, low-carb substitute for rice.

Canned Vegetables:

20. Canned Spinach, Green Beans, or Asparagus: Convenient and keto-friendly.

Herbs, Spices, and Seasonings:

21. Sea Salt and Himalayan Salt: Essential for seasoning dishes.

22. Black Pepper, Garlic Powder, Onion Powder: Adds flavor without carbs.

23. Dried Herbs (Thyme, Rosemary, Basil): Enhances the taste of meals.

Keto-Friendly Snacks:

24. Pork Rinds: A crunchy, low-carb alternative to chips.

25. Cheese Crisps or Cheese Strings: Convenient and satisfying snacks.

Low-Carb Baking Ingredients:

26. Baking Powder and Baking Soda: Essential for keto baking.

27. Xanthan Gum: Improves the texture of gluten-free and keto recipes.

Beverages:

28. Coffee and Tea: Unsweetened options are keto-friendly.

29. Almond Milk or Coconut Milk (Unsweetened): Low-carb milk alternatives.

Proteins:

30. Grass-Fed Beef or Lamb: Excellent sources of high-quality protein and fats.

Miscellaneous:

31. Nutritional Yeast: Adds a cheesy flavor to dishes.

32. Psyllium Husk: A fiber supplement often used in keto baking.

This list provides a solid foundation for a keto-friendly pantry, but individual preferences may vary. Always check labels for hidden sugars and carb content, and aim for whole, minimally processed foods to support a healthy ketogenic lifestyle.

Cooking Tools

Efficient keto cooking requires some essential kitchen equipment to help prepare and cook low-carb meals with ease. Here's a list of recommended kitchen equipment for efficient keto cooking:

1. High-Quality Chef's Knife:

A sharp, sturdy chef's knife is essential for cutting vegetables, meats, and other ingredients quickly and precisely.

2. Cutting Boards:

Invest in durable cutting boards to protect your countertops and provide a clean surface for food preparation.

3. Non-Stick Skillet or Frying Pan:

A non-stick skillet or frying pan is versatile for cooking everything from eggs to meats without excessive oil.

4. Stainless Steel Saute Pan:
Ideal for sautéing vegetables, frying meats, and making sauces.

5. Baking Sheets:
Use baking sheets for roasting vegetables, baking keto-friendly desserts, and making sheet pan meals.

6. Cast Iron Skillet:
A cast iron skillet provides even heat distribution and is perfect for searing meats and making one-pan meals.

7. Blender or Food Processor:
Essential for making keto smoothies, sauces, soups, and nut butters.

8. Spiralizer:
Use a spiralizer to make low-carb vegetable noodles from zucchini, squash, or sweet potatoes.

9. Instant Pot or Pressure Cooker:
Cook meats, soups, stews, and even keto-friendly desserts quickly and conveniently.

10. Slow Cooker or Crock-Pot:
Perfect for preparing tender, flavorful meats, broths, and keto-friendly chili with minimal effort.

11. Kitchen Scale:
A kitchen scale helps accurately measure ingredients, especially for precise portion control on the keto diet.

12. Measuring Cups and Spoons:
Essential for measuring liquids, dry ingredients, and spices for accurate recipes.

13. Vegetable Steamer:
Steam vegetables quickly and retain their nutrients for a healthy side dish.

14. Air Fryer:
Enjoy crispy, low-carb versions of your favorite fried foods without excess oil.

15. Silicone Baking Mats:
Replace parchment paper with reusable silicone baking mats for easy cleanup and non-stick baking.

16. Quality Mixing Bowls:
Use mixing bowls for combining ingredients, marinating meats, and storing leftovers.

17. Kitchen Thermometer:
Ensure meats are cooked to the proper internal temperature for safety and optimal flavor.

18. Grilling Tools:
If you have outdoor space, invest in high-quality grilling tools for cooking keto-friendly BBQ meats and vegetables.

Having these essential kitchen tools on hand will streamline your keto cooking process, making it easier to prepare delicious and nutritious low-carb meals at home.

Tips on Meal Prep and Planning

Meal prep and planning are crucial for staying on track with a ketogenic diet and ensuring you have healthy, low-carb meals

readily available. Here are some tips to help you streamline your meal prep and planning process:

1. Set Aside Dedicated Time:
Choose a day or two each week to dedicate to meal prep and planning. This could be a weekend day or any day that works best for your schedule.

2. Plan Your Meals:
Take some time to plan out your meals for the week, including breakfast, lunch, dinner, and snacks. Consider using a meal planning app or printable template to help organize your menu.

3. Create a Shopping List:
Based on your meal plan, make a list of all the ingredients you'll need for the week. Stick to your list to avoid impulse purchases and ensure you have everything on hand when it's time to cook.

4. Prep Ingredients in Advance:
Wash, chop, and portion out ingredients ahead of time to save time during the week. This could include cutting up vegetables, marinating meats, or pre-cooking staples like cauliflower rice.

5. Cook in Batch:
Cook large batches of proteins, such as chicken breasts or ground beef, and portion them out for multiple meals. This makes it easy to assemble quick meals throughout the week.

6. Utilize Make-Ahead Recipes:
Look for keto-friendly recipes that can be prepared in advance and stored in the fridge or freezer. Soups, casseroles, and egg muffins are great options for make-ahead meals.

7. Invest in Meal Prep Containers:
Purchase a set of reusable meal prep containers in various sizes to portion out your meals and keep them organized in the fridge.

8. Mix and Match Ingredients:
Keep your meals interesting by mixing and matching different proteins, vegetables, and fats throughout the week. This prevents meal fatigue and ensures you're getting a variety of nutrients.

9. Label and Date Containers:
To avoid confusion and waste, label your meal prep containers with the contents and date prepared. This helps you keep track of how long each meal will last in the fridge or freezer.

10. Schedule Time for Replenishing:
Set aside a regular time each week to replenish your meal prep supplies, such as fresh produce, proteins, and pantry staples. This ensures you always have what you need for successful meal prep sessions.

11. Stay Flexible:
Be flexible with your meal plan and adapt as needed based on your schedule, preferences, and any leftovers you have on hand. Don't be afraid to swap out planned meals or repurpose ingredients to minimize waste.

12. Enjoy the Process:
Meal prep and planning can be a fun and rewarding part of your keto journey. Put on some music or a podcast, and make it a relaxing and enjoyable experience.

By following these meal prep and planning tips, you'll save time, reduce stress, and set yourself up for success on your ketogenic diet journey. With a little effort upfront, you'll have delicious and nutritious meals ready to enjoy throughout the week.

30-Day Meal Plan

DAYS	BREAKFAST	LUNCH	DINNER	SNACK/DESSERT
1	Cheesy Bell Pepper Eggs 14	Coconut Shrimp Curry 29	Fried Chicken Breasts 38	Parmesan Crisps 79
2	BLT Breakfast Salad 14	Spinach-Artichoke Stuffed Mushrooms 67	Mouthwatering Cod over Creamy Leek Noodles 30	Buffalo Chicken Meatballs 76
3	Breakfast Roll-Ups 15	Simple Buttery Cod 25	Cheesy Broccoli Casserole 67	Cheesy Spinach Puffs 78
4	Egg-Stuffed Avocados 15	Cheese Stuffed Zucchini 71	Tilapia Bake 29	Spicy Baked Feta in Foil 85
5	BLT Breakfast Wrap 14	Ahi Tuna Steaks 29	Roasted Spaghetti Squash 71	Avocado Salsa 78
6	Coffee Shake 14	Cauliflower Rice-Stuffed Peppers 70	Fried Chicken Breasts 38	Pimento Cheese 83
7	Cheesy Cauliflower "Hash Browns" 16	Buttered Duck Breast 35	Broccoli-Cheese Fritters 67	Goat Cheese-Stuffed Jalapeño Poppers 76
8	Smoked Sausage and Mushroom Breakfast Skillet 16	Herbed Ricotta–Stuffed Mushrooms 71	Chicken Rollatini with Ricotta, Prosciutto, and Spinach 35	Lemon-Pepper Chicken Drumsticks 86
9	Greek Yogurt Parfait 16	Classic Chicken Salad 36	Peruvian Chicken with Green Herb Sauce 36	Cheese Stuffed Bell Peppers 84
10	Pancakes 17	Cheese Stuffed Chicken 37	Crispy Tofu 73	Devilish Eggs 78
11	Sausage Egg Cup 19	Beef Zucchini Boats 49	Garlicky Chicken Soup 58	Baked Brie with Pecans 87
12	Italian Sausage Stacks 17	Beef and Okra Stew 58	Pork Meatballs with Thyme 49	Sweet Pepper Poppers 79
13	Avocado Breakfast Sandwich 16	Beef and Broccoli Roast 53	Beef and Eggplant Tagine 58	Chocolate Soft-Serve Ice Cream 84
14	Baked Eggs in Avocados 19	Beef Chili 61	Easy Zucchini Beef Lasagna 49	Avocado Feta Dip 79
15	Meat Waffles/Bagels 19	Herbed Lamb Shank 50	Sausage Zoodle Soup 58	EL Presidente Guac 79
16	Southwestern Frittata with Avocados 20	Chicken Paella with Chorizo 40	Clam Chowder 31	Five-Minute Keto Cookie Dough 90

DAYS	BREAKFAST	LUNCH	DINNER	SNACK/DESSERT
17	No-Nuts Granola with Clusters 20	Tuna Steak 26	Poulet en Papillote 39	Vanilla-Almond Ice Pops 89
18	Spicy Egg Muffins with Bacon & Cheese 21	Roasted Chicken Breasts with Capers 41	Basil Alfredo Sea Bass 26	Pecan Butter Cookies 89
19	Pumpkin Coconut Flour Pancakes 15	Oregano Tilapia Fingers 31	Herby Chicken Meatballs 39	Glazed Coconut Bundt Cake 89
20	Bacon Egg Cups 15	Turkey Taco Boats 37	Caprese Salmon 26	Lemon Drops 92
21	All Day Any Day Hash 17	Cheese Stuffed Peppers 69	Beery Boston-Style Butt 53	Vanilla Crème Brûlée 94
22	Golden Gate Granola 19	Grilled Lamb on Lemony Sauce 51	Asparagus and Fennel Frittata 72	Lemon Bars with Cashew Crust 94
23	Green Eggs and Ham 22	Vegetable Vodka Sauce Bake 70	Beef Tripe in Vegetable Sauté 51	Pumpkin Spice Fat Bombs 90
24	Bacon Spaghetti Squash Fritters 23	Chipotle-Spiced Meatball Subs 54	Cauliflower Steak with Gremolata 69	Vanilla Cream Pie 92
25	Avocado and Eggs 18	Broccoli Crust Pizza 69	BBQ Beef & Slaw 54	Stu Can't Stop Bark 92
26	Western Frittata 20	Grilled Calamari 31	Chicken and Zoodles Soup 65	Coconut Whipped Cream 90
27	Dreamy Matcha Latte 18	Keto Pho with Shirataki Noodles 64	Mahi-Mahi Fillets with Peppers 33	Lime Muffins 93
28	Cranberry-Orange Scones 18	Almond Pesto Salmon 33	Tomato-Basil Parmesan Soup 63	Lemon Vanilla Cheesecake 95
29	Savory Zucchini Cheddar Waffles 21	Power Green Soup 64	Salmon Fritters with Zucchini 33	Coconut Muffins 91
30	Classic Cinnamon Roll Coffee Cake 23	Dill Lemon Salmon 32	Miso Magic 60	Fruit Pizza 91

Chapter 2
Breakfasts

Chapter 2 Breakfasts

Cheesy Bell Pepper Eggs

Prep time: 10 minutes | Cook time: 15 minutes | Serves 4

- 4 medium green bell peppers
- 3 ounces (85 g) cooked ham, chopped
- ¼ medium onion, peeled and
- chopped
- 8 large eggs
- 1 cup mild Cheddar cheese

1. Cut the tops off each bell pepper. Remove the seeds and the white membranes with a small knife. Place ham and onion into each pepper. 2. Crack 2 eggs into each pepper. Top with ¼ cup cheese per pepper. Place into the air fryer basket. 3. Adjust the temperature to 390°F (199°C) and air fry for 15 minutes. 4. When fully cooked, peppers will be tender and eggs will be firm. Serve immediately.

Per Serving:

calories: 314 | fat: 20g | protein: 25g | carbs: 7g | net carbs: 5g | fiber: 2g

BLT Breakfast Salad

Prep time: 10 minutes | Cook time: 5 minutes | Serves 2

- 2 large eggs
- 5 ounces organic mixed greens
- 2 tablespoons olive oil
- Pink Himalayan salt
- Freshly ground black pepper
- 1 avocado, thinly sliced
- 5 grape tomatoes, halved
- 6 bacon slices, cooked and chopped

1. In a small saucepan filled with water over high heat, bring the water to a boil. Put the eggs on to softboil, turn the heat down to medium-high, and cook for about 6 minutes. 2. While the eggs are cooking, toss the mixed greens with the olive oil and season with pink Himalayan salt and pepper. Divide the dressed greens between two bowls. 3. Top the greens with the avocado slices, grape tomatoes, and bacon. 4. When the eggs are done, peel them, halve them, and place two halves on top of each salad. Season with more pink Himalayan salt and pepper and serve.

Per Serving:

calories: 445 | fat: 39g | protein: 18g | carbs: 18g | net carbs: 4g | fiber: 6g

BLT Breakfast Wrap

Prep time: 5 minutes | Cook time: 10 minutes | Serves 4

- 8 ounces (227 g) reduced-sodium bacon
- 8 tablespoons mayonnaise
- 8 large romaine lettuce leaves
- 4 Roma tomatoes, sliced
- Salt and freshly ground black pepper, to taste

1. Arrange the bacon in a single layer in the air fryer basket. (It's OK if the bacon sits a bit on the sides.) Set the air fryer to 350°F (177°C) and air fry for 10 minutes. Check for crispiness and air fry for 2 to 3 minutes longer if needed. Cook in batches, if necessary, and drain the grease in between batches. 2. Spread 1 tablespoon of mayonnaise on each of the lettuce leaves and top with the tomatoes and cooked bacon. Season to taste with salt and freshly ground black pepper. Roll the lettuce leaves as you would a burrito, securing with a toothpick if desired.

Per Serving:

calories: 343 | fat: 32g | protein: 10g | carbs: 5g | net carbs: 4g | fiber: 1g

Coffee Shake

Prep time: 5 minutes | Cook time: 0 minutes | Makes 1

- 1 cup (240 ml) full-fat coconut milk
- ½ cup (120 ml) water
- 4 ice cubes
- 2 tablespoons coconut oil, unflavored MCT oil powder,
- or ghee
- 1½ tablespoons cocoa powder
- 1½ teaspoons erythritol, or 2 drops liquid stevia
- ½ teaspoon instant coffee granules

1. Place all the ingredients in a blender or food processor. Blend on high until the ice is broken up completely and the texture of the shake is smooth. 2. Transfer to a 14-ounce (415-ml) or larger glass. Best enjoyed immediately.

Per Serving:

calories: 757 | fat: 76g | protein: 6g | carbs: 12g | net carbs: 10g | fiber: 3g

Bacon Egg Cups

Prep time: 5 minutes | Cook time: 7 minutes | Serves 4

- 6 large eggs
- 2 strips cooked bacon, sliced in ¼-inch wide pieces
- ½ cup Cheddar cheese, divided
- ¼ teaspoon sea salt
- ¼ teaspoon black pepper
- 1 cup water
- 1 tablespoon chopped fresh flat leaf parsley

1. In a small bowl, beat the eggs. Stir in the cooked bacon, ¼ cup of the cheese, sea salt and pepper. Divide the egg mixture equally among four ramekins and loosely cover with aluminum foil. 2. Pour the water and place the trivet in the Instant Pot. Place two ramekins on the trivet and stack the other two on the top. 3. Lock the lid. Select the Manual mode and set the cooking time for 7 minutes at High Pressure. When the timer goes off, use a natural pressure release for 10 minutes, then release any remaining pressure. Carefully open the lid. 4. Top each ramekin with the remaining ¼ cup of the cheese. Lock the lid and melt the cheese for 2 minutes. Garnish with the chopped parsley and serve immediately.

Per Serving:

calories: 168 | fat: 12g | protein: 13g | carbs: 1g | net carbs: 1g | fiber: 0g

Pumpkin Coconut Flour Pancakes

Prep time: 5 minutes | Cook time: 10 minutes | Serves 6

- 6 large eggs
- ½ cup canned unsweetened pumpkin purée
- 6 tablespoons (1½ ounces / 43 g) coconut flour
- ¼ cup unsweetened coconut milk
- ⅓ cup avocado oil
- ½ cup erythritol
- 1½ tablespoons pumpkin pie spice
- 1 teaspoon baking powder
- 1 teaspoon vanilla extract

1. In a blender, combine all the ingredients and purée until smooth. 2. Let the batter sit for 15 to 20 minutes to thicken and stabilize. (This will help with consistency and make the pancakes easier to flip.) 3. Heat an oiled skillet over medium heat. Working in batches, add 2 tablespoons (⅛ cup) batter for each pancake. Don't make them larger than 3 inches across, otherwise they will be hard to flip. Cover with a lid and when bubbles form on the edges, 1 to 2 minutes, flip and cook on the second side for 1 to 2 minutes. 4. Repeat with the remaining batter.

Per Serving:

calories: 234 | fat: 18g | protein: 8g | carbs: 12g | net carbs: 4g | fiber: 8g

Breakfast Roll-Ups

Prep time: 5 minutes | Cook time: 11 minutes | Makes 3 roll-ups

- 4 large eggs
- ¼ cup heavy whipping cream
- ½ teaspoon pink Himalayan salt
- 6 ounces fresh spinach
- 6 slices bacon, cooked
- 2 ounces fresh (soft) goat cheese

1. Heat a 12-inch skillet over low heat and grease with coconut oil spray. 2. Put the eggs, cream, and salt in a medium-sized bowl and whisk to combine. 3. Using a ⅓ cup measuring cup, scoop out some of the egg mixture and place it in the center of the hot skillet. Tilt the pan so that the mixture coats the entire flat surface. Cover with a lid and cook for 2 to 3 minutes, until cooked through. Repeat with the rest of the egg mixture to make a total of 3 egg wraps. 4. Turn the heat up to medium-high, grease the skillet with coconut oil spray, and add the spinach. Cover with the lid and cook for 1 to 2 minutes, until the spinach has wilted and cooked down. Remove from the skillet. 5. Divide the cooked spinach among the 3 egg wraps, placing it along the edge of each wrap. Place 2 slices of bacon on top of the spinach in each wrap and divide the goat cheese evenly among the wraps. 6. Starting at the edge with the fillings, roll each egg wrap into a burrito, folding in the ends, or simply roll it up like crepe. Serve warm.

Per Serving:

calories: 299 | fat: 24g | protein: 20g | carbs: 4g | net carbs: 2g | fiber: 2g

Egg-Stuffed Avocados

Prep time: 5 minutes | Cook time: 35 minutes | Serves 2

- 1 large avocado, halved and pitted
- 2 small eggs
- Pink Himalayan sea salt
- Freshly ground black pepper
- 1 bacon slice, cooked until crispy and crumbled

1. Preheat the oven to 375°F (190°C). 2. Using a small spoon, enlarge the hole of the avocado left by the pit so it is roughly 2 inches in diameter. 3. Place the avocado halves cut-side up on a baking sheet. 4. Crack an egg into the well of each half. Season with salt and pepper. 5. Bake for 30 to 35 minutes, until the yolk reaches your preferred texture, 30 minutes for soft and 35 minutes for hard. 6. Sprinkle the bacon crumbles on top and enjoy!

Per Serving:

calories: 264 | fat: 21g | protein: 10g | carbs: 12g | net carbs: 3g | fiber: 9g

Smoked Sausage and Mushroom Breakfast Skillet

Prep time: 15 minutes | Cook time: 35 minutes | serves 6

- 8 large eggs
- ¼ cup heavy whipping cream
- 1 cup shredded cheddar cheese
- Pinch of salt
- Pinch of ground black pepper
- 12 ounces smoked sausage, sliced
- 1 cup diced white mushrooms
- ¼ cup sliced green onions, plus extra for garnish if desired

1. In a medium-sized bowl, whisk together the eggs and cream, then stir in the cheese, salt, and pepper. Set aside. 2. Preheat the oven to 400°F. 3. Heat a 12-inch cast-iron skillet or other ovenproof skillet over medium heat. Cook the sausage slices until browned on both sides, 5 to 6 minutes. Add the mushrooms and green onions and continue cooking until the mushrooms are tender, about 5 minutes. Turn off the heat. 4. Pour the egg mixture evenly over the sausage and vegetables in the skillet. Bake for 25 minutes or until the eggs are set. 5. Run a knife around the edge of the skillet before slicing. Garnish with more green onions, if desired, and serve immediately. Leftovers can be stored in the refrigerator for up to 5 days. Reheat just until warmed; be careful not to overheat or the eggs will become rubbery.

Per Serving:

calories: 281 | fat: 23g | protein: 16g | carbs: 3g | net carbs: 2g | fiber: 0g

Cheesy Cauliflower "Hash Browns"

Prep time: 30 minutes | Cook time: 24 minutes | Makes 6 hash browns

- 2 ounces (57 g) 100% cheese crisps
- 1 (12-ounce / 340-g) steamer bag cauliflower, cooked according to package
- instructions
- 1 large egg
- ½ cup shredded sharp Cheddar cheese
- ½ teaspoon salt

1. Let cooked cauliflower cool 10 minutes. 2. Place cheese crisps into food processor and pulse on low 30 seconds until crisps are finely ground. 3. Using a kitchen towel, wring out excess moisture from cauliflower and place into food processor. 4. Add egg to food processor and sprinkle with Cheddar and salt. Pulse five times until mixture is mostly smooth. 5. Cut two pieces of parchment to fit air fryer basket. Separate mixture into six even scoops and place three on each piece of ungreased parchment, keeping at least 2 inch of space between each scoop. Press each into a hash brown shape, about ¼ inch thick. 6. Place one batch on parchment into air fryer basket. Adjust the temperature to 375°F (191°C) and air fry for 12 minutes, turning hash browns halfway through cooking. Hash browns will be golden brown when done. Repeat with second batch. 7. Allow 5 minutes to cool. Serve warm.

Per Serving:

calories: 100 | fat: 7g | protein: 7g | carbs: 3g | net carbs: 2g | fiber: 1g

Greek Yogurt Parfait

Prep time: 5 minutes | Cook time: 0 minutes | Serves 1

- ½ cup plain whole-milk Greek yogurt
- 2 tablespoons heavy whipping cream
- ¼ cup frozen berries, thawed with juices
- ½ teaspoon vanilla or almond
- extract (optional)
- ¼ teaspoon ground cinnamon (optional)
- 1 tablespoon ground flaxseed
- 2 tablespoons chopped nuts (walnuts or pecans)

1. In a small bowl or glass, combine the yogurt, heavy whipping cream, thawed berries in their juice, vanilla or almond extract (if using), cinnamon (if using), and flaxseed and stir well until smooth. Top with chopped nuts and enjoy.

Per Serving:

calories: 401 | fat: 32g | protein: 15g | carbs: 16g | net carbs: 11g | fiber: 5g

Avocado Breakfast Sandwich

Prep time: 5 minutes | Cook time: 15 minutes | Serves 1

- 2 slices bacon
- 2 eggs
- 1 avocado

1. Press the Sauté button. Press the Adjust button to set heat to Low. Add bacon to Instant Pot and cook until crispy. Remove and set aside. 2. Crack egg over Instant Pot slowly, into bacon grease. Repeat with second egg. When edges become golden, after 2 to 3 minutes, flip. Press the Cancel button. 3. Cut avocado in half and scoop out half without seed. Place in small bowl and mash with fork. Spread on one egg. Place bacon on top and top with second egg. Let cool 5 minutes before eating.

Per Serving:

calories: 489 | fat: 39g | protein: 21g | carbs: 7g | net carbs: 2g | fiber: 5g

Italian Sausage Stacks

Prep time: 10 minutes | Cook time: 10 minutes | Serves 6

- ◆ 6 Italian sausage patties
- ◆ 4 tablespoons olive oil
- ◆ 2 ripe avocados, pitted
- ◆ 2 teaspoons fresh lime juice
- ◆ Salt and black pepper to taste
- ◆ 6 fresh eggs
- ◆ Red pepper flakes to garnish

1. In a skillet, warm the oil over medium heat and fry the sausage patties about 8 minutes until lightly browned and firm. Remove the patties to a plate. 2. Spoon the avocado into a bowl, mash with the lime juice, and season with salt and black pepper. Spread the mash on the sausages. 3. Boil 3 cups of water in a wide pan over high heat, and reduce to simmer (don't boil). 4. Crack each egg into a small bowl and gently put the egg into the simmering water; poach for 2 to 3 minutes. Use a perforated spoon to remove from the water on a paper towel to dry. Repeat with the other 5 eggs. Top each stack with a poached egg, sprinkle with chili flakes, salt, black pepper, and chives. Serve with turnip wedges.

Per Serving:

calories: 537 | fat: 45g | protein: 22g | carbs: 12g | net carbs: 7g | fiber: 8g

Pancakes

Prep time: 10 minutes | Cook time: 40 minutes | Makes 4 pancakes

Pancakes:
- ◆ 2.8 ounces (80 g) unseasoned pork rinds
- ◆ 2 teaspoons ground cinnamon, plus more for garnish (optional)
- ◆ ½ teaspoon baking powder

Sauce:
- ◆ 2 tablespoons coconut oil
- ◆ 2 tablespoons unsweetened
- ◆ 4 large eggs
- ◆ ½ cup (120 ml) full-fat coconut milk
- ◆ ¼ scant teaspoon liquid stevia
- ◆ 2 tablespoons coconut oil, divided, for the pan

smooth almond butter

1. Place the pork rinds in a spice grinder or blender. Grind to a very fine but clumping powder (it will clump together when pinched because of the fat content in the pork rinds). 2. Transfer the ground pork rinds to a small bowl and add the cinnamon and baking powder. Stir to combine. 3. In a larger bowl, whisk together the eggs, coconut milk, and stevia. Add the pork rind mixture and stir to incorporate. 4. In an 8-inch (20 cm) nonstick frying pan, melt ½ tablespoon of coconut oil over medium-low heat. 5. Preheat your oven to the lowest temperature possible. 6. Pour a quarter of the batter into the hot oiled pan and spread the batter evenly into

a circle with the back of a spoon or by rotating the pan. Do not allow the batter to migrate too far up the sides of the pan, or it will burn. Cook the pancake for 4 to 5 minutes, until bubbles form all over. Flip carefully and cook for another 4 to 5 minutes. 7. Transfer the completed pancake to a clean oven-safe plate and place in the preheated oven. 8. Add another ½ tablespoon of coconut oil to the pan. The batter may have thickened while sitting. If so, add water, a splash at a time, and mix until the batter returns to its original consistency, being careful not to add too much water. 9. Pour another quarter of the batter into the pan, form it into a circle, and cook, following Step 6. Repeat with the remaining coconut oil and batter. 10. While the last pancake is cooking, prepare the sauce: Melt the 2 tablespoons of coconut oil and put it in a small bowl along with the almond butter. Stir to combine. 11. When the pancakes are ready, divide between 2 plates and drizzle with the almond butter sauce. Sprinkle with additional cinnamon, if desired.

Per Serving:

calories: 885 | fat: 71g | protein: 53g | carbs: 8g | net carbs: 5g | fiber: 3g

All Day Any Day Hash

Prep time: 10 minutes | Cook time: 25 minutes | Serves 4

- ◆ ¼ cup (55 g) coconut oil or ghee
- ◆ ⅔ cup (100 g) sliced white onions
- ◆ 3 cloves garlic, minced
- ◆ 3 medium turnips (about 1 pound/455 g), peeled and cubed
- ◆ 2 medium carrots (about 5 ounces/140 g), diced
- ◆ 1 red bell pepper, diced
- ◆ 8 ounces (225 g) boneless
- steak, thinly sliced
- ◆ ⅓ cup (25 g) crushed pork rinds
- ◆ 2 tablespoons chopped fresh parsley leaves
- ◆ 1 teaspoon fresh thyme leaves
- ◆ ¼ teaspoon finely ground sea salt
- ◆ ⅛ teaspoon ground black pepper
- ◆ ½ cup (120 ml) creamy Italian dressing

1. Heat the oil in a large frying pan over medium heat. Add the onions and garlic and cook until the onions are translucent, 5 to 7 minutes. 2. Add the turnips, carrots, bell pepper, and steak. Toss to coat, cover, and cook for 15 to 18 minutes, stirring every 3 minutes, until the turnips are fork-tender and the steak is cooked to your liking. Remove the pan from the heat. 3. Add the crushed pork rinds, parsley, thyme, salt, and pepper and toss to coat. 4. Divide the hash evenly among 4 bowls and drizzle each bowl with 2 tablespoons of dressing just before serving.

Per Serving:

calories: 512 | fat: 37g | protein: 27g | carbs: 17g | net carbs: 13g | fiber: 4g

Cranberry-Orange Scones

Prep time: 5 minutes | Cook time: 22 minutes | Makes 8 scones

- 2 cups (8 ounces / 227 g) blanched almond flour
- ⅓ cup erythritol
- ½ teaspoon baking powder
- ¼ teaspoon sea salt
- ¼ cup coconut oil, melted
- 2 tablespoons orange zest
- ½ teaspoon vanilla extract
- 1 large egg
- ½ cup (2 ounces / 57 g) cranberries, fresh or frozen

1. Preheat the oven to 350°F (180°C). Line a baking sheet with parchment paper. 2. In a medium bowl, combine the almond flour, erythritol, baking powder, and sea salt. 3. In a small bowl, whisk together the melted coconut oil, orange zest, vanilla, and egg. Stir the wet mixture into the almond flour mixture, pressing with a spoon or spatula, until a uniform dough forms. (The dough should be pliable and dense, but not crumbly; add a little more coconut oil, a teaspoon at a time, if it's very dry.) Stir and press the cranberries into the dough. 4. Place the dough onto the lined pan and form a disc shape, about 1 inch thick and 6 inches in diameter. Cut into 8 wedges, like a pie or pizza. Move the pieces about 1 inch apart. Bake for 18 to 22 minutes, until golden. 5. Cool completely on the pan to firm up. (Scones will fall apart if you move them before cooling.)

Per Serving:

calories: 232 | fat: 21g | protein: 6g | carbs: 9g | net carbs: 4g | fiber: 5g

Western Frittata

Prep time: 10 minutes | Cook time: 19 minutes | Serves 1 to 2

- ½ red or green bell pepper, cut into ½-inch chunks
- 1 teaspoon olive oil
- 3 eggs, beaten
- ¼ cup grated Cheddar cheese
- ¼ cup diced cooked ham
- Salt and freshly ground black pepper, to taste
- 1 teaspoon butter
- 1 teaspoon chopped fresh parsley

1. Preheat the air fryer to 400°F (204°C). 2. Toss the peppers with the olive oil and air fry for 6 minutes, shaking the basket once or twice during the cooking process to redistribute the ingredients. 3. While the vegetables are cooking, beat the eggs well in a bowl, stir in the Cheddar cheese and ham, and season with salt and freshly ground black pepper. Add the air-fried peppers to this bowl when they have finished cooking. 4. Place a cake pan into the air fryer basket with the butter using an aluminum sling to lower the pan into

the basket. Air fry for 1 minute at 380°F (193°C) to melt the butter. Remove the cake pan and rotate the pan to distribute the butter and grease the pan. Pour the egg mixture into the cake pan and return the pan to the air fryer, using the aluminum sling. 5. Air fry at 380°F (193°C) for 12 minutes, or until the frittata has puffed up and is lightly browned. Let the frittata sit in the air fryer for 5 minutes to cool to an edible temperature and set up. Remove the cake pan from the air fryer, sprinkle with parsley and serve immediately.

Per Serving:

calories: 221 | fat: 16g | protein: 16g | carbs: 3g | net carbs: 2g | fiber: 1g

Dreamy Matcha Latte

Prep time: 2 minutes | Cook time: 0 minutes | Serves 1

- 1 cup hot water
- ⅓ cup full-fat coconut, nut, or dairy milk
- 1 tablespoon cacao butter
- 1 scoop grass-fed collagen
- peptides
- ½ to 1 teaspoon matcha powder
- 2 or 3 drops stevia extract (optional)

1. Place all the ingredients in a blender and blend until smooth.

Per Serving:

calories: 261 | fat: 23g | protein: 13g | carbs: 2g | net carbs: 2g | fiber: 0g

Avocado and Eggs

Prep time: 10 minutes | Cook time: 20 minutes | Serves 4

- 2 avocados, peeled, halved lengthwise, and pitted
- 4 large eggs
- 1 (4-ounce) chicken breast,
- cooked and shredded
- ¼ cup Cheddar cheese
- Sea salt
- Freshly ground black pepper

1. Preheat the oven to 425°F. 2. Take a spoon and hollow out each side of the avocado halves until the hole is about twice the original size. 3. Place the avocado halves in an 8-by-8-inch baking dish, hollow-side up. 4. Crack an egg into each hollow and divide the shredded chicken between each avocado half. Sprinkle the cheese on top of each and season lightly with the salt and pepper. 5. Bake the avocados until the eggs are cooked through, about 15 to 20 minutes. 6. Serve immediately.

Per Serving:

calories: 324 | fat: 25g | protein: 19g | carbs: 8g | net carbs: 3g | fiber: 5g

Baked Eggs in Avocados

Prep time: 10 minutes | Cook time: 10 minutes | Serves 4

- 2 large avocados, halved and pitted
- 4 small eggs
- Salt and black pepper to season
- Chopped parsley to garnish

1. Preheat the oven to 400°F. 2. Crack each egg into each avocado half and place them on a greased baking sheet. Bake the filled avocados in the oven for 8 or 10 minutes or until eggs are cooked. 3. Season with salt and pepper, and garnish with parsley.

Per Serving:

calories: 221 | fat: 18g | protein: 7g | carbs: 9g | net carbs: 3g | fiber: 6g

Meat Waffles/Bagels

Prep time: 5 minutes | Cook time: 5 to 20 minutes | Serves 4

- Avocado oil, coconut oil, or butter, for greasing
- 1 pound (454 g) ground beef, turkey, pork, or bison
- ½ tablespoon garlic powder
- ½ tablespoon dried oregano
- ½ tablespoon paprika
- Salt and freshly ground black
- pepper, to taste
- 4 eggs, sunny-side-up or over-easy, for serving (optional)
- Sliced cheese, for serving (optional)
- (You can use any other herbs/ spices you like)

1. First, determine if you're making meat waffles or meat bagels. Once you figure that out, grab your waffle maker or your bagel baking dish. (If you have neither, perhaps you have a muffin tin? If you have one of those, then you can cook your meat the same way you would the bagels.) Grease the waffle maker or baking dish with oil or butter; if making bagels, preheat the oven to 380°F (193°C). 2. In a bowl, mix the meat with the garlic, oregano, paprika, salt, and pepper. Separate the meat mixture into 4 equal portions and press into the waffle maker or baking dish. 3. The meat will cook 3 to 5 minutes in your waffle maker or 15 to 20 minutes in the oven. (If you're cooking poultry, obviously you need to cook it until completely done.) 4. Once done cooking, let cool slightly, but they should still be slightly warm when you serve them. 5. When ready to serve, place a slice of cheese and an egg on top of each waffle, if desired, and poke the yolk for some extreme yolk porn. Slice the meat bagels in half and place a slice of cheese and an egg inside, if desired. Take a bite like you would a regular bagel, but, warning, yolk may dribble down your face!

Per Serving:

calories: 294 | fat: 19g | protein: 29g | carbs: 2g | net carbs: 2g | fiber: 0g

Sausage Egg Cup

Prep time: 10 minutes | Cook time: 15 minutes | Serves 6

- 12 ounces (340 g) ground pork breakfast sausage
- 6 large eggs
- ½ teaspoon salt
- ¼ teaspoon ground black pepper
- ½ teaspoon crushed red pepper flakes

1. Place sausage in six 4-inch ramekins (about 2 ounces / 57 g per ramekin) greased with cooking oil. Press sausage down to cover bottom and about ½-inch up the sides of ramekins. Crack one egg into each ramekin and sprinkle evenly with salt, black pepper, and red pepper flakes. 2. Place ramekins into air fryer basket. Adjust the temperature to 350°F (177°C) and set the timer for 15 minutes. Egg cups will be done when sausage is fully cooked to at least 145°F (63°C) and the egg is firm. Serve warm.

Per Serving:

calories: 268 | fat: 23g | protein: 14g | carbs: 1g | net carbs: 1g | fiber: 0g

Golden Gate Granola

Prep time: 10 minutes | Cook time: 1 hour | Makes 4 cups

- ¼ cup (½ stick) unsalted butter
- ¼ cup powdered erythritol
- ¼ teaspoon plus 10 drops of liquid stevia
- 1 teaspoon ground cinnamon
- ½ teaspoon vanilla extract
- 1 cup raw almonds
- 1 cup raw hazelnuts
- 1 cup unsweetened coconut flakes
- ½ cup raw pumpkin seeds
- ¼ cup hemp hearts

1. Preheat the oven to 275°F and line a rimmed baking sheet with parchment paper or a silicone baking mat. 2. In a small saucepan over medium heat, combine the butter, erythritol, stevia, cinnamon, and vanilla extract. Stirring occasionally, heat until the butter and erythritol are melted and dissolved. Remove from the heat and set aside. 3. In a large bowl, combine the nuts, coconut flakes, pumpkin seeds, and hemp hearts. Pour the melted butter mixture over the nut mixture and toss using a rubber spatula, making sure that everything is well coated. 4. Pour the granola onto the lined baking sheet and spread it out into an even layer. Bake for 1 hour, stirring every 15 minutes or so, until dark golden brown. 5. Let the granola cool in the pan for at least 1 hour to allow it to harden and form clumps. Store in a sealed jar or zip-top plastic bag for up to 3 weeks. It does not need to be refrigerated.

Per Serving:

calories: 200 | fat: 18g | protein: 5g | carbs: 5g | net carbs: 2g | fiber: 3g

Southwestern Frittata with Avocados

Prep time: 5 minutes | Cook time: 20 minutes | Serves 4

- 2 tablespoons coconut oil
- ¼ cup diced onion
- ¼ cup diced green chilies
- ½ green bell pepper, diced
- 8 eggs
- 1 teaspoon salt
- ½ teaspoon chili powder
- ¼ teaspoon garlic powder
- ¼ teaspoon pepper
- ¼ cup heavy cream
- 4 tablespoons melted butter
- ½ cup shredded Cheddar cheese
- 1 cup water
- 2 avocados
- ¼ cup sour cream

1. Press the Sauté button and add coconut oil to Instant Pot. Add onion, chilies, and bell pepper. Sauté until onion is translucent and peppers begin to soften, approximately 3 minutes. While sautéing, whisk eggs, seasoning, heavy cream, and butter in large bowl. Pour into 7-inch round baking pan. 2. Press the Cancel button. Add onion and pepper mixture to egg mixture. Mix in Cheddar. Cover pan with aluminum foil. 3. Pour water into Instant Pot, and scrape bottom of pot if necessary to remove any stuck-on food. Place steam rack into pot and put in baking dish with eggs on top. Click lid closed. 4. Press the Manual button and set time for 25 minutes. 5. While food is cooking, cut avocados in half, remove pit, scoop out of shell and slice thinly. When timer beeps, quick-release the pressure. Serve with avocado slices and a spoonful of sour cream.

Per Serving:

calories: 563 | fat: 6g | protein: 19g | carbs: 10g | net carbs: 5g | fiber: 5g

Bacon-and-Eggs Avocado

Prep time: 5 minutes | Cook time: 17 minutes | Serves 1

- 1 large egg
- 1 avocado, halved, peeled, and pitted
- 2 slices bacon
- Fresh parsley, for serving (optional)
- Sea salt flakes, for garnish (optional)

1. Spray the air fryer basket with avocado oil. Preheat the air fryer to 320ºF (160ºC). Fill a small bowl with cool water. 2. Soft-boil the egg: Place the egg in the air fryer basket. Air fry for 6 minutes for a soft yolk or 7 minutes for a cooked yolk. Transfer the egg to the bowl of cool water and let sit for 2 minutes. Peel and set aside. 3. Use a spoon to carve out extra space in the center of the avocado halves until the cavities are big enough to fit the soft-boiled egg. Place the soft-boiled egg in the center of one half of the avocado and replace the other half of the avocado on top, so the avocado appears whole on the outside. 4. Starting at one end of the avocado, wrap the bacon around the avocado to completely cover it. Use toothpicks to hold the bacon in place. 5. Place the bacon-wrapped avocado in the air fryer basket and air fry for 5 minutes. Flip the avocado over and air fry for another 5 minutes, or until the bacon is cooked to your liking. Serve on a bed of fresh parsley, if desired, and sprinkle with salt flakes, if desired. 6. Best served fresh. Store extras in an airtight container in the fridge for up to 4 days. Reheat in a preheated 320ºF (160ºC) air fryer for 4 minutes, or until heated through.

Per Serving:

calories: 380 | fat: 32g | protein: 13g | carbs: 14g | net carbs: 2g | fiber: 12g

No-Nuts Granola with Clusters

Prep time: 20 minutes | Cook time: 50 minutes | Makes 6 cups

- ½ cup (120 ml) melted coconut oil, plus more for the pan
- ½ cup (80 g) collagen peptides
- 1 large egg
- 3 tablespoons ground cinnamon
- 2 teaspoons vanilla extract
- ¼ teaspoon liquid stevia
- ¼ teaspoon finely ground
- gray sea salt
- 2 cups (200 g) shredded unsweetened coconut
- 1 cup (150 g) sesame seeds
- 1 cup (150 g) hulled hemp seeds
- ¼ cup (38 g) chia seeds
- Serving Suggestions:
- Full-fat coconut milk
- Fresh berries or stevia-sweetened chocolate chips

1. Preheat the oven to 300°F (150°C) and grease a 13 by 9-inch (33 by 23-cm) baking pan with a dab of coconut oil. 2. Place the melted coconut oil, collagen, egg, cinnamon, vanilla, stevia, and salt in a medium-sized bowl and whisk until combined. The consistency will be a bit odd, but don't worry, keep going! 3. In a separate large bowl, combine the shredded coconut, sesame seeds, hemp seeds, and chia seeds. Pour the liquid mixture into the bowl with the seed mixture and stir with a spatula until all the seeds are coated. 4. Transfer the mixture to the prepared pan and press it down firmly with your hands. Really pressing it in there is what creates those yummy clusters. 5. Bake for 30 minutes, or until the top and corners begin to turn golden. 6. Break the granola into large pieces with a metal spatula, keeping as many clusters intact as possible. Flip the pieces over and return the pan to the oven for another 15 to 20 minutes, until the pieces are golden. 7. Allow the clusters to cool in the pan for 1 hour before using. 8. When ready to serve, place ½ cup (60 g) of granola in a bowl and pour coconut milk over the top. Fresh berries or chocolate chips are a nice touch. 9. Enjoy!

Per Serving:

calories: 384 | fat: 32g | protein: 14g | carbs: 10g | net carbs: 3g | fiber: 6g

Spicy Egg Muffins with Bacon & Cheese

Prep time: 10 minutes | Cook time: 20 minutes | Serves 6

- 12 eggs
- ¼ cup coconut milk
- Salt and black pepper to taste
- 1 cup grated cheddar cheese
- 12 slices bacon
- 4 jalapeño peppers, seeded and minced

1. Preheat oven to 370ºF. 2. Crack the eggs into a bowl and whisk with coconut milk until combined. Season with salt and pepper, and evenly stir in the cheddar cheese. 3. Line each hole of a muffin tin with a slice of bacon and fill each with the egg mixture twothirds way up. Top with the jalapeno peppers and bake in the oven for 18 to 20 minutes or until puffed and golden. 4.Remove, allow cooling for a few minutes, and serve with arugula salad.

Per Serving:

calories: 440 | fat: 38g | protein: 22g | carbs: 2g | net carbs: 1g | fiber: 1g

Zesty Nacho Cabbage Chips

Prep time: 30 minutes | Cook time: 4 minutes | Serves 8

- 2 medium heads green cabbage

Sauce:
- ¼ cup (60 ml) refined avocado oil or extra-virgin olive oil
- ½ cup (75 g) raw hulled sunflower seeds, soaked for 8 hours, then drained and rinsed
- ½ white onion, roughly chopped
- 2 small carrots (about 2 ounces/55 g), roughly chopped
- 2 tablespoons tahini
- 2 tablespoons apple cider vinegar
- 3 small cloves garlic
- 2 teaspoons fresh lemon juice
- 2 teaspoons chipotle powder
- 3 drops liquid stevia

1. Preheat the oven to 170°F (77°C) and line 3 rimmed baking sheets with parchment paper or silicone baking mats. 2. Place one of the cabbages on a cutting board and cut it in half crosswise. Lay one half flat side down and cut it into quarters. Begin peeling off the leaves, being careful not to rip them. When it gets too difficult to access flatter, easy-to-remove leaves, continue with the next quarter. Place the usable leaves in a large bowl and the excess that you can't work with in a sealable container for use in another recipe. Repeat this process with the other half, then with the second head of cabbage. When done, you should have 1⅓ pounds (600 g) of leaves.

3. Prepare the sauce: Place the ingredients for the sauce in a high-powered blender or food processor and blend or pulse on high for 1 minute, or until smooth. 4. Pour the sauce over the cabbage leaves and massage it into the leaves with your hands, coating each leaf in sauce. 5. Transfer the coated leaves to the prepared baking sheets, laying them in a single layer, close together. 6. Place the baking sheets in the oven, layering them on top of one another if needed, crisscrossing them so the bottom of one sheet isn't touching the tops of the cabbage chips in the tray below it, but the edge of the bottom tray is holding up the second tray over the top of it. 7. Bake for 2 hours before checking on the chips. If any are crisp, transfer them to a cooling rack, then continue to cook for an additional 2 hours, checking for completed chips every 30 minutes. 8. Allow the chips to cool for 5 to 10 minutes before enjoying.

Per Serving:

calories: 120 | fat: 8g | protein: 4g | carbs: 9g | net carbs: 5g | fiber: 4g

Savory Zucchini Cheddar Waffles

Prep time: 10 minutes | Cook time: 18 minutes | Makes 4 medium-sized waffles

Waffles:
- 2 large zucchini
- 2 large eggs
- ⅔ cup shredded cheddar cheese (about 2⅔ ounces)
- 2 tablespoons coconut flour
- ½ teaspoon garlic powder
- ½ teaspoon red pepper flakes
- ¼ teaspoon pink Himalayan salt

For garnish (optinal):
- Sour cream
- Shredded cheddar cheese
- Minced fresh chives

1. Preheat a waffle iron on the medium setting. 2. Using a vegetable or cheese grater, grate the zucchini into a large colander set inside of a bowl. Squeeze the excess water out of the grated zucchini using your hands and drain. 3. Add the eggs and cheese to the drained zucchini and combine with a fork. Add the coconut flour, garlic powder, red pepper flakes, and salt and use the fork to combine once more. 4. Open the waffle iron and grease the top and bottom with coconut oil spray. 5. Using a ⅓-cup measuring cup, scoop out some of the batter, place it in the center of the waffle iron, and close the lid. Cook the waffle for 4 to 4½ minutes, until golden brown and fully cooked through. Use a fork to lift it off the iron and set on a plate. 6. Repeat with the remaining batter, making a total of 4 waffles. Garnish with sour cream, shredded cheddar cheese, and/or minced chives, if desired.

Per Serving:

calories: 292 | fat: 19g | protein: 20g | carbs: 14g | net carbs: 9g | fiber: 5g

Green Eggs and Ham

Prep time: 5 minutes | Cook time: 10 minutes | Serves 2

- 1 large Hass avocado, halved and pitted
- 2 thin slices ham
- 2 large eggs
- 2 tablespoons chopped green onions, plus more for garnish
- ½ teaspoon fine sea salt
- ¼ teaspoon ground black pepper
- ¼ cup shredded Cheddar cheese (omit for dairy-free)

1. Preheat the air fryer to 400ºF (204ºC). 2. Place a slice of ham into the cavity of each avocado half. Crack an egg on top of the ham, then sprinkle on the green onions, salt, and pepper. 3. Place the avocado halves in the air fryer cut side up and air fry for 10 minutes, or until the egg is cooked to your desired doneness. Top with the cheese (if using) and air fry for 30 seconds more, or until the cheese is melted. Garnish with chopped green onions. 4. Best served fresh. Store extras in an airtight container in the fridge for up to 4 days. Reheat in a preheated 350ºF (177ºC) air fryer for a few minutes, until warmed through.

Per Serving:

calories: 401 | fat: 30g | protein: 21g | carbs: 12g | net carbs: 6g | fiber: 9g

No-Bake Keto Power Bars

Prep time: 10 minutes | Cook time: 0 minutes | Makes 12 bars

- ½ cup pili nuts
- ½ cup whole hazelnuts
- ½ cup walnut halves
- ¼ cup hulled sunflower seeds
- ¼ cup unsweetened coconut flakes or chips
- ¼ cup hulled hemp seeds
- 2 tablespoons unsweetened cacao nibs
- 2 scoops collagen powder (I use 1 scoop Perfect Keto vanilla collagen and 1 scoop Perfect Keto unflavored collagen powder)
- ½ teaspoon ground cinnamon
- ½ teaspoon sea salt
- ¼ cup coconut oil, melted
- 1 teaspoon vanilla extract
- Stevia or monk fruit to sweeten (optional if you are using unflavored collagen powder)

1. Line a 9-inch square baking pan with parchment paper. 2. In a food processor or blender, combine the pili nuts, hazelnuts, walnuts, sunflower seeds, coconut, hemp seeds, cacao nibs, collagen powder, cinnamon, and salt and pulse a few times. 3. Add the coconut oil, vanilla extract, and sweetener (if using). Pulse again until the ingredients are combined. Do not over pulse or it will turn to mush. You want the nuts and seeds to still have some texture. 4. Pour the mixture into the prepared pan and press it into an even layer. Cover with another piece of parchment (or fold over extra from the first piece) and place a heavy pan or dish on top to help press the bars together. 5. Refrigerate overnight and then cut into 12 bars. Store the bars in individual storage bags in the refrigerator for a quick grab-and-go breakfast.

Per Serving:

calories: 242 | fat: 22g | protein: 6g | carbs: 4g | net carbs: 2g | fiber: 2g

Rocket Fuel Hot Chocolate

Prep time: 5 minutes | Cook time: 0 minutes | Makes 2

- 2 cups (475 ml) milk (nondairy or regular), hot
- 2 tablespoons cocoa powder
- 2 tablespoons collagen peptides or protein powder
- 2 tablespoons coconut oil, MCT oil, unflavored MCT oil powder, or ghee
- 1 tablespoon coconut butter
- 1 tablespoon erythritol, or 4 drops liquid stevia
- Pinch of ground cinnamon (optional)

1. Place all the ingredients in a blender and blend for 10 seconds, or until the ingredients are fully incorporated. 2. Divide between 2 mugs, sprinkle with cinnamon if you'd like, and enjoy!

Per Serving:

calories: 357 | fat: 29g | protein: 13g | carbs: 11g | net carbs: 7g | fiber: 4g

Jelly-Filled Breakfast Strudels

Prep time: 10 minutes | Cook time: 25 minutes | Serves 2

Pastry:
- ¾ cup shredded low-moisture mozzarella cheese
- 2 ounces (57 g) full-fat cream cheese, at room temperature

Frosting:
- ¼ cup powdered erythritol
- 2 ounces (57 g) full-fat cream cheese, at room temperature
- 1 tablespoon butter, at room
- 1 cup almond flour
- 1 large egg
- 4 tablespoons stevia-sweetened jelly

- temperature
- 2 teaspoons heavy (whipping) cream
- ¼ teaspoon vanilla extract

1. Preheat the oven to 325ºF (163ºC). Have a silicone-lined baking sheet nearby. 2. To make the dough: In a large, microwave-safe bowl, combine the mozzarella and cream cheese. 3. Microwave for 1 minute, until the cheese is melted. Then stir to combine. 4. Add the almond flour and egg to the melted cheese. Combine using a rubber scraper, working quickly so the cheese does not cool and harden. (If it starts to harden, reheat in the microwave for 20 seconds, being careful not to cook the egg.) 5. Roll out the dough between 2 pieces of parchment paper to a large rectangle that is between ¼ and ⅛ inch thick. 6. Make 3 even cuts widthwise to form 4 long rectangles of dough. 7. Place 1 tablespoon of jelly in the top half of each rectangle, leaving a little room on the sides. 8. Puncture the non-jellied bottom of each rectangle with a fork. Then, fold this bottom half over the top jellied half. 9. Seal the edges all the way around the square by pressing down with a fork. Transfer the squares to the baking sheet. 10. Bake for 20 to 25 minutes, until the pastry is golden brown. 11. Remove from the oven, and allow to cool for 10 minutes. 12. To make the frosting: In a small bowl, combine the erythritol, cream cheese, butter, cream, and vanilla and mix until smooth. 13. With a knife or the back of a spoon, coat the strudels with frosting and enjoy.

Per Serving:

calories: 702 | fat: 61g | protein: 27g | carbs: 16g | net carbs: 10g | fiber: 6g

Classic Cinnamon Roll Coffee Cake

Prep time: 10 minutes | Cook time: 45 minutes | Serves 8

Cake:
- 2 cups almond flour
- 1 cup granulated erythritol
- 1 teaspoon baking powder
- Pinch of salt
- 2 eggs
- ½ cup sour cream
- 4 tablespoons butter, melted
- 2 teaspoons vanilla extract
- 2 tablespoons Swerve
- 1½ teaspoons ground cinnamon
- Cooking spray
- ½ cup water

Icing:
- 2 ounces (56 g) cream cheese, softened
- 1 cup powdered erythritol
- 1 tablespoon heavy cream
- ½ teaspoon vanilla extract

1. In the bowl of a stand mixer, combine the almond flour, granulated erythritol, baking powder and salt. Mix until no lumps remain. Add the eggs, sour cream, butter and vanilla to the mixer bowl and mix until well combined. 2. In a separate bowl, mix together the Swerve and cinnamon. 3. Spritz the baking pan with cooking spray. Pour in the cake batter and use a knife to make sure it is level around the pan. Sprinkle the cinnamon mixture on top. Cover the pan tightly with aluminum foil. 4. Pour the water and insert the trivet in the Instant Pot. Put the pan on the trivet. 5. Set the lid in place. Select the Manual mode and set the cooking time for 45 minutes on High Pressure. When the timer goes off, do a quick pressure release. Carefully open the lid. 6. Remove the cake from the pot and remove the foil. Blot off any moisture on top of the cake with a paper towel, if necessary. Let rest in the pan for 5 minutes. 7. Meanwhile, make the icing: In a small bowl, use a mixer to whip the cream cheese until it is light and fluffy. Slowly fold in the powdered erythritol and mix until well combined. Add the heavy cream and vanilla extract and mix until thoroughly combined. 8. When the cake is cooled, transfer it to a platter and drizzle the icing all over.

Per Serving:

calories: 313 | fat: 27g | protein: 9g | carbs: 7g | net carbs: 4g | fiber: 3g

Eggs & Crabmeat with Creme Fraiche Salsa

Prep time: 10 minutes | Cook time: 10 minutes | Serves 3

- 1 tablespoon olive oil
- 6 eggs, whisked
- 1 (6 ounces) can crabmeat, flaked
- Salt and black pepper to taste
- For the Salsa:
- ¾ cup crème fraiche
- ½ cup scallions, chopped
- ½ teaspoon garlic powder
- Salt and black pepper to taste
- ½ teaspoon fresh dill, chopped

1. Set a sauté pan over medium heat and warm olive oil. Crack in eggs and scramble them. Stir in crabmeat and season with salt and black pepper; cook until cooked thoroughly. 2. In a mixing dish, combine all salsa ingredients. Equally, split the egg/crabmeat mixture among serving plates; serve alongside the scallions and salsa to the side.

Per Serving:

calories: 364 | fat: 26g | protein: 25g | carbs: 5g | net carbs: 5g | fiber: 0g

Bacon Spaghetti Squash Fritters

Prep time: 20 minutes | Cook time: 15 minutes | Serves 4

- ½ cooked spaghetti squash
- 2 tablespoons cream cheese
- ½ cup shredded whole-milk Mozzarella cheese
- 1 egg
- ½ teaspoon salt
- ¼ teaspoon pepper
- 1 stalk green onion, sliced
- 4 slices cooked bacon, crumbled
- 2 tablespoons coconut oil

1. Remove seeds from cooked squash and use fork to scrape strands out of shell. Place strands into cheesecloth or kitchen towel and squeeze to remove as much excess moisture as possible. 2. Place cream cheese and Mozzarella in small bowl and microwave for 45 seconds to melt together. Mix with spoon and place in large bowl. Add all ingredients except coconut oil to bowl. Mixture will be wet like batter. 3. Press the Sauté button and then press the Adjust button to set heat to Less. Add coconut oil to Instant Pot. When fully preheated, add 2 to 3 tablespoons of batter to pot to make a fritter. Let fry until firm and completely cooked through.

Per Serving:

calories: 202 | fat: 16g | protein: 9g | carbs: 2g | net carbs: 1g | fiber: 1g

Keto Egg "Mcmuffins"

Prep time: 5 minutes | Cook time: 10 minutes | Makes 2 sandwiches

- 1 tablespoon butter
- 4 eggs
- 2 cooked breakfast sausage patties
- 2 slices Cheddar cheese
- Salt and freshly ground black pepper, to taste

1. Heat a large nonstick skillet over medium heat. Add the butter and let it melt. 2. Crack each egg into a round metal biscuit cutter, silicone mold, or just the ring of a mason jar lid, and give it a quick stir as it cooks, gently breaking the yolk. Cook for 3 to 4 minutes or until set. Remove from the mold. Repeat until all the eggs are cooked. 3. In the same skillet, heat the sausage for 1 to 2 minutes to warm. Top each piece with 1 slice of cheese. You can cover the skillet to help the cheese melt more quickly. 4. Assemble the sandwiches by placing a cheesy sausage on 1 egg and topping it with a second egg. Repeat with the remaining sandwich ingredients and serve immediately.

Per Serving:

1 sandwich: calories: 397 | fat: 34g | protein: 23g | carbs: 1g | net carbs: 1g | fiber: 0g

Chapter 3

Fish and Seafood

Chapter 3 Fish and Seafood

Cod with Parsley Pistou

Prep time: 15 minutes | Cook time: 10 minutes | Serves 4

- 1 cup packed roughly chopped fresh flat-leaf Italian parsley
- 1 to 2 small garlic cloves, minced
- Zest and juice of 1 lemon
- 1 teaspoon salt
- ½ teaspoon freshly ground black pepper
- 1 cup extra-virgin olive oil, divided
- 1 pound (454 g) cod fillets, cut into 4 equal-sized pieces

1. In a food processor, combine the parsley, garlic, lemon zest and juice, salt, and pepper. Pulse to chop well. 2. While the food processor is running, slowly stream in ¾ cup olive oil until well combined. Set aside. 3. In a large skillet, heat the remaining ¼ cup olive oil over medium-high heat. Add the cod fillets, cover, and cook 4 to 5 minutes on each side, or until cooked through. Thicker fillets may require a bit more cooking time. Remove from the heat and keep warm. 4. Add the pistou to the skillet and heat over medium-low heat. Return the cooked fish to the skillet, flipping to coat in the sauce. Serve warm, covered with pistou.

Per Serving:

calories: 550 | fat: 50g | protein: 21g | carbs: 4g | net carbs: 3g | fiber: 1g

Sicilian-Style Zoodle Spaghetti

Prep time: 10 minutes | Cook time: 11 minutes | Serves 2

- 4 cups zoodles (spiralled zucchini)
- 2 ounces cubed bacon
- 4 ounces canned sardines, chopped
- ½ cup canned chopped tomatoes
- 1 tablespoon capers
- 1 tablespoon parsley
- 1 teaspoon minced garlic

1. Pour some of the sardine oil in a pan. Add garlic and cook for 1 minute. Add the bacon and cook for 2 more minutes. Stir in the tomatoes and let simmer for 5 minutes. Add zoodles and sardines and cook for 3 minutes.

Per Serving:

calories: 290 | fat: 18g | protein: 22g | carbs: 13g | net carbs: 9g | fiber: 4g

Tuna with Herbs

Prep time: 20 minutes | Cook time: 17 minutes | Serves 4

- 1 tablespoon butter, melted
- 1 medium-sized leek, thinly sliced
- 1 tablespoon chicken stock
- 1 tablespoon dry white wine
- 1 pound (454 g) tuna
- ½ teaspoon red pepper flakes, crushed
- Sea salt and ground black pepper, to taste
- ½ teaspoon dried rosemary
- ½ teaspoon dried basil
- ½ teaspoon dried thyme
- 2 small ripe tomatoes, puréed
- 1 cup Parmesan cheese, grated

1. Melt ½ tablespoon of butter in a sauté pan over medium-high heat. Now, cook the leek and garlic until tender and aromatic. Add the stock and wine to deglaze the pan. 2. Preheat the air fryer to 370ºF (188ºC). 3. Grease a casserole dish with the remaining ½ tablespoon of melted butter. Place the fish in the casserole dish. Add the seasonings. Top with the sautéed leek mixture. Add the tomato purée. Cook for 10 minutes in the preheated air fryer. Top with grated Parmesan cheese; cook an additional 7 minutes until the crumbs are golden. Bon appétit!

Per Serving:

calories: 450 | fat: 22g | protein: 56g | carbs: 8g | net carbs: 6g | fiber: 2g

Simple Buttery Cod

Prep time: 5 minutes | Cook time: 8 minutes | Serves 2

- 2 (4-ounce / 113-g) cod fillets
- 2 tablespoons salted butter, melted
- 1 teaspoon Old Bay seasoning
- ½ medium lemon, sliced

1. Place cod fillets into a round baking dish. Brush each fillet with butter and sprinkle with Old Bay seasoning. Lay two lemon slices on each fillet. Cover the dish with foil and place into the air fryer basket. 2. Adjust the temperature to 350ºF (177ºC) and bake for 8 minutes. 3. Flip halfway through the cooking time. When cooked, internal temperature should be at least 145ºF (63ºC). Serve warm.

Per Serving:

calories: 294 | fat: 16g | protein: 31g | carbs: 3g | net carbs: 3g | fiber: 0g

Caprese Salmon

Prep time: 10 minutes | Cook time: 15 minutes | Serves 2

- 10 ounces (283 g) salmon fillet (2 fillets)
- 4 ounces (113 g) Mozzarella, sliced
- 4 cherry tomatoes, sliced
- 1 teaspoon erythritol
- 1 teaspoon dried basil
- ½ teaspoon ground black pepper
- 1 tablespoon apple cider vinegar
- 1 tablespoon butter
- 1 cup water, for cooking

1. Grease the mold with butter and put the salmon inside. 2. Sprinkle the fish with erythritol, dried basil, ground black pepper, and apple cider vinegar. 3. Then top the salmon with tomatoes and Mozzarella. 4. Pour water and insert the steamer rack in the instant pot. 5. Put the fish on the rack. 6. Close and seal the lid. 7. Cook the meal on Manual mode at High Pressure for 15 minutes. Make a quick pressure release.

Per Serving:

calories: 447 | fat: 25g | protein: 46g | carbs: 15g | net carbs: 12g | fiber: 3g

Basil Alfredo Sea Bass

Prep time: 15 minutes | Cook time: 30 minutes | Serves 4

Sea Bass:
- 4 (6-ounce / 170-g) sea bass pieces

Pesto:
- 1 cup tightly packed fresh basil leaves
- ¼ cup grated Parmesan cheese
- 3 tablespoons pine nuts, or walnuts

Alfredo Sauce:
- 2 tablespoons butter
- 1 tablespoon olive oil
- 1 garlic clove, minced
- 1 cup heavy (whipping) cream

- 2 tablespoons olive oil

- 1 tablespoon water
- ½ teaspoon salt
- Freshly ground black pepper, to taste
- 3 tablespoons olive oil

- ¾ cup Parmesan cheese
- Salt, to taste
- Freshly ground black pepper, to taste

Make the Sea Bass 1. Preheat the oven to 375ºF (190ºC). 2. Rub the sea bass with the olive oil and place it in a baking dish or on a rimmed baking sheet. Bake for 20 to 25 minutes or until the fish is completely opaque and the flesh flakes easily with a fork. Make the Pesto 1. In a blender or food processor (I prefer a blender because I like this very finely chopped/blended), combine the basil, Parmesan, pine nuts, water, and salt. Season with pepper. 2. With the blender running, stream the olive oil in. Set aside. Make the Alfredo Sauce 1. In a small saucepan over medium heat, melt the butter and olive oil together. 2. Stir in the garlic and cream. Bring to a low simmer and cook for 5 to 7 minutes until thickened. 3. Slowly add the Parmesan, stirring well to mix as it melts. Continue to stir until smooth. Season with salt and pepper. Set aside. 4. In a small bowl, stir together ½ cup of pesto and ½ cup of Alfredo sauce. Spoon over the fish before serving. Refrigerate leftovers in an airtight container for up to 4 days.

Per Serving:

calories: 768 | fat: 64g | protein: 45g | carbs: 4g | net carbs: 4g | fiber: 0g

Chili and Turmeric Haddock

Prep time: 10 minutes | Cook time: 5 minutes | Serves 4

- 1 chili pepper, minced
- 1 pound (454 g) haddock, chopped
- ½ teaspoon ground turmeric
- ½ cup fish stock
- 1 cup water

1. In the mixing bowl mix up chili pepper, ground turmeric, and fish stock. 2. Then add chopped haddock and transfer the mixture in the baking mold. 3. Pour water in the instant pot and insert the trivet. 4. Place the baking mold with fish on the trivet and close the lid. 5. Cook the meal on Manual (High Pressure) for 5 minutes. Make a quick pressure release.

Per Serving:

calories: 130 | fat: 1g | protein: 28g | carbs: 0g | net carbs: 0g | fiber: 0g

Tuna Steak

Prep time: 10 minutes | Cook time: 12 minutes | Serves 4

- 1 pound (454 g) tuna steaks, boneless and cubed
- 1 tablespoon mustard
- 1 tablespoon avocado oil
- 1 tablespoon apple cider vinegar

1. Mix avocado oil with mustard and apple cider vinegar. 2. Then brush tuna steaks with mustard mixture and put in the air fryer basket. 3. Cook the fish at 360ºF (182ºC) for 6 minutes per side.

Per Serving:

calories: 180 | fat: 9g | protein: 25g | carbs: 1g | net carbs: 1g | fiber: 0g

Spicy Sea Bass with Hazelnuts

Prep time: 5 minutes | Cook time: 15 minutes | Serves 2

- 2 sea bass fillets
- 2 tablespoons butter
- ⅓ cup roasted hazelnuts
- A pinch of cayenne pepper

1. Preheat your oven to 425°F. Line a baking dish with waxed paper. Melt the butter and brush it over the fish. Process the cayenne pepper and hazelnuts in a food processor to achieve a smooth consistency. Coat the sea bass with the hazelnut mixture. Place in the oven and bake for about 15 minutes.

Per Serving:

calories: 403 | fat: 27g | protein: 37g | carbs: 3g | net carbs: 3g | fiber: 0g

Parchment-Baked Cod and Asparagus with Beurre Blanc

Prep time: 15 minutes | Cook time: 15 minutes | Serves 4

- 1 pound (454 g) skinless cod, halibut, or other white flaky fish
- 1 teaspoon salt, divided
- ½ teaspoon freshly ground black pepper, divided
- 2 garlic cloves, thinly sliced
- 1 lemon, thinly sliced
- ½ pound (227 g) asparagus spears, rough ends trimmed
- 4 tablespoons extra-virgin olive oil, divided
- 1 tablespoon finely chopped red onion
- ¼ cup white wine vinegar
- ¼ cup heavy cream
- ½ cup (1 stick) chilled unsalted butter, cut into tablespoon-size pieces

1. Preheat the oven to 375°F (190°C). 2. Place 1 large sheet of parchment paper (about twice the size of the fish fillet) on a rimmed baking sheet. Place the fish in the center of the parchment and sprinkle with ½ teaspoon of the salt and ¼ teaspoon of the pepper. 3. Top the fish with the garlic and lemon slices. Top with the asparagus spears and drizzle with 2 tablespoons of olive oil. 4. Top the fish with a second large piece of parchment. Starting on a long side, fold the paper up to about 1 inch from the fish and vegetables. Repeat on the remaining sides, going in a clockwise direction. Fold in each corner once to secure. 5. Bake for 10 to 12 minutes, until the fish is cooked through and flakes easily when poked with a paring knife. 6. Meanwhile, prepare the sauce. Heat the remaining 2 tablespoons of olive oil over medium heat. Add the red onion and sauté until tender, 3 to 4 minutes. Add the vinegar, cream, remaining ½ teaspoon of salt, and ¼ teaspoon of pepper. Bring to a simmer and reduce heat to low. 7. Whisking constantly, add the butter, a couple tablespoons at a time, until melted and creamy. Remove the sauce from the heat and serve warm, poured over the fish and asparagus.

Per Serving:

calories: 472 | fat: 43g | protein: 19g | carbs: 4g | net carbs: 3g | fiber: 1g

Aromatic Monkfish Stew

Prep time: 5 minutes | Cook time: 6 minutes | Serves 6

- Juice of 1 lemon
- 1 tablespoon fresh basil
- 1 tablespoon fresh parsley
- 1 tablespoon olive oil
- 1 teaspoon garlic, minced
- 1½ pounds (680 g) monkfish
- 1 tablespoon butter
- 1 bell pepper, chopped
- 1 onion, sliced
- ½ teaspoon cayenne pepper
- ½ teaspoon mixed peppercorns
- ¼ teaspoon turmeric powder
- ¼ teaspoon ground cumin
- Sea salt and ground black pepper, to taste
- 2 cups fish stock
- ½ cup water
- ¼ cup dry white wine
- 2 bay leaves
- 1 ripe tomato, crushed

1. Stir together the lemon juice, basil, parsley, olive oil, and garlic in a ceramic dish. Add the monkfish and marinate for 30 minutes. 2. Set your Instant Pot to Sauté. Add and melt the butter. Once hot, cook the bell pepper and onion until fragrant. 3. Stir in the remaining ingredients. 4. Lock the lid. Select the Manual mode and set the cooking time for 6 minutes at High Pressure. 5. When the timer beeps, perform a quick pressure release. Carefully remove the lid. 6. Discard the bay leaves and divide your stew into serving bowls. Serve hot.

Per Serving:

calories: 153 | fat: 7g | protein: 19g | carbs: 4g | net carbs: 3g | fiber: 1g

Mascarpone Tilapia with Nutmeg

Prep time: 10 minutes | Cook time: 20 minutes | Serves 2

- 10 ounces (283 g) tilapia
- ½ cup mascarpone
- 1 garlic clove, diced
- 1 teaspoon ground nutmeg
- 1 tablespoon olive oil
- ½ teaspoon salt

1. Pour olive oil in the instant pot. 2. Add diced garlic and sauté it for 4 minutes. 3. Add tilapia and sprinkle it with ground nutmeg. Sauté the fish for 3 minutes per side. 4. Add mascarpone and close the lid. 5. Sauté tilapia for 10 minutes.

Per Serving:

calories: 293 | fat: 17g | protein: 33g | carbs: 3g | net carbs: 2g | fiber: 1g

Rainbow Trout with Mixed Greens

Prep time: 5 minutes | Cook time: 12 minutes | Serves 4

- 1 cup water
- 1½ (680 g) pounds rainbow trout fillets
- 4 tablespoons melted butter, divided
- Sea salt and ground black pepper, to taste
- 1 pound (454 g) mixed greens, trimmed and torn into pieces
- 1 bunch of scallions
- ½ cup chicken broth
- 1 tablespoon apple cider vinegar
- 1 teaspoon cayenne pepper

1. Pour the water into your Instant Pot and insert a steamer basket. 2. Add the fish to the basket. Drizzle with 1 tablespoon of the melted butter and season with the salt and black pepper. 3. Lock the lid. Select the Manual mode and set the cooking time for 12 minutes at Low pressure. 4. When the timer beeps, perform a quick pressure release. Carefully remove the lid. 5. Wipe down the Instant Pot with a damp cloth. 6. Add and warm the remaining 3 tablespoons of butter. Once hot, add the greens, scallions, broth, vinegar, and cayenne pepper and cook until the greens are wilted, stirring occasionally. 7. Serve the prepared trout fillets with the greens on the side.

Per Serving:

calories: 349 | fat: 18g | protein: 39g | carbs: 8g | net carbs: 3g | fiber: 4g

Garam Masala Fish

Prep time: 10 minutes | Cook time: 10 minutes | Serves 4

- 2 tablespoons sesame oil
- ½ teaspoon cumin seeds
- ½ cup chopped leeks
- 1 teaspoon ginger-garlic paste
- 1 pound (454 g) cod fillets, boneless and sliced
- 2 ripe tomatoes, chopped
- 1½ tablespoons fresh lemon juice
- ½ teaspoon garam masala
- ½ teaspoon turmeric powder
- 1 tablespoon chopped fresh dill leaves
- 1 tablespoon chopped fresh curry leaves
- 1 tablespoon chopped fresh parsley leaves
- Coarse sea salt, to taste
- ½ teaspoon smoked cayenne pepper
- ¼ teaspoon ground black pepper, or more to taste

1. Set the Instant Pot to Sauté. Add and heat the sesame oil until hot. Sauté the cumin seeds for 30 seconds. 2. Add the leeks and cook for another 2 minutes until translucent. Add the ginger-garlic paste and cook for an additional 40 seconds. 3. Stir in the remaining ingredients. 4. Lock the lid. Select the Manual mode and set the cooking time for 6 minutes at Low Pressure. 5. When the timer

beeps, perform a quick pressure release. Carefully remove the lid. 6. Serve immediately.

Per Serving:

calories: 166 | fat: 8g | protein: 18g | carbs: 6g | net carbs: 4g | fiber: 2g

Baked Coconut Haddock

Prep time: 10 minutes | Cook time: 12 minutes | Serves 4

- 4 (5-ounce) boneless haddock fillets
- Sea salt
- Freshly ground black pepper
- 1 cup shredded unsweetened coconut
- ¼ cup ground hazelnuts
- 2 tablespoons coconut oil, melted

1. Preheat the oven to 400°F. Line a baking sheet with parchment paper and set aside. 2. Pat the fillets very dry with paper towels and lightly season them with salt and pepper. 3. Stir together the shredded coconut and hazelnuts in a small bowl. 4. Dredge the fish fillets in the coconut mixture so that both sides of each piece are thickly coated. 5. Place the fish on the baking sheet and lightly brush both sides of each piece with the coconut oil. 6. Bake the haddock until the topping is golden and the fish flakes easily with a fork, about 12 minutes total. 7. Serve.

Per Serving:

calories: 299 | fat: 24g | protein: 20g | carbs: 4g | net carbs: 1g | fiber: 4g

Coconut Shrimp

Prep time: 5 minutes | Cook time: 6 minutes | Serves 2

- 8 ounces (227 g) medium shelled and deveined shrimp
- 2 tablespoons salted butter, melted
- ½ teaspoon Old Bay seasoning
- ¼ cup unsweetened shredded coconut

1. In a large bowl, toss the shrimp in butter and Old Bay seasoning. 2. Place shredded coconut in bowl. Coat each piece of shrimp in the coconut and place into the air fryer basket. 3. Adjust the temperature to 400°F (204°C) and air fry for 6 minutes. 4. Gently turn the shrimp halfway through the cooking time. Serve immediately.

Per Serving:

calories: 197 | fat: 13g | protein: 16g | carbs: 2g | net carbs: 1g | fiber: 1g

Coconut Shrimp Curry

Prep time: 10 minutes | Cook time: 4 minutes | Serves 5

- 15 ounces (425 g) shrimp, peeled
- 1 teaspoon chili powder
- 1 teaspoon garam masala
- 1 cup coconut milk
- 1 teaspoon olive oil
- ½ teaspoon minced garlic

1. Heat up the instant pot on Sauté mode for 2 minutes. 2. Then add olive oil. Cook the ingredients for 1 minute. 3. Add shrimp and sprinkle them with chili powder, garam masala, minced garlic, and coconut milk. 4. Carefully stir the ingredients and close the lid. 5. Cook the shrimp curry on Manual mode for 1 minute. Make a quick pressure release.

Per Serving:

calories: 222 | fat: 14g | protein: 21g | carbs: 4g | net carbs: 3g | fiber: 1g

Tilapia Bake

Prep time: 5 minutes | Cook time: 30 minutes | Serves 4

- 3 medium or 4 small tilapia fillets (approximately 1 pound / 454 g total)
- 1 teaspoon kosher salt
- 1 teaspoon black pepper
- 2 tablespoons plus 1 teaspoon butter
- 1 medium leek, white part
- thinly sliced (¾ cup)
- 10 ounces (283 g) baby spinach
- ¼ cup heavy cream
- ½ teaspoon dried parsley
- ½ teaspoon dried oregano
- ¼ teaspoon red pepper flakes
- 1 cup crumbled feta cheese

1. Preheat the oven to 425°F (220°C). Season the tilapia fillets with ½ teaspoon each of the salt and pepper. 2. In a large skillet, melt 2 tablespoons of the butter over medium-high heat. Add the leeks and sauté a few minutes, until soft but not brown. Add the spinach a handful at a time; the spinach will reduce in volume by a lot. Add the cream and the parsley, oregano, and red pepper flakes, as well as the remaining ½ teaspoon each salt and pepper. Reduce the heat to medium low and simmer, stirring frequently, until the mixture thickens a bit. 3. Use the remaining 1 teaspoon butter to lightly grease a small glass baking dish. Transfer three-fourths of the spinach mixture to the baking dish and arrange the fish in a single layer on top. Layer the rest of the spinach on top. Sprinkle the feta evenly over and bake for 20 to 25 minutes, or until the fish is cooked through.

Per Serving:

calories: 318 | fat: 20g | protein: 27g | carbs: 5g | net carbs: 3g | fiber: 2g

Grilled Salmon with Caponata

Prep time: 15 minutes | Cook time: 20 minutes | Serves 4

- ¼ cup good-quality olive oil, divided
- 1 onion, chopped
- 2 celery stalks, chopped
- 1 tablespoon minced garlic
- 2 tomatoes, chopped
- ½ cup chopped marinated artichoke hearts
- ¼ cup pitted green olives,
- chopped
- ¼ cup cider vinegar
- 2 tablespoons white wine
- 2 tablespoons chopped pecans
- 4 (4-ounce) salmon fillets
- Freshly ground black pepper, for seasoning
- 2 tablespoons chopped fresh basil

1. Make the caponata. In a large skillet over medium heat, warm 3 tablespoons of the olive oil. Add the onion, celery, and garlic, and sauté until they've softened, about 4 minutes. Stir in the tomatoes, artichoke hearts, olives, vinegar, white wine, and pecans. Bring the mixture to a boil, then reduce the heat to low and simmer until the liquid has reduced, 6 to 7 minutes. Remove the skillet from the heat and set it aside. 2. Grill the fish. Preheat a grill to medium-high heat. Pat the fish dry with paper towels and rub it with the remaining 1 tablespoon of olive oil and season lightly with black pepper. Grill the salmon, turning once, until it is just cooked through, about 8 minutes total. 3. Serve. Divide the salmon between four plates, top with a generous scoop of the caponata, and serve immediately with fresh basil.

Per Serving:

calories: 348 | fat: 25g | protein: 24g | carbs: 7g | net carbs: 4g | fiber: 3g

Ahi Tuna Steaks

Prep time: 5 minutes | Cook time: 14 minutes | Serves 2

- 2 (6 ounces / 170 g) ahi tuna steaks
- 2 tablespoons olive oil
- 3 tablespoons everything bagel seasoning

1. Drizzle both sides of each steak with olive oil. Place seasoning on a medium plate and press each side of tuna steaks into seasoning to form a thick layer. 2. Place steaks into ungreased air fryer basket. Adjust the temperature to 400°F (204°C) and air fry for 14 minutes, turning steaks halfway through cooking. Steaks will be done when internal temperature is at least 145°F (63°C) for well-done. Serve warm.

Per Serving:

calories: 488 | fat: 33g | protein: 44g | carbs: 5g | net carbs: 2g | fiber: 3g

Tuna-Stuffed Tomatoes

Prep time: 5 minutes | Cook time: 5 minutes | Serves 2

- 2 medium beefsteak tomatoes, tops removed, seeded, membranes removed
- 2 (2.6-ounce / 74-g) pouches tuna packed in water, drained
- 1 medium stalk celery, trimmed and chopped
- 2 tablespoons mayonnaise
- ¼ teaspoon salt
- ¼ teaspoon ground black pepper
- 2 teaspoons coconut oil
- ¼ cup shredded mild Cheddar cheese

1. Scoop pulp out of each tomato, leaving ½-inch shell. 2. In a medium bowl, mix tuna, celery, mayonnaise, salt, and pepper. Drizzle with coconut oil. Spoon ½ mixture into each tomato and top each with 2 tablespoons Cheddar. 3. Place tomatoes into ungreased air fryer basket. Adjust the temperature to 320ºF (160ºC) and air fry for 5 minutes. Cheese will be melted when done. Serve warm.

Per Serving:

calories: 232 | fat: 15g | protein: 20g | carbs: 6g | net carbs: 4g | fiber: 2g

Mouthwatering Cod over Creamy Leek Noodles

Prep time: 10 minutes | Cook time: 24 minutes | Serves 4

- 1 small leek, sliced into long thin noodles (about 2 cups)
- ½ cup heavy cream
- 2 cloves garlic, minced
- 1 teaspoon fine sea salt, Coating:
- ¼ cup grated Parmesan cheese
- 2 tablespoons mayonnaise
- 2 tablespoons unsalted butter, softened
- divided
- 4 (4-ounce / 113-g) cod fillets (about 1 inch thick)
- ½ teaspoon ground black pepper
- 1 tablespoon chopped fresh thyme, or ½ teaspoon dried thyme leaves, plus more for garnish

1. Preheat the air fryer to 350ºF (177ºC). 2. Place the leek noodles in a casserole dish or a pan that will fit in your air fryer. 3. In a small bowl, stir together the cream, garlic, and ½ teaspoon of the salt. Pour the mixture over the leeks and cook in the air fryer for 10 minutes, or until the leeks are very tender. 4. Pat the fish dry and season with the remaining ½ teaspoon of salt and the pepper. When the leeks are ready, open the air fryer and place the fish fillets on top of the leeks. Air fry for 8 to 10 minutes, until the fish flakes easily with a fork (the thicker the fillets, the longer this will take). 5. While the fish cooks, make the coating: In a small bowl,

combine the Parmesan, mayo, butter, and thyme. 6. When the fish is ready, remove it from the air fryer and increase the heat to 425ºF (218ºC) (or as high as your air fryer can go). Spread the fillets with a ½-inch-thick to ¾-inch-thick layer of the coating. 7. Place the fish back in the air fryer and air fry for 3 to 4 minutes, until the coating browns. 8. Garnish with fresh or dried thyme, if desired. Store leftovers in an airtight container in the refrigerator for up to 3 days. Reheat in a casserole dish in a preheated 350ºF (177ºC) air fryer for 6 minutes, or until heated through.

Per Serving:

calories: 380 | fat: 28g | protein: 24g | carbs: 6g | net carbs: 5g | fiber: 1g

Apple Cider Mussels

Prep time: 10 minutes | Cook time: 2 minutes | Serves 5

- 2 pounds (907 g) mussels, cleaned, peeled
- 1 teaspoon onion powder
- 1 teaspoon ground cumin
- 1 tablespoon avocado oil
- ¼ cup apple cider vinegar
-

1. Mix mussels with onion powder, ground cumin, avocado oil, and apple cider vinegar. 2. Put the mussels in the air fryer and cook at 395ºF (202ºC) for 2 minutes.

Per Serving:

calories: 210 | fat: 9g | protein: 23g | carbs: 7g | net carbs: 6g | fiber: 1g

Perch Fillets with Red Curry

Prep time: 5 minutes | Cook time: 6 minutes | Serves 4

- 1 cup water
- 2 sprigs rosemary
- 1 large-sized lemon, sliced
- 1 pound (454 g) perch fillets
- 1 teaspoon cayenne pepper
- Sea salt and ground black pepper, to taste
- 1 tablespoon red curry paste
- 1 tablespoons butter

1. Add the water, rosemary, and lemon slices to the Instant Pot and insert a trivet. 2. Season the perch fillets with the cayenne pepper, salt, and black pepper. Spread the red curry paste and butter over the fillets. 3. Arrange the fish fillets on the trivet. 4. Lock the lid. Select the Manual mode and set the cooking time for 6 minutes at Low Pressure. 5. When the timer beeps, perform a quick pressure release. Carefully remove the lid. Serve with your favorite keto sides.

Per Serving:

calories: 142 | fat: 4g | protein: 23g | carbs: 3g | net carbs: 2g | fiber: 2g

Clam Chowder

Prep time: 5 minutes | Cook time: 15 minutes | Serves 4

- 4 slices bacon, chopped into ½-inch squares
- 2 tablespoons unsalted butter
- ½ small yellow onion, chopped
- 4 ribs celery, cut into ¼-inch-thick half-moons
- 1 cup chopped cauliflower florets, cut to about ½ inch thick
- 4 ounces (113 g) chopped mushrooms
- 4 cloves garlic, minced
- 1 teaspoon dried tarragon
- 1 teaspoon salt
- ¼ teaspoon freshly ground black pepper
- 8 ounces (227 g) bottled clam juice
- 1 cup vegetable stock or broth
- ½ cup heavy cream
- 8 ounces (227 g) cream cheese, room temperature
- 3 (6½-ounce / 184-g) cans chopped clams, with juice
- ¼ cup freshly chopped Italian parsley

1. Place the bacon in a medium saucepan over medium heat. Fry until just browned and most of the fat has been rendered, 3 to 4 minutes. Remove the bacon with a slotted spoon, reserving the rendered fat. 2. Add the butter to the pan with the fat and melt over medium heat. Add the onion, celery, cauliflower, and mushrooms and sauté until vegetables are just tender, 4 to 5 minutes. Add the garlic, tarragon, salt, and pepper and sauté for another 30 seconds or until fragrant. 3. Add the clam juice, stock, cream, and cream cheese and whisk until the cheese is melted and creamy, 2 to 3 minutes. Add the clams and their juice, bring to a simmer, and cook for 1 to 2 minutes so the flavors meld. Stir in the parsley and serve warm.

Per Serving:

calories: 671 | fat: 54g | protein: 34g | carbs: 15g | net carbs: 13g | fiber: 2g

Oregano Tilapia Fingers

Prep time: 15 minutes | Cook time: 9 minutes | Serves 4

- 1 pound (454 g) tilapia fillet
- ½ cup coconut flour
- 2 eggs, beaten
- ½ teaspoon ground paprika
- 1 teaspoon dried oregano
- 1 teaspoon avocado oil

1. Cut the tilapia fillets into fingers and sprinkle with ground paprika and dried oregano. 2. Then dip the tilapia fingers in eggs and coat in the coconut flour. 3. Sprinkle fish fingers with avocado oil and cook in the air fryer at 370°F (188°C) for 9 minutes.

Per Serving:

calories: 230 | fat: 8g | protein: 32g | carbs: 10g | net carbs: 7g | fiber: 3g

Grilled Calamari

Prep time: 10 minutes | Cook time: 5 minutes | Serves 4

- 2 pounds calamari tubes and tentacles, cleaned
- ½ cup good-quality olive oil
- Zest and juice of 2 lemons
- 2 tablespoons chopped fresh oregano
- 1 tablespoon minced garlic
- ¼ teaspoon sea salt
- ⅛ teaspoon freshly ground black pepper

1. Prepare the calamari. Score the top layer of the calamari tubes about 2 inches apart. 2. Marinate the calamari. In a large bowl, stir together the olive oil, lemon zest, lemon juice, oregano, garlic, salt, and pepper. Add the calamari and toss to coat it well, then place it in the refrigerator to marinate for at least 30 minutes and up to 1 hour. 3. Grill the calamari. Preheat a grill to high heat. Grill the calamari, turning once, for about 3 minutes total, until it's tender and lightly charred. 4. Serve. Divide the calamari between four plates and serve it hot.

Per Serving:

calories: 455 | fat: 30g | protein: 35g | carbs: 8g | net carbs: 7g | fiber: 1g

Shrimp in Creamy Pesto over Zoodles

Prep time: 10 minutes | Cook time: 10 minutes | Serves 4

- 1 pound (454 g) peeled and deveined fresh shrimp
- Salt
- Freshly ground black pepper
- 2 tablespoons extra-virgin olive oil
- ½ small onion, slivered
- 8 ounces (227 g) store-bought jarred pesto
- ¾ cup crumbled goat or feta cheese, plus more for serving
- 6 cups zucchini noodles (from about 2 large zucchini), for serving
- ¼ cup chopped flat-leaf Italian parsley, for garnish

1. In a bowl, season the shrimp with salt and pepper and set aside. 2. In a large skillet, heat the olive oil over medium-high heat. Sauté the onion until just golden, 5 to 6 minutes. 3. Reduce the heat to low and add the pesto and cheese, whisking to combine and melt the cheese. Bring to a low simmer and add the shrimp. Reduce the heat back to low and cover. Cook until the shrimp is cooked through and pink, another 3 to 4 minutes. 4. Serve warm over zucchini noodles, garnishing with chopped parsley and additional crumbled cheese, if desired.

Per Serving:

calories: 550 | fat: 37g | protein: 41g | carbs: 13g | net carbs: 9g | fiber: 4g

Crab au Gratin

Prep time: 10 minutes | Cook time: 35 minutes | Serves 4

- ½ cup (1 stick) butter
- 1 (8-ounce / 227-g) container crab claw meat
- 2 ounces (57 g) full-fat cream cheese
- ½ cup heavy (whipping) cream
- 2 tablespoons freshly squeezed lemon juice
- 1 tablespoon white wine vinegar
- 1 teaspoon pink Himalayan sea salt
- ½ teaspoon freshly ground black pepper
- ½ teaspoon onion powder
- 1 cup shredded Cheddar cheese, divided
- 1 (12-ounce / 340-g) package cauliflower rice, cooked and drained

1. Preheat the oven to 350ºF (180ºC). 2. In a medium sauté pan or skillet, melt the butter over medium heat. Add the crab and cook until warmed through. 3. Add the cream cheese, cream, lemon juice, vinegar, salt, pepper, and onion powder. Keep stirring until the cream cheese fully melts into the sauce. 4. Add ½ cup of Cheddar cheese and stir it into the sauce. 5. Spread the cauliflower rice on the bottom of an 8-inch square baking dish. 6. Pour the crab and sauce over, then sprinkle with the remaining ½ cup of Cheddar cheese. 7. Bake for 25 to 30 minutes, until the sauce is bubbling. Turn the broiler on to high. 8. Broil for an additional 2 to 3 minutes, until the cheese topping is slightly browned. 9. Allow to cool for 5 to 10 minutes, then serve.

Per Serving:

calories: 555 | fat: 49g | protein: 23g | carbs: 7g | net carbs: 5g | fiber: 2g

Lemony Salmon

Prep time: 30 minutes | Cook time: 10 minutes | Serves 4

- 1½ pounds (680 g) salmon steak
- ½ teaspoon grated lemon zest
- Freshly cracked mixed peppercorns, to taste
- ⅓ cup lemon juice
- Fresh chopped chives, for garnish
- ½ cup dry white wine
- ½ teaspoon fresh cilantro, chopped
- Fine sea salt, to taste

1. To prepare the marinade, place all ingredients, except for salmon steak and chives, in a deep pan. Bring to a boil over medium-high flame until it has reduced by half. Allow it to cool down. 2. After that, allow salmon steak to marinate in the refrigerator approximately 40 minutes. Discard the marinade and transfer the fish steak to the preheated air fryer. 3. Air fry at 400ºF (204ºC) for 9 to 10 minutes. To finish, brush hot fish steaks with the reserved marinade, garnish with fresh chopped chives, and serve right away!

Per Serving:

calories: 319 | fat: 17g | protein: 37g | carbs: 3g | net carbs: 2g | fiber: 1g

Dill Lemon Salmon

Prep time: 10 minutes | Cook time: 4 minutes | Serves 4

- 1 pound (454 g) salmon fillet
- 1 tablespoon butter, melted
- 2 tablespoons lemon juice
- 1 teaspoon dried dill
- 1 cup water

1. Cut the salmon fillet on 4 servings. 2. Line the instant pot baking pan with foil and put the salmon fillets inside in one layer. 3. Then sprinkle the fish with dried dill, lemon juice, and butter. 4. Pour water in the instant pot and insert the rack. 5. Place the baking pan with salmon on the rack and close the lid. 6. Cook the meal on Manual mode (High Pressure) for 4 minutes. Allow the natural pressure release for 5 minutes and remove the fish from the instant pot.

Per Serving:

calories: 178 | fat: 10g | protein: 22g | carbs: 0g | net carbs: 0g | fiber: 0g

Parmesan-Garlic Salmon with Asparagus

Prep time: 10 minutes | Cook time: 15 minutes | Serves 2

- 2 (6-ounce) salmon fillets, skin on
- Pink Himalayan salt
- Freshly ground black pepper
- 1 pound fresh asparagus, ends snapped off
- 3 tablespoons butter
- 2 garlic cloves, minced
- ¼ cup grated Parmesan cheese

1. Preheat the oven to 400°F. Line a baking sheet with aluminum foil or a silicone baking mat. 2. Pat the salmon dry with a paper towel, and season both sides with pink Himalayan salt and pepper. 3. Place the salmon in the middle of the prepared pan, and arrange the asparagus around the salmon. 4. In a small saucepan over medium heat, melt the butter. Add the minced garlic and stir until the garlic just begins to brown, about 3 minutes. 5. Drizzle the garlic-butter sauce over the salmon and asparagus, and top both with the Parmesan cheese. 6. Bake until the salmon is cooked and the asparagus is crisp-tender, about 12 minutes. You can switch the oven to broil at the end of cooking time for about 3 minutes to get a nice char on the asparagus. 7. Serve hot.

Per Serving:

calories: 434 | fat: 26g | protein: 42g | carbs: 10g | net carbs: 6g | fiber: 5g

Coconut Shrimp with Spicy Dipping Sauce

Prep time: 15 minutes | Cook time: 8 minutes | Serves 4

- 1 (2½-ounce / 71-g) bag pork rinds
- ¾ cup unsweetened shredded coconut flakes
- ¾ cup coconut flour
- 1 teaspoon onion powder
- 1 teaspoon garlic powder
- 2 eggs
- 1½ pounds (680 g) large shrimp, peeled and deveined
- ½ teaspoon salt
- ¼ teaspoon freshly ground black pepper

Spicy Dipping Sauce:
- ½ cup mayonnaise
- 2 tablespoons Sriracha
- Zest and juice of ½ lime
- 1 clove garlic, minced

1. Preheat the air fryer to 390ºF (199ºC). 2. In a food processor fitted with a metal blade, combine the pork rinds and coconut flakes. Pulse until the mixture resembles coarse crumbs. Transfer to a shallow bowl. 3. In another shallow bowl, combine the coconut flour, onion powder, and garlic powder; mix until thoroughly combined. 4. In a third shallow bowl, whisk the eggs until slightly frothy. 5. In a large bowl, season the shrimp with the salt and pepper, tossing gently to coat. 6. Working a few pieces at a time, dredge the shrimp in the flour mixture, followed by the eggs, and finishing with the pork rind crumb mixture. Arrange the shrimp on a baking sheet until ready to air fry. 7. Working in batches if necessary, arrange the shrimp in a single layer in the air fryer basket. Pausing halfway through the cooking time to turn the shrimp, air fry for 8 minutes until cooked through. 8. To make the sauce: In a small bowl, combine the mayonnaise, Sriracha, lime zest and juice, and garlic. Whisk until thoroughly combined. Serve alongside the shrimp.

Per Serving:

calories: 473 | fat: 33g | protein: 30g | carbs: 13g | net carbs: 7g | fiber: 6g

Mahi-Mahi Fillets with Peppers

Prep time: 10 minutes | Cook time: 3 minutes | Serves 3

- 2 sprigs fresh rosemary
- 2 sprigs dill, tarragon
- 1 sprig fresh thyme
- 1 cup water
- 1 lemon, sliced
- 3 mahi-mahi fillets
- 2 tablespoons coconut oil,
- melted
- Sea salt and ground black pepper, to taste
- 1 serrano pepper, seeded and sliced
- 1 green bell pepper, sliced
- 1 red bell pepper, sliced

1. Add the herbs, water, and lemon slices to the Instant Pot and insert a steamer basket. 2. Arrange the mahi-mahi fillets in the steamer basket. 3. Drizzle the melted coconut oil over the top and season with the salt and black pepper. 4. Lock the lid. Select the Manual mode and set the cooking time for 3 minutes at Low Pressure. 5. When the timer beeps, perform a natural pressure release for 10 minutes, then release any remaining pressure. Carefully remove the lid. 6. Place the peppers on top. Select the Sauté mode and let it simmer for another 1 minute. 7. Serve immediately.

Per Serving:

calories: 454 | fat: 15g | protein: 76g | carbs: 4g | net carbs: 4g | fiber: 1g

Almond Pesto Salmon

Prep time: 5 minutes | Cook time: 12 minutes | Serves 2

- ¼ cup pesto
- ¼ cup sliced almonds, roughly chopped
- 2 (1½-inch-thick) salmon
- fillets (about 4 ounces / 113 g each)
- 2 tablespoons unsalted butter, melted

1. In a small bowl, mix pesto and almonds. Set aside. 2. Place fillets into a round baking dish. 3. Brush each fillet with butter and place half of the pesto mixture on the top of each fillet. Place dish into the air fryer basket. 4. Adjust the temperature to 390ºF (199ºC) and set the timer for 12 minutes. 5. Salmon will easily flake when fully cooked and reach an internal temperature of at least 145ºF (63ºC). Serve warm.

Per Serving:

calories: 610 | fat: 50g | protein: 33g | carbs: 6g | net carbs: 5g | fiber: 1g

Salmon Fritters with Zucchini

Prep time: 15 minutes | Cook time: 12 minutes | Serves 4

- 2 tablespoons almond flour
- 1 zucchini, grated
- 1 egg, beaten
- 6 ounces (170 g) salmon
- fillet, diced
- 1 teaspoon avocado oil
- ½ teaspoon ground black pepper

1. Mix almond flour with zucchini, egg, salmon, and ground black pepper. 2. Then make the fritters from the salmon mixture. 3. Sprinkle the air fryer basket with avocado oil and put the fritters inside. 4. Cook the fritters at 375ºF (191ºC) for 6 minutes per side.

Per Serving:

calories: 115 | fat: 6g | protein: 9g | carbs: 7g | net carbs: 4g | fiber: 3g

Chapter 4

Poultry

Chapter 4 Poultry

Buttered Duck Breast

Prep time: 10 minutes | Cook time: 12 minutes | Serves 1

- 1 medium duck breast, skin scored
- 1 tablespoon heavy cream
- 2 tablespoons butter
- Salt and black pepper, to taste
- 1 cup kale
- ¼ teaspoon fresh sage

1. Set the pan over medium heat and warm half of the butter. Place in sage and heavy cream, and cook for 2 minutes. Set another pan over medium heat. Place in the remaining butter and duck breast as the skin side faces down, cook for 4 minutes, flip, and cook for 3 more minutes. 2. Place the kale to the pan containing the sauce, cook for 1 minute. Set the duck breast on a flat surface and slice. Arrange the duck slices on a platter and drizzle over the sauce.

Per Serving:

calories: 485 | fat: 37g | protein: 35g | carbs: 3g | net carbs: 2g | fiber: 1g

Chicken Rollatini with Ricotta, Prosciutto, and Spinach

Prep time: 15 minutes | Cook time: 35 minutes | Serves 4

- 4 (3-ounce) boneless skinless chicken breasts, pounded to about ⅓ inch thick
- 4 ounces ricotta cheese
- 4 slices prosciutto (4 ounces)
- 1 cup fresh spinach
- ½ cup almond flour
- ½ cup grated Parmesan cheese
- 2 eggs, beaten
- ¼ cup good-quality olive oil

1. Preheat the oven. Set the oven temperature to 400°F. 2. Prepare the chicken. Pat the chicken breasts dry with paper towels. Spread ¼ of the ricotta in the middle of each breast. Place the prosciutto over the ricotta and ¼ cup of the spinach on the prosciutto. Fold the long edges of the chicken breast over the filling, then roll the chicken breast up to enclose the filling. Place the rolls seam-side down on your work surface. 3. Bread the chicken. On a plate, stir together the almond flour and Parmesan and set it next to the beaten eggs. Carefully dip a chicken roll in the egg, then roll it in the almond-flour mixture until it is completely covered. Set the rolls seam-side down on your work surface. Repeat with the other rolls. 4. Brown the rolls. In a medium skillet over medium heat, warm the olive oil. Place the rolls seam-side down in the skillet and brown them on all sides, turning them carefully, about 10 minutes in total. Transfer the rolls, seam-side down, to a 9-by-9-inch baking dish. 5. Bake. Bake the chicken rolls for 25 minutes, or until they're cooked through. 6. Serve. Place one chicken roll on each of four plates and serve them immediately.

Per Serving:

calories: 438 | fat: 30g | protein: 40g | carbs: 2g | net carbs: 2g | fiber: 0g

Silky Chicken with Mushroom Sauce

Prep time: 10 minutes | Cook time: 20 minutes | Serves 4

- 4 (4.2-ounce) boneless, skinless chicken breasts
- 4 tablespoons olive oil, divided
- 2 cups sliced mushrooms
- ½ cup diced onion
- 2 tablespoons unblanched almond flour
- 1 clove garlic, peeled and minced
- ½ cup half and half, divided
- 2 tablespoons chopped dried thyme
- ¼ teaspoon salt
- ¼ teaspoon black pepper

1. Pound chicken breasts to even thickness, about ¼" thick. 2. In a large sauté pan over medium heat, heat 2 tablespoons olive oil and then add chicken. Cook 1–2 minutes until brown on each side. Reduce heat to low. 3. Cover with secure lid and let cook additional 15 minutes (flipping at 7½ minutes). After 15 minutes, remove chicken from pan, and cover to keep warm. 4. In same pan, add mushrooms, 2 tablespoons oil, and onion. Cook over medium heat 10–15 minutes, stirring regularly. Stir in almond flour to thicken and cook an additional 2–3 minutes. 5. Add garlic, ¼ cup half and half, thyme, salt, and pepper. Keep stirring, adding more half and half if needed until the desired consistency is achieved. 6. Serve warm chicken on a plate topped with mushroom sauce.

Per Serving:

calories: 444 | fat: 29g | protein: 37g | carbs: 9g | net carbs: 7g | fiber: 2g

Chicken Scarpariello with Spicy Sausage

Prep time: 10 minutes | Cook time: 45 minutes | Serves 6

- 1 pound boneless chicken thighs
- Sea salt, for seasoning
- Freshly ground black pepper, for seasoning
- 3 tablespoons good-quality olive oil, divided
- ½ pound Italian sausage
- (sweet or hot)
- 1 tablespoon minced garlic
- 1 pimiento, chopped
- ¼ cup dry white wine
- 1 cup chicken stock
- 2 tablespoons chopped fresh parsley

1. Preheat the oven. Set the oven temperature to 425°F. 2. Brown the chicken and sausage. Pat the chicken thighs dry with paper towels and season them lightly with salt and pepper. In a large oven-safe skillet over medium-high heat, warm 2 tablespoons of the olive oil. Add the chicken thighs and sausage to the skillet and brown them on all sides, turning them carefully, about 10 minutes. 3. Bake the chicken and sausage. Place the skillet in the oven and bake for 25 minutes or until the chicken is cooked through. Take the skillet out of the oven, transfer the chicken and sausage to a plate, and put the skillet over medium heat on the stovetop. 4. Make the sauce. Warm the remaining 1 tablespoon of olive oil, add the garlic and pimiento, and sauté for 3 minutes. Add the white wine and deglaze the skillet by using a spoon to scrape up any browned bits from the bottom of the skillet. Pour in the chicken stock and bring it to a boil, then reduce the heat to low and simmer until the sauce reduces by about half, about 6 minutes. 5. Finish and serve. Return the chicken and sausage to the skillet, toss it to coat it with the sauce, and serve it topped with the parsley.

Per Serving:

calories: 370 | fat: 30g | protein: 19g | carbs: 3g | net carbs: 3g | fiber: 0g

Classic Chicken Salad

Prep time: 5 minutes | Cook time: 12 minutes | Serves 8

- 2 pounds (907 g) chicken breasts
- 1 cup vegetable broth
- 2 sprigs fresh thyme
- 1 teaspoon granulated garlic
- 1 teaspoon onion powder
- 1 bay leaf
- ½ teaspoon ground black
- pepper
- 1 cup mayonnaise
- 2 stalks celery, chopped
- 2 tablespoons chopped fresh chives
- 1 teaspoon fresh lemon juice
- 1 teaspoon Dijon mustard
- ½ teaspoon coarse sea salt

1. Combine the chicken, broth, thyme, garlic, onion powder, bay

leaf, and black pepper in the Instant Pot. 2. Lock the lid. Select the Poultry mode and set the cooking time for 12 minutes at High Pressure. 3. When the timer beeps, perform a natural pressure release for 10 minutes, then release any remaining pressure. Carefully remove the lid. 4. Remove the chicken from the Instant Pot and let rest for a few minutes until cooled slightly. 5. Slice the chicken breasts into strips and place in a salad bowl. Add the remaining ingredients and gently stir until well combined. Serve immediately.

Per Serving:

calories: 348 | fat: 27g | protein: 25g | carbs: 2g | net carbs: 1g | fiber: 0g

Peruvian Chicken with Green Herb Sauce

Prep time: 30 minutes | Cook time: 15 minutes | Serves 4

Chicken:
- 4 boneless, skinless chicken thighs (about 1½ pounds / 680 g)
- 2 teaspoons grated lemon zest
- 2 tablespoons fresh lemon juice
- 1 tablespoon extra-virgin

Sauce:
- 1 cup fresh cilantro leaves
- 1 jalapeño, seeded and coarsely chopped
- 1 garlic clove, minced
- 1 tablespoon extra-virgin

- olive oil
- 1 serrano chile, seeded and minced
- 1 teaspoon ground cumin
- ½ teaspoon dried oregano, crushed
- ½ teaspoon kosher salt

- olive oil
- 2½ teaspoons fresh lime juice
- ¼ teaspoon kosher salt
- ⅓ cup mayonnaise

1. For the chicken: Use a fork to pierce the chicken all over to allow the marinade to penetrate better. In a small bowl, combine the lemon zest, lemon juice, olive oil, serrano, cumin, oregano, and salt. Place the chicken in a large bowl or large resealable plastic bag. Pour the marinade over the chicken. Toss to coat. Marinate at room temperature for 30 minutes, or cover and refrigerate for up to 24 hours. 2. Place the chicken in the air fryer basket. (Discard remaining marinade.) Set the air fryer to 350ºF (177ºC) for 15 minutes, turning halfway through the cooking time. 3. Meanwhile, for the sauce: Combine the cilantro, jalapeño, garlic, olive oil, lime juice, and salt in a blender. Blend until combined. Add the mayonnaise and blend until puréed. Transfer to a small bowl. Cover and chill until ready to serve. 4. At the end of the cooking time, use a meat thermometer to ensure the chicken has reached an internal temperature of 165ºF (74ºC). Serve the chicken with the sauce.

Per Serving:

calories: 384 | fat: 28g | protein: 24g | carbs: 7g | net carbs: 6g | fiber: 1g

Cheese Stuffed Chicken

Prep time: 15 minutes | Cook time: 20 minutes | Serves 4

- 12 ounces (340 g) chicken fillet
- 4 ounces (113 g) provolone cheese, sliced
- 1 tablespoon cream cheese
- ½ teaspoon dried cilantro
- ½ teaspoon smoked paprika
- 1 cup water, for cooking

1. Beat the chicken fillet well and rub it with dried cilantro and smoked paprika. 2. Then spread it with cream cheese and top with Provolone cheese. 3. Roll the chicken fillet into the roll and wrap in the foil. 4. Pour water and insert the rack in the instant pot. 5. Place the chicken roll on the rack. Close and seal the lid. 6. Cook it on Manual mode (High Pressure) for 20 minutes. 7. Make a quick pressure release and slice the chicken roll into the servings.

Per Serving:

calories: 271 | fat: 15g | protein: 32g | carbs: 1g | net carbs: 1g | fiber: 0g

Chicken Strips with Satay Sauce

Prep time: 15 minutes | Cook time: 10 minutes | Serves 4

- 4 (6-ounce / 170-g) boneless, skinless chicken breasts, sliced into 16 (1-inch) strips

Sauce:
- ¼ cup creamy almond butter (or sunflower seed butter for nut-free)
- 2 tablespoons chicken broth
- 1½ tablespoons coconut vinegar or unseasoned rice vinegar

For Garnish/Serving (Optional):
- ¼ cup chopped cilantro leaves
- Red pepper flakes
- Sea salt flakes
- Thinly sliced red, orange, and

- 1 teaspoon fine sea salt
- 1 teaspoon paprika

- 1 clove garlic, minced
- 1 teaspoon peeled and minced fresh ginger
- ½ teaspoon hot sauce
- ⅛ teaspoon stevia glycerite, or 2 to 3 drops liquid stevia

yellow bell peppers
- Special Equipment:
- 16 wooden or bamboo skewers, soaked in water for 15 minutes

1. Spray the air fryer basket with avocado oil. Preheat the air fryer to 400°F (204°C). 2. Thread the chicken strips onto the skewers. Season on all sides with the salt and paprika. Place the chicken skewers in the air fryer basket and air fry for 5 minutes, flip, and cook for another 5 minutes, until the chicken is cooked through and the internal temperature reaches 165°F (74°C). 3. While the chicken skewers cook, make the sauce: In a medium-sized bowl, stir together all the sauce ingredients until well combined. Taste and

adjust the sweetness and heat to your liking. 4. Garnish the chicken with cilantro, red pepper flakes, and salt flakes, if desired, and serve with sliced bell peppers, if desired. Serve the sauce on the side. 5. Store leftovers in an airtight container in the fridge for up to 4 days or in the freezer for up to a month. Reheat in a preheated 350°F (177°C) air fryer for 3 minutes per side, or until heated through.

Per Serving:

calories: 440 | fat: 22g | protein: 52g | carbs: 9g | net carbs: 5g | fiber: 2g

Turkey Taco Boats

Prep time: 10 minutes | Cook time: 30 minutes | Serves 4

- 1 pound lean ground turkey
- 1 (1-ounce) package taco seasoning
- ¾ cup water
- ½ small onion, peeled and finely chopped
- ½ large green bell pepper, seeded and chopped
- 1 (4-ounce) can tomato sauce
- 8 large romaine lettuce leaves
- 1 small tomato, diced

1. In a medium pan over medium heat, brown turkey. (There shouldn't be any fat to drain.) Stir in seasoning packet and water. 2. Add onion, bell pepper, and tomato sauce to meat and stir. Cover and reduce heat to low for 15 minutes. 3. Add two lettuce "boats" per plate and fill one-eighth of the meat mixture into each boat. 4. Top with fresh tomato and serve.

Per Serving:

calories: 220 | fat: 9g | protein: 23g | carbs: 10g | net carbs: 7g | fiber: 3g

Paprika Chicken Wings

Prep time: 10 minutes | Cook time: 13 minutes | Serves 4

- 1 pound (454 g) boneless chicken wings
- 1 teaspoon ground paprika
- 1 teaspoon avocado oil
- ¼ teaspoon minced garlic
- ¾ cup beef broth

1. Pour the avocado oil in the instant pot. 2. Rub the chicken wings with ground paprika and minced garlic and put them in the instant pot. 3. Cook the chicken on Sauté mode for 4 minutes from each side. 4. Then add beef broth and close the lid. 5. Sauté the meal for 5 minutes more.

Per Serving:

calories: 226 | fat: 9g | protein: 34g | carbs: 1g | net carbs: 1g | fiber: 0g

Crunchy Chicken Tacos

Prep time: 5 minutes | Cook time: 30 minutes to 8 hours | Serves 4

- 1 pound (454 g) frozen boneless, skinless chicken thighs
- 1 cup chicken broth
- 1 cup low-carb green salsa
- ½ medium onion, chopped
- 2 teaspoons minced garlic
- 8 slices provolone cheese
- 1 cup shredded lettuce
- ¼ cup chopped ripe tomato
- ½ cup sour cream

1. In a slow cooker or electric pressure cooker, combine the chicken thighs, broth, salsa, onion, and garlic. 2. Place the lid on the pot. If using a slow cooker, cook on the low setting for 7 to 8 hours or on high for 3 to 4 hours. If using a pressure cooker, cook for 20 minutes on high pressure, then quick-release the pressure. 3. Place a slice of the provolone on a piece of parchment paper (not wax paper). Microwave on high power for 45 seconds; the cheese should just begin to turn a brownish orange in a few spots. 4. Quickly and carefully remove the parchment paper from the microwave. Holding opposite edges of the paper, form the melted cheese into a U shape. Hold it in this position for about 10 seconds, until it cools enough to hold its shape. (You can also hang the microwaved cheese slice over a wooden spoon handle to form the shape.) Remove the taco from the parchment paper. Repeat with the remaining 7 cheese slices. 5. Using a slotted spoon, remove the chicken from the cooker. Using 2 forks, shred the chicken, then return it to the cooker. 6. Use tongs or a slotted spoon to fill the tacos with equal portions of the chicken, being careful to drain off some of the liquid so the tacos don't get soggy. 7. Top the chicken filling with shredded lettuce, tomato, and sour cream, then serve.

Per Serving:

calories: 528 | fat: 40g | protein: 35g | carbs: 8g | net carbs: 6g | fiber: 2g

Italian Chicken with Sauce

Prep time: 15 minutes | Cook time: 20 minutes | Serves 4

- 2 large skinless chicken breasts (about 1¼ pounds / 567 g)
- Salt and freshly ground black pepper
- ½ cup almond meal
- ½ cup grated Parmesan cheese
- 2 teaspoons Italian seasoning
- 1 egg, lightly beaten
- 1 tablespoon olive oil
- 1 cup no-sugar-added marinara sauce
- 4 slices Mozzarella cheese or ½ cup shredded Mozzarella

1. Preheat the air fryer to 360°F (182°C). 2. Slice the chicken breasts in half horizontally to create 4 thinner chicken breasts. Working with one piece at a time, place the chicken between two pieces of parchment paper and pound with a meat mallet or rolling pin to flatten to an even thickness. Season both sides with salt and freshly ground black pepper. 3. In a large shallow bowl, combine the almond meal, Parmesan, and Italian seasoning; stir until thoroughly combined. Place the egg in another large shallow bowl. 4. Dip the chicken in the egg, followed by the almond meal mixture, pressing the mixture firmly into the chicken to create an even coating. 5. Working in batches if necessary, arrange the chicken breasts in a single layer in the air fryer basket and coat both sides lightly with olive oil. Pausing halfway through the cooking time to flip the chicken, air fry for 15 minutes, or until a thermometer inserted into the thickest part registers 165°F (74°C). 6. Spoon the marinara sauce over each piece of chicken and top with the Mozzarella cheese. Air fry for an additional 3 to 5 minutes until the cheese is melted.

Per Serving:

calories: 462 | fat: 27g | protein: 46g | carbs: 9g | net carbs: 7g | fiber: 2g

Fried Chicken Breasts

Prep time: 30 minutes | Cook time: 12 to 14 minutes | Serves 4

- 1 pound (454 g) boneless, skinless chicken breasts
- ¾ cup dill pickle juice
- ¾ cup finely ground blanched almond flour
- ¾ cup finely grated Parmesan
- cheese
- ½ teaspoon sea salt
- ½ teaspoon freshly ground black pepper
- 2 large eggs
- Avocado oil spray

1. Place the chicken breasts in a zip-top bag or between two pieces of plastic wrap. Using a meat mallet or heavy skillet, pound the chicken to a uniform ½-inch thickness. 2. Place the chicken in a large bowl with the pickle juice. Cover and allow to brine in the refrigerator for up to 2 hours. 3. In a shallow dish, combine the almond flour, Parmesan cheese, salt, and pepper. In a separate, shallow bowl, beat the eggs. 4. Drain the chicken and pat it dry with paper towels. Dip in the eggs and then in the flour mixture, making sure to press the coating into the chicken. Spray both sides of the coated breasts with oil. 5. Spray the air fryer basket with oil and put the chicken inside. Set the temperature to 400°F (204°C) and air fry for 6 to 7 minutes. 6. Carefully flip the breasts with a spatula. Spray the breasts again with oil and continue cooking for 6 to 7 minutes more, until golden and crispy.

Per Serving:

calories: 450 | fat: 27g | protein: 44g | carbs: 6g | net carbs: 4g | fiber: 2g

Chicken and Scallions Stuffed Peppers

Prep time: 5 minutes | Cook time: 20 minutes | Serves 5

- 1 tablespoon butter, at room temperature
- ½ cup scallions, chopped
- 1 pound (454 g) ground chicken
- ½ teaspoon sea salt
- ½ teaspoon chili powder
- ⅓ teaspoon paprika
- ⅓ teaspoon ground cumin
- ¼ teaspoon shallot powder
- 6 ounces (170 g) goat cheese, crumbled
- 1½ cups water
- 5 bell peppers, tops, membrane, and seeds removed
- ½ cup sour cream

1. Set your Instant Pot to Sauté and melt the butter. 2. Add the scallions and chicken and sauté for 2 to 3 minutes. 3. Stir in the sea salt, chili powder, paprika, cumin, and shallot powder. Add the crumbled goat cheese, stir, and reserve the mixture in a bowl. 4. Clean your Instant Pot. Pour the water into the Instant Pot and insert the trivet. 5. Stuff the bell peppers with enough of the chicken mixture, and don't pack the peppers too tightly. Put the peppers on the trivet. 6. Lock the lid. Select the Poultry mode and set the cooking time for 15 minutes at High Pressure. 7. When the timer beeps, perform a natural pressure release for 10 minutes, then release any remaining pressure. Carefully remove the lid. 8. Remove from the Instant Pot and serve with the sour cream.

Per Serving:

calories: 338 | fat: 20g | protein: 30g | carbs: 9g | net carbs: 7g | fiber: 1g

Poulet en Papillote

Prep time: 10 minutes | Cook time: 45 minutes | Serves 4

- 4 chicken breasts, skinless, scored
- 4 tablespoons white wine
- 2 tablespoons olive oil + extra for drizzling
- 4 tablespoons butter
- 3 cups mixed mushrooms, teared up
- 1 medium celeriac, peeled, chopped
- 2 cups water
- 3 cloves garlic, minced
- 4 sprigs thyme, chopped
- 3 lemons, juiced
- Salt and black pepper to taste
- 2 tablespoons Dijon mustard

1. Preheat the oven to 450°F. 2. Arrange the celeriac on a baking sheet, drizzle it with a little oil, and bake for 20 minutes; set aside. 3. In a bowl, evenly mix the chicken, roasted celeriac, mushrooms, garlic, thyme, lemon juice, salt, black pepper, and mustard. Make 4 large cuts of foil, fold them in half, and then fold them in half again. Tightly fold the two open edges together to create a bag. 4.

Now, share the chicken mixture into each bag, top with the white wine, olive oil, and a tablespoon of butter. Seal the last open end securely making sure not to pierce the bag. Put the bag on a baking tray and bake the chicken in the middle of the oven for 25 minutes.

Per Serving:

calories: 333 | fat: 21g | protein: 29g | carbs: 7g | net carbs: 3g | fiber: 4g

Herby Chicken Meatballs

Prep time: 10 minutes | Cook time: 16 minutes | Serves 3

- 1 pound ground chicken
- Salt and black pepper, to taste
- 2 tablespoons ranch dressing
- ½ cup almond flour
- ¼ cup mozzarella cheese, grated
- 1 tablespoon dry Italian seasoning
- ¼ cup hot sauce + more for serving
- 1 egg

1. In a bowl, combine chicken meat, pepper, ranch dressing, Italian seasoning, flour, hot sauce, mozzarella cheese, salt, and the egg. Form 9 meatballs, arrange them on a lined baking tray and cook for 16 minutes at 480°F. Place the chicken meatballs in a bowl and serve with the hot sauce.

Per Serving:

calories: 390 | fat: 26g | protein: 36g | carbs: 3g | net carbs: 2g | fiber: 1g

Cilantro Lime Chicken Thighs

Prep time: 15 minutes | Cook time: 22 minutes | Serves 4

- 4 bone-in, skin-on chicken thighs
- 1 teaspoon baking powder
- ½ teaspoon garlic powder
- 2 teaspoons chili powder
- 1 teaspoon cumin
- 2 medium limes
- ¼ cup chopped fresh cilantro

1. Pat chicken thighs dry and sprinkle with baking powder. 2. In a small bowl, mix garlic powder, chili powder, and cumin and sprinkle evenly over thighs, gently rubbing on and under chicken skin. 3. Cut one lime in half and squeeze juice over thighs. Place chicken into the air fryer basket. 4. Adjust the temperature to 380°F (193°C) and roast for 22 minutes. 5. Cut other lime into four wedges for serving and garnish cooked chicken with wedges and cilantro.

Per Serving:

calories: 287 | fat: 20g | protein: 23g | carbs: 4g | net carbs: 3g | fiber: 1g

Rotisserie Chicken

Prep time: 5 minutes | Cook time: 8 hours | Serves 2

- Nonstick cooking spray
- 3 garlic cloves, crushed
- 1 teaspoon salt
- 1½ teaspoons ground smoked paprika
- 1 teaspoon dried thyme leaves
- ¼ teaspoon freshly ground black pepper
- 1 (2½ to 3 pounds / 1.1 to 1.4 kg) roasting or broiler chicken
- 1 lemon

1. Spray the slow cooker with nonstick cooking spray. Tear off 4 (18-inch-long) pieces of foil. Scrunch the foil into balls and place in the slow cooker. 2. In a small bowl, mix the crushed garlic, salt, paprika, thyme, and pepper until well combined. Sprinkle one-quarter of this mixture inside the chicken; rub the rest onto the chicken skin. 3. Roll the lemon on the counter beneath your palm to soften it. Quarter the lemon. Put 2 quarters inside the chicken. Squeeze the remaining 2 quarters over the chicken, and put those pieces in the slow cooker between the foil balls. 4. Place the chicken, breast-side down, on top of the foil balls. 5. Cover and cook on low for 8 hours, or until the chicken registers 165ºF (74ºC) on a meat thermometer and is very tender. 6. Carve and serve.

Per Serving:

calories: 547 | fat: 13g | protein: 98g | carbs: 4g | net carbs: 3g | fiber: 1g

Chicken Patties

Prep time: 15 minutes | Cook time: 12 minutes | Serves 4

- 1 pound (454 g) ground chicken thigh meat
- ½ cup shredded Mozzarella cheese
- 1 teaspoon dried parsley
- ½ teaspoon garlic powder
- ¼ teaspoon onion powder
- 1 large egg
- 2 ounces (57 g) pork rinds, finely ground

1. In a large bowl, mix ground chicken, Mozzarella, parsley, garlic powder, and onion powder. Form into four patties. 2. Place patties in the freezer for 15 to 20 minutes until they begin to firm up. 3. Whisk egg in a medium bowl. Place the ground pork rinds into a large bowl. 4. Dip each chicken patty into the egg and then press into pork rinds to fully coat. Place patties into the air fryer basket. 5. Adjust the temperature to 360ºF (182ºC) and air fry for 12 minutes. 6. Patties will be firm and cooked to an internal temperature of 165ºF (74ºC) when done. Serve immediately.

Per Serving:

calories: 334 | fat: 21g | protein: 32g | carbs: 2g | net carbs: 1g | fiber: 1g

Chicken Paella with Chorizo

Prep time: 15 minutes | Cook time: 45 minutes | Serves 6

- 18 chicken drumsticks
- 12 ounces chorizo, chopped
- 1 white onion, chopped
- 4 ounces jarred piquillo peppers, finely diced
- 2 tablespoons olive oil
- ½ cup chopped parsley
- 1 teaspoon smoked paprika
- 2 tablespoons tomato puree
- ½ cup white wine
- 1 cup chicken broth
- 2 cups cauli rice
- 1 cup chopped green beans
- 1 lemon, cut in wedges
- Salt and pepper, to taste

1. Preheat the oven to 350ºF. 2. Heat the olive oil in a cast iron pan over medium heat, meanwhile season the chicken with salt and black pepper, and fry in the hot oil on both sides for 10 minutes to lightly brown. After, remove onto a plate with a perforated spoon. 3. Then, add the chorizo and onion to the hot oil, and sauté for 4. minutes. Include the tomato puree, piquillo peppers, and paprika, and let simmer for 2 minutes. Add the broth, and bring the ingredients to boil for 6 minutes until slightly reduced. 4Stir in the cauli rice, white wine, green beans, half of the parsley, and lay the chicken on top. Transfer the pan to the oven and continue cooking for 20 to 25 minutes. Let the paella sit to cool for 10 minutes before serving garnished with the remaining parsley and lemon wedges.

Per Serving:

calories: 736 | fat: 46g | protein: 56g | carbs: 15g | net carbs: 11g | fiber: 4g

Parmesan Carbonara Chicken

Prep time: 15 minutes | Cook time: 25 minutes | Serves 5

- 1 pound (454 g) chicken, skinless, boneless, chopped
- 1 cup heavy cream
- 1 cup chopped spinach
- 2 ounces (57 g) Parmesan, grated
- 1 teaspoon ground black pepper
- 1 tablespoon coconut oil
- 2 ounces (57 g) bacon, chopped

1. Put the coconut oil and chopped chicken in the instant pot. 2. Sauté the chicken for 10 minutes. Stir it from time to time. 3. Then add ground black pepper, and spinach. Stir the mixture well and sauté for 5 minutes more. 4. Then add heavy cream and Parmesan. Close and seal the lid. 5. Cook the meal on Manual mode (High Pressure) for 10 minutes. Allow the natural pressure release for 10 minutes.

Per Serving:

calories: 343 | fat: 22g | protein: 35g | carbs: 2g | net carbs: 2g | fiber: 0g

Roasted Chicken Breasts with Capers

Prep time: 10 minutes | Cook time: 55 minutes | Serves 6

- 3 medium lemons, sliced
- ½ teaspoon salt
- 1 teaspoon olive oil
- 3 chicken breasts, halved
- Salt and black pepper to season
- ¼ cup almond flour
- 2 teaspoons olive oil
- 2 tablespoons capers, rinsed
- 1¼ cup chicken broth
- 2 teaspoons butter
- 1½ tablespoons chopped fresh parsley
- Parsley for garnish

1. Preheat the oven to 350ºF and lay a piece of parchment paper on a baking sheet. 2. Lay the lemon slices on the baking sheet, drizzle with olive oil and sprinkle with salt. Roast in the oven for 25 minutes to brown the lemon rinds. 3. Cover the chicken with plastic wrap, place them on a flat surface, and gently pound with the rolling pin to flatten to about ½ -inch thickness. Remove the plastic wraps and season with salt and pepper. 4. Next, dredge the chicken in the almond flour on each side, and shake off any excess flour. Set aside. 5. Heat the olive oil in a skillet over medium heat and fry the chicken on both sides to a golden brown, for about 8 minutes in total. Pour the chicken broth in, shake the skillet, and let the broth boil and reduce to a thick consistency, about 12 minutes. 6. Lightly stir in the capers, roasted lemon, pepper, butter, and parsley, and simmer on low heat for 10 minutes. Turn the heat off and serve the chicken with the sauce hot, an extra garnish of parsley with a creamy squash mash.

Per Serving:

calories: 366 | fat: 26g | protein: 27g | carbs: 6g | net carbs: 4g | fiber: 2g

Herbed Turkey Breast

Prep time: 10 minutes | Cook time: 9 hours | Serves 2

- 1 (2½- to 3-pound / 1.1- to 1.4-kg) bone-in half turkey breast
- 3 garlic cloves, cut into slivers
- 2 tablespoons chopped fresh flat-leaf parsley
- 2 tablespoons butter, at room temperature
- 1 teaspoon dried basil
- 1 teaspoon dried thyme
- ½ teaspoon dried sage leaves
- 1 teaspoon salt
- ⅛ teaspoon freshly ground black pepper
- 2 onions, sliced
- 1 cup chicken stock

1. Using a sharp knife, poke holes in the turkey breast. Push the garlic slivers and the parsley into the holes. 2. On a platter, rub the turkey with the butter and sprinkle it with the basil, thyme, sage, salt, and pepper. 3. In the slow cooker, set the turkey on top of the onions and pour the stock over everything. 4. Cover and cook on low for 8 to 9 hours, or until the turkey registers 160ºF (71ºC) on a meat thermometer. 5. Remove the turkey from the slow cooker to a clean platter and cover it with foil; let stand for 10 minutes. 6. In a saucepan over high heat, boil the liquid and onions from the slow cooker until slightly reduced, 6 to 8 minutes. 7. Slice the turkey and serve it with the gravy.

Per Serving:

calories: 968 | fat: 34g | protein: 174g | carbs: 4g | net carbs: 3g | fiber: 1g

Rubbed Whole Chicken

Prep time: 20 minutes | Cook time: 25 minutes | Serves 4

- 1½ pound (680 g) whole chicken
- 1 tablespoon poultry
- seasoning
- 2 tablespoons avocado oil
- 2 cups water

1. Pour water in the instant pot. 2. Then rub the chicken with poultry seasoning and avocado oil. 3. Put the chicken in the instant pot. Close and seal the lid. 4. Cook the meal in Manual mode for 25 minutes. When the time is finished, allow the natural pressure release for 10 minutes.

Per Serving:

calories: 335 | fat: 14g | protein: 49g | carbs: 1g | net carbs: 1g | fiber: 0g

Chicken Legs with Leeks

Prep time: 30 minutes | Cook time: 18 minutes | Serves 6

- 2 leeks, sliced
- 2 large-sized tomatoes, chopped
- 3 cloves garlic, minced
- ½ teaspoon dried oregano
- 6 chicken legs, boneless and
- skinless
- ½ teaspoon smoked cayenne pepper
- 2 tablespoons olive oil
- A freshly ground nutmeg

1. In a mixing dish, thoroughly combine all ingredients, minus the leeks. Place in the refrigerator and let it marinate overnight. 2. Lay the leeks onto the bottom of the air fryer basket. Top with the chicken legs. 3. Roast chicken legs at 375ºF (191ºC) for 18 minutes, turning halfway through. Serve with hoisin sauce.

Per Serving:

calories: 275 | fat: 15g | protein: 25g | carbs: 10g | net carbs: 8g | fiber: 2g

Chicken Wings with Thyme Chutney

Prep time: 10 minutes | Cook time: 25 minutes | Serves 4

- 12 chicken wings, cut in half
- 1 tablespoon turmeric
- 1 tablespoon cumin
- 3 tablespoons fresh ginger, grated
- 1 tablespoon cilantro, chopped
- 2 tablespoons paprika
- Salt and ground black pepper, to taste
- 3 tablespoons olive oil
- Juice of ½ lime
- 1 cup thyme leaves
- ¾ cup cilantro, chopped
- 1 tablespoon water
- 1 jalapeño pepper

1. In a bowl, stir together 1 tablespoon ginger, cumin, paprika, salt, 2 tablespoons olive oil, black pepper, and turmeric. Place in the chicken wings pieces, toss to coat, and refrigerate for 20 minutes. 2. Heat the grill, place in the marinated wings, cook for 25 minutes, turning from time to time, remove and set to a serving plate. 3. Using a blender, combine thyme, remaining ginger, salt, jalapeno pepper, black pepper, lime juice, cilantro, remaining olive oil, and water, and blend well. Drizzle the chicken wings with the sauce to serve.

Per Serving:

calories: 479 | fat: 27g | protein: 45g | carbs: 10g | net carbs: 6g | fiber: 3g

Keto Greek Avgolemono

Prep time: 10 minutes | Cook time: 30 minutes | Serves 4

- 4 bone-in, skin-on chicken thighs
- ¼ cup diced onions
- 1 sprig fresh thyme
- 4 cups chicken bone broth, homemade or store-bought, plus more if needed
- Fine sea salt and freshly
Cracklings:
- Chicken skin (from above)
- ½ teaspoon fine sea salt
- ½ teaspoon freshly ground black pepper

- ground black pepper, to taste
- 2 large eggs
- 2 tablespoons lemon juice
- 4 tablespoons extra-virgin olive oil or MCT oil, for drizzling (optional)

- 1½ teaspoons Paleo fat, such as lard, tallow, or avocado oil

1. Remove the skin from the chicken thighs and set aside (you will use it to make cracklings). Place the skinless chicken, diced onions, and thyme in a large pot and fill with broth so that the broth covers the thighs by 1 inch. Add a couple pinches each of salt and pepper. Bring to a boil and cook for 20 minutes, or until the chicken is tender and easily falls off the bone. 2. While the chicken is cooking, make the cracklings: Cut the chicken skin into ¼-inch pieces and season with the ½ teaspoon each of salt and pepper. Heat the Paleo fat in a skillet over medium-high heat, then add the chicken skin and fry until golden brown and crispy, about 8 minutes. Set the cracklings aside on a paper towel to drain. 3. When the chicken thighs are done, place them in individual serving bowls and set aside. 4. In a medium bowl, whisk the eggs and lemon juice. While whisking, very slowly pour in ½ cup of the hot broth (if you add the hot broth too quickly, the eggs will curdle). Slowly whisk another cup of hot soup into the egg mixture. 5. Pour the hot egg mixture into the pot while stirring to create a creamy soup without the cream. Reduce the heat and simmer for 10 minutes, stirring constantly. The soup will thicken slightly as it cooks. 6. Pour one-quarter (about 1 cup) of the creamy soup over each chicken thigh. Top with the cracklings. Drizzle each bowl with 1 tablespoon of olive oil, if desired. 7. This dish is best served fresh to avoid curdled eggs from reheating, but leftovers can be stored in an airtight container in the fridge for up to 2 days. Reheat in a saucepan over medium-low heat until warmed, stirring constantly to keep the eggs from curdling.

Per Serving:

calories: 275 | fat: 20g | protein: 22g | carbs: 2g | net carbs: 1g | fiber: 1g

Tangy Meatballs

Prep time: 10 minutes | Cook time: 10 minutes | Makes 20 meatballs

- 1 pound (454 g) ground chicken
- 1 egg, lightly beaten
- ½ medium onion, diced
Sauce:
- 2 teaspoons erythritol
- 1 teaspoon rice vinegar
- 1 teaspoon garlic powder
- 1 teaspoon pepper
- 1 teaspoon salt
- 1 cup water
- ½ teaspoon sriracha

1. Stir together the ground chicken, beaten egg, onion, garlic powder, salt, and pepper in a large bowl. Shape into bite-sized balls with your hands. 2. Pour the water into Instant Pot and insert a steamer basket. Put the meatballs in the basket. 3. Secure the lid. Select the Manual mode and set the cooking time for 10 minutes at High Pressure. 4. Meanwhile, whisk together all ingredients for the sauce in a separate bowl. 5. Once cooking is complete, do a quick pressure release. Carefully open the lid. 6. Toss the meatballs in the prepared sauce and serve.

Per Serving:

calories: 151 | fat: 8g | protein: 18g | carbs: 3g | net carbs: 3g | fiber: 1g

Chicken Alfredo

Prep time: 5 minutes | Cook time: 20 minutes | Serves 2

- 2 teaspoons extra-virgin olive oil, divided
- 8 ounces (227 g) boneless, skinless chicken thighs, cubed
- 2 tablespoons butter
- ½ teaspoon minced garlic
- ½ cup heavy (whipping) cream
- ⅔ cup grated Parmesan cheese
- ¼ cup shredded low-moisture mozzarella cheese
- Pinch of red pepper flakes
- Pink Himalayan sea salt
- Freshly ground black pepper
- 1 (7-ounce / 198-g) package shirataki noodles, drained, or 7 ounces / 198 g zoodles (spiralized zucchini)

1. In a small sauté pan or skillet, heat 1 teaspoon of olive oil over medium heat and cook the chicken for 10 to 12 minutes, until cooked through. 2. In a medium saucepan, melt the butter over medium heat. Add the garlic and cook for 1 to 2 minutes, until slightly browned. Add the cream and bring to a simmer. 3. Slowly add the Parmesan and mozzarella while stirring. The cheese should melt into the sauce. 4. Reduce the heat, add the chicken, and heat through, without allowing the sauce to boil. Season with the salt and pepper. 5. In the same skillet as you cooked the chicken, add the remaining 1 teaspoon of olive oil and drop in the shirataki noodles. Cook the noodles over medium heat for 2 to 3 minutes, until heated through. 6. Spoon the noodles onto 2 serving plates and top with the sauce.

Per Serving:

calories: 810 | fat: 70g | protein: 36g | carbs: 11g | net carbs: 9g | fiber: 2g

Crackling Creole Crispy Chicken Thighs

Prep time: 10 minutes | Cook time: 50 minutes | Serves 4

- Coconut or olive oil, for greasing
- ¼ teaspoon paprika
- ¼ teaspoon onion powder
- ¼ teaspoon garlic powder
- ⅛ teaspoon dried oregano
- ⅛ teaspoon dried basil
- ⅛ teaspoon dried thyme
- ⅛ teaspoon dried rosemary
- ⅛ teaspoon dried parsley
- ⅛ teaspoon cayenne pepper
- 4 skin-on, bone-in chicken thighs
- 1 yellow onion, quartered
- 8 garlic cloves, peeled and left whole
- ¼ cup extra-virgin olive oil
- 1 tablespoon freshly squeezed lemon juice

1. Preheat the oven to 350ºF (180ºC). Grease a cast iron (or other oven-safe) skillet with oil. 2. In a large bowl, stir together the paprika, onion powder, garlic powder, oregano, basil, thyme, rosemary, parsley, and cayenne. Add the chicken and toss to coat. Place the chicken in the prepared skillet, skin-side up. 3. Separate the thighs with the quartered onion and then sprinkle the whole garlic cloves throughout the skillet, preferably so that they are touching the bottom. 4. Drizzle the oil over the chicken and then the lemon juice. 5. Bake in the oven for 30 to 40 minutes until cooked through and the juices run clear. Baste the breasts with juice from the bottom of the skillet. 6. Turn the oven to broil and broil for 5 to 10 minutes, watching closely, until the skin has crisped up to your liking. 7. Remove from the oven, break apart the onion, and enjoy the chicken with the onions and caramelized garlic cloves alongside your favorite vegetable.

Per Serving:

1 thigh: calories: 392 | fat: 32g | protein: 20g | carbs: 6g | net carbs: 5g | fiber: 1g

Jamaican Jerk Chicken

Prep time: 10 minutes | Cook time: 45 minutes | Serves 4

- ¼ medium white onion
- ¼ cup extra-virgin olive oil
- 1 to 3 habanero chiles
- 2 tablespoons granulated erythritol
- 2 tablespoons jerk seasoning
- 1 tablespoon coconut aminos
- or soy sauce
- Juice of 1 lime
- 1 tablespoon minced garlic
- 4 chicken leg quarters (thighs and drumsticks)
- 2 scallions, white and green parts, sliced

1. In a food processor, combine the onion, olive oil, chiles, erythritol, jerk seasoning, coconut aminos, lime juice, and garlic. Purée on high until the mixture is smooth. Transfer this marinade to a resealable 1-gallon plastic bag. 2. Add the chicken to the bag, then seal and shake the bag until the chicken is well coated with the seasoning. Allow to marinate in the refrigerator for 12 to 24 hours, preferably 24. 3. Set a grill to high or preheat the oven to 425ºF (220ºC). 4. Remove the chicken from the marinade bag and place it on the grill or on a rack set on a baking sheet. Reserve the marinade. Cook the chicken for 30 to 35 minutes, flipping the pieces every 15 minutes. An instant-read thermometer inserted between the thigh and drumstick should read 165ºF (74ºC), and the juices should run clear when the chicken is pierced. 5. Transfer the marinade to a small saucepan and set it over high heat. Cook for about 10 minutes, or until it reaches just over 165ºF (74ºC). 6. Place the chicken on a serving platter. Top with the scallions and serve with the jerk sauce on the side.

Per Serving:

calories: 884 | fat: 68g | protein: 58g | carbs: 7g | net carbs: 6g | fiber: 1g

Chicken Piccata

Prep time: 5 minutes | Cook time: 25 minutes | Serves 4

- 4 (6-ounce / 170-g) boneless, skinless chicken breasts
- ½ teaspoon salt
- ½ teaspoon garlic powder
- ¼ teaspoon pepper
- 2 tablespoons coconut oil
- 1 cup water
- 2 cloves garlic, minced
- 4 tablespoons butter
- Juice of 1 lemon
- ¼ teaspoon xanthan gum

1. Sprinkle the chicken with salt, garlic powder, and pepper. 2. Set your Instant Pot to Sauté and melt the coconut oil. 3. Add the chicken and sear each side for about 5 to 7 minutes until golden brown. 4. Remove the chicken and set aside on a plate. 5. Pour the water into the Instant Pot. Using a wooden spoon, scrape the bottom if necessary to remove any stuck-on seasoning or meat. Insert the trivet and place the chicken on the trivet. 6. Secure the lid. Select the Manual mode and set the cooking time for 10 minutes at High Pressure. 7. Once cooking is complete, do a natural pressure release for 10 minutes, then release any remaining pressure. Carefully open the lid. 8. Remove the chicken and set aside. Strain the broth from the Instant Pot into a large bowl and return to the pot. 9. Set your Instant Pot to Sauté again and add the remaining ingredients. Cook for at least 5 minutes, stirring frequently, or until the sauce is cooked to your desired thickness. 10. Pour the sauce over the chicken and serve warm.

Per Serving:

calories: 338 | fat: 20g | protein: 32g | carbs: 2g | net carbs: 1g | fiber: 1g

Pancetta & Chicken Casserole

Prep time: 10 minutes | Cook time: 25 minutes | Serves 3

- 8 pancetta strips, chopped
- ⅓ cup Dijon mustard
- Salt and black pepper, to taste
- 1 onion, chopped
- 1 tablespoon olive oil
- 1½ cups chicken stock
- 3 chicken breasts, skinless and boneless
- ¼ teaspoon sweet paprika

1. In a bowl, combine paprika, black pepper, salt, and mustard. Sprinkle this on chicken breasts and massage. Set a pan over medium heat, stir in the pancetta, cook until it browns, and remove to a plate. 2Place oil in the same pan and heat over medium heat, add in the chicken breasts, cook for each side for 2 minutes and set aside. Put in the stock, and bring to a simmer. Stir in black pepper, pancetta, salt, and onion. Return the chicken to the pan as well, stir gently, and simmer for 20 minutes over medium heat, turning the meat halfway through. Split the chicken on serving plates, sprinkle the sauce over it to serve.

Per Serving:

calories: 438 | fat: 23g | protein: 47g | carbs: 8g | net carbs: 7g | fiber: 2g

Buttered Chicken

Prep time: 15 minutes | Cook time: 15 minutes | Serves 4

- 1 (14½-ounce / 411-g) can diced tomatoes, undrained
- 5 or 6 garlic cloves, minced
- 1 tablespoon minced fresh ginger
- 1 teaspoon ground turmeric
- 1 teaspoon cayenne
- 1 teaspoon smoked paprika
- 2 teaspoons garam masala, divided
- 1 teaspoon ground cumin
- 1 teaspoon salt
- 1 pound (454 g) boneless, skinless chicken breasts or thighs
- ½ cup unsalted butter, cut into cubes, or ½ cup coconut oil
- ½ cup heavy (whipping) cream or full-fat coconut milk
- ¼ to ½ cup chopped fresh cilantro
- 4 cups cauliflower rice or cucumber noodles

1. Put the tomatoes, garlic, ginger, turmeric, cayenne, paprika, 1 teaspoon of garam masala, cumin, and salt in the inner cooking pot of the Instant Pot. Mix thoroughly, then place the chicken pieces on top of the sauce. 2. Lock the lid into place. Select Manual and adjust the pressure to High. Cook for 10 minutes. When the cooking is complete, let the pressure release naturally. Unlock the lid. Carefully remove the chicken and set aside. 3. Using an immersion blender in the pot, blend together all the ingredients into a smooth sauce. (Or use a stand blender, but be careful with the hot sauce and be sure to leave the inside lid open to vent.) After blending, let the sauce cool before adding the remaining ingredients or it will be thinner than is ideal. 4. Add the butter cubes, cream, remaining 1 teaspoon of garam masala, and cilantro. Stir until well incorporated. The sauce should be thick enough to coat the back of a spoon when you're done. 5. Remove half the sauce and freeze it for later or refrigerate for up to 2 to 3 days. 6. Cut the chicken into bite-size pieces. Add it back to the sauce. 7. Preheat the Instant Pot by selecting Sauté and adjust to Less for low heat. Let the chicken heat through. Break it up into smaller pieces if you like, but don't shred it. 8. Serve over cauliflower rice or raw cucumber noodles.

Per Serving:

calories: 512 | fat: 36g | protein: 31g | carbs: 16g | net carbs: 10g | fiber: 6g

Brazilian Tempero Baiano Chicken Drumsticks

Prep time: 30 minutes | Cook time: 20 minutes | Serves 4

- 1 teaspoon cumin seeds
- 1 teaspoon dried oregano
- 1 teaspoon dried parsley
- 1 teaspoon ground turmeric
- ½ teaspoon coriander seeds
- 1 teaspoon kosher salt
- ½ teaspoon black peppercorns
- ½ teaspoon cayenne pepper
- ¼ cup fresh lime juice
- 2 tablespoons olive oil
- 1½ pounds (680 g) chicken drumsticks

1. In a clean coffee grinder or spice mill, combine the cumin, oregano, parsley, turmeric, coriander seeds, salt, peppercorns, and cayenne. Process until finely ground. 2. In a small bowl, combine the ground spices with the lime juice and oil. Place the chicken in a resealable plastic bag. Add the marinade, seal, and massage until the chicken is well coated. Marinate at room temperature for 30 minutes or in the refrigerator for up to 24 hours. 3. When you are ready to cook, place the drumsticks skin side up in the air fryer basket. Set the air fryer to 400°F (204°C) for 20 to 25 minutes, turning the legs halfway through the cooking time. Use a meat thermometer to ensure that the chicken has reached an internal temperature of 165°F (74°C). 4. Serve with plenty of napkins.

Per Serving:

calories: 317 | fat: 19g | protein: 29g | carbs: 5g | net carbs: 4g | fiber: 1g

Classic Whole Chicken

Prep time: 5 minutes | Cook time: 50 minutes | Serves 4

- Oil, for spraying
- 1 (4-pound / 1.8-kg) whole chicken, giblets removed
- 1 tablespoon olive oil
- 1 teaspoon paprika
- ½ teaspoon granulated garlic
- ½ teaspoon salt
- ½ teaspoon freshly ground black pepper
- ¼ teaspoon finely chopped fresh parsley, for garnish

1. Line the air fryer basket with parchment and spray lightly with oil. 2. Pat the chicken dry with paper towels. Rub it with the olive oil until evenly coated. 3. In a small bowl, mix together the paprika, garlic, salt, and black pepper and sprinkle it evenly over the chicken. 4. Place the chicken in the prepared basket, breast-side down. 5. Air fry at 360°F (182°C) for 30 minutes, flip, and cook for another 20 minutes, or until the internal temperature reaches 165°F (74°C) and the juices run clear. 6. Sprinkle with the parsley before serving.

Per Serving:

calories: 372 | fat: 23g | protein: 38g | carbs: 0g | net carbs: 0g | fiber: 0g

Caprese Chicken Thighs

Prep time: 10 minutes | Cook time: 28 minutes | Serves 4

- ⅓ cup olive oil
- 3 tablespoons balsamic vinegar, divided into 2 tablespoons and 1 tablespoon
- 1 teaspoon Italian seasoning
- ½ teaspoon garlic powder
- ½ teaspoon sea salt
- ¼ teaspoon black pepper
- 8 boneless, skinless chicken
- thighs (2½ ounces / 71 g each)
- 4 ounces (113 g) fresh Mozzarella cheese, cut into 8 slices
- 2 medium Roma (plum) tomatoes, thinly sliced
- 2 tablespoons fresh basil, cut into ribbons

1. In a large bowl, whisk together the oil, 2 tablespoons of balsamic vinegar, the Italian seasoning, garlic powder, sea salt, and black pepper. 2. Add the chicken thighs and push down into the marinade. Set aside for 20 minutes, or refrigerate until ready to use. 3. Meanwhile, preheat the oven to 375°F (190°C). Line a sheet pan with foil or parchment paper. 4. Shake off any excess marinade from each piece of chicken and arrange on the baking sheet in a single layer without touching. 5. Top each chicken thigh with a slice of Mozzarella, covering most of it. You may need to cut a piece in half to cover the chicken better. Place 2 slices of tomato on top of the Mozzarella. 6. Roast for 23 to 28 minutes, until the chicken is cooked through. You may need to pour off extra liquid from the pan at the end. 7. Drizzle the chicken with the remaining 1 tablespoon balsamic vinegar (or with a reduction by simmering more balsamic vinegar in a small saucepan). Garnish with basil ribbons.

Per Serving:

calories: 564 | fat: 46g | protein: 31g | carbs: 4g | net carbs: 4g | fiber: 0g

Chapter 5

Beef, Pork, and Lamb

Chapter 5 Beef, Pork, and Lamb

Caribbean Beef

Prep time: 20 minutes | Cook time: 1 hour 10 minutes | Serves 8

- 2 onions, chopped
- 2 tablespoons avocado oil
- 2 pounds beef stew meat, cubed
- 2 red bell peppers, seeded and chopped
- 1 habanero pepper, chopped
- 4 green chilies, chopped
- 14½ ounces canned diced

- tomatoes
- 2 tablespoons fresh cilantro, chopped
- 4 garlic cloves, minced
- ½ cup vegetable broth
- Salt and black pepper, to taste
- 1½ teaspoons cumin
- ½ cup black olives, chopped
- 1 teaspoon dried oregano

1. Set a pan over medium heat and warm avocado oil. Brown the beef on all sides; remove and set aside. Stir-fry in the red bell peppers, green chilies, oregano, garlic, habanero pepper, onions, and cumin, for about 5-6 minutes. Pour in the tomatoes and broth, and cook for 1 hour. Stir in the olives, adjust the seasonings and serve in bowls sprinkled with fresh cilantro.

Per Serving:

calories: 295 | fat: 17g | protein: 25g | carbs: 12g | net carbs: 9g | fiber: 3g

Beef Steak with Cheese Mushroom Sauce

Prep time: 6 minutes | Cook time: 30 minutes | Serves 6

- 1 tablespoon olive oil
- 1½ pounds (680 g) beef blade steak
- 1 cup stock
- 2 garlic cloves, minced

Sauce:
- 1 tablespoon butter, softened
- 2 cups sliced Porcini mushrooms
- ½ cup thinly sliced onions

- Sea salt and ground black pepper, to taste
- ½ teaspoon cayenne pepper
- 1 tablespoon coconut aminos

- ½ cup sour cream
- 4 ounces (113 g) goat cheese, crumbled

1. Press the Sauté button to heat up the Instant Pot. Then, heat the olive oil until sizzling. Once hot, cook the blade steak approximately 3 minutes or until delicately browned. 2. Add the stock, garlic, salt, black pepper, cayenne pepper, and coconut aminos. 3. Secure the lid. Choose Manual mode and High Pressure; cook for 20 minutes. Once cooking is complete, use a quick pressure release; carefully remove the lid. 4. Take the meat out of the Instant Pot. Allow it to cool slightly and then, slice it into strips. 5. Press the Sauté button again and add the butter, mushrooms and onions to the Instant Pot. Let it cook for 5 minutes longer or until the mushrooms are fragrant and the onions are softened. 6. Add sour cream and goat cheese; continue to simmer for a couple of minutes more or until everything is thoroughly heated. 7. Return the meat to the Instant Pot and serve. Bon appétit!

Per Serving:

calories: 311 | fat: 20g | protein: 31g | carbs: 3g | net carbs: 3g | fiber: 0g

Cilantro Lime Shredded Pork

Prep time: 5 minutes | Cook time: 30 minutes | Serves 4

- 1 tablespoon chili adobo sauce
- 1 tablespoon chili powder
- 2 teaspoons salt
- 1 teaspoon garlic powder
- 1 teaspoon cumin
- ½ teaspoon pepper

- 1 (2½ to 3 pounds / 1.1 to 1.4 kg) cubed pork butt
- 1 tablespoon coconut oil
- 2 cups beef broth
- 1 lime, cut into wedges
- ¼ cup chopped cilantro

1. In a small bowl, mix adobo sauce, chili powder, salt, garlic powder, cumin, and pepper. 2. Press the Sauté button on Instant Pot and add coconut oil to pot. Rub spice mixture onto cubed pork butt. Place pork into pot and sear for 3 to 5 minutes per side. Add broth. 3. Press the Cancel button. Lock Lid. Press the Manual button and adjust time to 30 minutes. 4. When timer beeps, let pressure naturally release until the float valve drops, and unlock lid. 5. Shred pork with fork. Pork should easily fall apart. For extra-crispy pork, place single layer in skillet on stove over medium heat. Cook for 10 to 15 minutes or until water has cooked out and pork becomes brown and crisp. Serve warm with fresh lime wedges and cilantro garnish.

Per Serving:

calories: 570 | fat: 36g | protein: 55g | carbs: 3g | net carbs: 2g | fiber: 1g

Beef Back Ribs with Barbecue Glaze

Prep time: 10 minutes | Cook time: 35 minutes | Serves 4

- ½ cup water
- 1 (3-pound / 1.4-kg) rack beef back ribs, prepared with rub of choice
- ¼ cup unsweetened tomato purée
- ¼ teaspoon Worcestershire sauce
- ¼ teaspoon garlic powder
- 2 teaspoons apple cider vinegar
- ¼ teaspoon liquid smoke
- ¼ teaspoon smoked paprika
- 3 tablespoons Swerve
- Dash of cayenne pepper

1. Pour the water in the pot and place the trivet inside. 2. Arrange the ribs on top of the trivet. 3. Close the lid. Select Manual mode and set cooking time for 25 minutes on High Pressure. 4. Meanwhile, prepare the glaze by whisking together the tomato purée, Worcestershire sauce, garlic powder, vinegar, liquid smoke, paprika, Swerve, and cayenne in a medium bowl. Heat the broiler. 5. When timer beeps, quick release the pressure. Open the lid. Remove the ribs and place on a baking sheet. 6. Brush a layer of glaze on the ribs. Put under the broiler for 5 minutes. 7. Remove from the broiler and brush with glaze again. Put back under the broiler for 5 more minutes, or until the tops are sticky. 8. Serve immediately.

Per Serving:

calories: 758 | fat: 27g | protein: 34g | carbs: 1g | net carbs: 1g | fiber: 0g

Pan-Seared Steak with Mushroom Sauce

Prep time: 10 minutes | Cook time: 20 minutes | Serves 4

- 4 top sirloin steaks (6 ounces / 170 g each), at room temperature
- ½ teaspoon sea salt, or more to taste
- ¼ teaspoon black pepper, or more to taste
- 4 tablespoons (½ stick) butter, divided into 2 tablespoons
- and 2 tablespoons
- 2 cloves garlic, minced
- 8 ounces (227 g) baby portobello mushrooms, thinly sliced
- ¼ cup beef broth
- 1 teaspoon fresh thyme, chopped
- ¼ cup heavy cream

1. Season the steaks on both sides with the sea salt and black pepper. Let rest at room temperature for 30 minutes. 2. Heat a large sauté pan over medium-high heat. Add 2 tablespoons of the butter

and melt. 3. Place the steaks in the pan in a single layer. Cook for the following number of minutes on each side, based on desired level of doneness (cook time will vary depending on the steak's thickness and the temperature of the pan). For best results, use a meat thermometer and remove the steak from the heat when it's 5ºF lower than the desired final temperature. Steaks will rise another 5ºF while resting. Rare: 2 to 4 minutes per side, or until 115ºF (46ºC) inside. Steak will reach 120ºF (49ºC) while resting afterward. Medium-rare: 3 to 5 minutes per side, or until 125ºF (52ºC) inside. Steak will reach 130ºF (54ºC) while resting afterward. Medium: 4 to 6 minutes per side, or until 135ºF (57ºC) inside. Steak will reach 140ºF (60ºC) while resting afterward. Medium-well: 5 to 7 minutes per side, or until 145ºF (63ºC) inside. Steak will reach 150ºF (66ºC) while resting afterward. Well-done: 7 to 9 minutes per side, or until 155ºF (68ºC) inside. Steak will reach 160ºF (71ºC) while resting afterward. 4. When the steaks in the pan reach the desired internal temperature, remove them from the pan, transfer to a plate, and cover with foil. Let the steaks rest without cutting: the steak's internal temperature will rise another 5ºF to the desired final temperature. 5. Return the sauté pan to medium heat. Melt the remaining 2 tablespoons butter. Add the garlic and sauté for about 1 minute, until fragrant. 6. Add the mushrooms, beef broth, and thyme. Scrape any browned bits from the bottom of the pan. Adjust the heat to bring to a simmer (typically at medium-high), cover, and simmer, stirring occasionally, for 5 to 8 minutes, until the mushrooms are soft. 7. Reduce the heat to medium, add the cream, and simmer for 1 to 3 minutes, until the sauce thickens. Adjust salt and pepper to taste, if needed. 8. Spoon the mushroom sauce over the steaks to serve.

Per Serving:

calories: 420 | fat: 27g | protein: 39g | carbs: 3g | net carbs: 3g | fiber: 0g

Mascarpone Pork Chops

Prep time: 10 minutes | Cook time: 12 minutes | Serves 3

- 3 pork chops
- 1 tablespoon mascarpone cheese
- 1 teaspoon ground
- peppercorns
- ½ teaspoon dried sage
- 1 tablespoon olive oil

1. In the shallow bowl, mix up peppercorns, dried sage, olive oil, and mascarpone cheese. 2. Brush the pork chops with the cheese mixture well and transfer in the instant pot. 3. Cook the meat on Sauté mode for 5 minutes from each side. 4. Then add the remaining cream cheese mixture and cook the pork chops for 2 minutes more.

Per Serving:

calories: 324 | fat: 18g | protein: 40g | carbs: 0g | net carbs: 0g | fiber: 0g

Beef Zucchini Boats

Prep time: 10 minutes | Cook time: 33 minutes | Serves 4

- 2 garlic cloves, minced
- 1 teaspoon cumin
- 1 tablespoon olive oil
- 1 pound ground beef
- ½ cup onions, chopped
- 1 teaspoon smoked paprika
- Salt and black pepper, to taste
- 4 zucchinis
- ¼ cup fresh cilantro, chopped
- ½ cup Monterey Jack cheese, shredded
- 1½ cups enchilada sauce
- 1 avocado, chopped, for serving
- Green onions, chopped, for serving
- Tomatoes, chopped, for serving

1. Set a pan over high heat and warm the oil. Add the onions, and cook for 2 minutes. Stir in the beef, and brown for 4-5 minutes. Stir in the paprika, pepper, garlic, cumin, and salt; cook for 2 minutes. 2. Slice the zucchini in half lengthwise and scoop out the seeds. Set the zucchini in a greased baking pan, stuff each with the beef, scatter enchilada sauce on top, and spread with the Monterey cheese. 3. Bake in the oven at 350ºF for 20 minutes while covered. Uncover, spread with cilantro, and bake for 5 minutes. Top with tomatoes, green onions and avocado, place on serving plates and enjoy.

Per Serving:

calories: 422 | fat: 33g | protein: 39g | carbs: 15g | net carbs: 8g | fiber: 7g

Easy Zucchini Beef Lasagna

Prep time: 10 minutes | Cook time: 45 minutes | Serves 4

- 1 pound ground beef
- 2 large zucchinis, sliced lengthwise
- 3 cloves garlic
- 1 medium white onion, finely chopped
- 3 tomatoes, chopped
- Salt and black pepper to taste
- 2 teaspoons sweet paprika
- 1 teaspoon dried thyme
- 1 teaspoon dried basil
- 1 cup shredded mozzarella cheese
- 1 tablespoon olive oil
- Cooking spray

1. Preheat the oven to 370ºF and lightly grease a baking dish with cooking spray. 2. Heat the olive oil in a skillet and cook the beef for 4 minutes while breaking any lumps as you stir. Top with onion, garlic, tomatoes, salt, paprika, and pepper. Stir and continue cooking for 5 minutes. 3. Then, lay ⅓ of the zucchini slices in the baking dish. Top with ⅓ of the beef mixture and repeat the layering process two more times with the same quantities. Season with basil and thyme. 4. Finally, sprinkle the mozzarella cheese on top and tuck the baking dish in the oven. Bake for 35 minutes. Remove the lasagna and let it rest for 10 minutes before serving.

Per Serving:

calories: 396 | fat: 27g | protein: 27g | carbs: 12g | net carbs: 9g | fiber: 3g

Pork Meatballs with Thyme

Prep time: 15 minutes | Cook time: 16 minutes | Serves 8

- 2 cups ground pork
- 1 teaspoon dried thyme
- ½ teaspoon chili flakes
- ½ teaspoon garlic powder
- 1 tablespoon coconut oil
- ¼ teaspoon ground ginger
- 3 tablespoons almond flour
- ¼ cup water

1. In the mixing bowl, mix up ground pork, dried thyme, chili flakes, garlic powder, ground ginger, and almond flour. 2. Make the meatballs. 3. Melt the coconut oil in the instant pot on Sauté mode. 4. Arrange the meatballs in the instant pot in one layer and cook them for 3 minutes from each side. 5. Then add water and cook the meatballs for 10 minutes.

Per Serving:

calories: 264 | fat: 19g | protein: 20g | carbs: 1g | net carbs: 1g | fiber: 0g

Herb Pork Chops with Raspberry Sauce

Prep time: 5 minutes | Cook time: 15 minutes | Serves 4

- 1 tablespoon olive oil + extra for brushing
- 2 pounds pork chops
- Pink salt and black pepper to taste
- 2 cups raspberries
- ¼ cup water
- 1½ tablespoons Italian Herb mix
- 3 tablespoons balsamic vinegar
- 2 teaspoons sugar-free Worcestershire sauce

1. Heat oil in a skillet over medium heat, season the pork with salt and black pepper and cook for 5 minutes on each side. Put on serving plates and reserve the pork drippings. 2. Mash the raspberries with a fork in a bowl until jam-like. Pour into a saucepan, add the water, and herb mix. Bring to boil on low heat for 4 minutes. Stir in pork drippings, vinegar, and Worcestershire sauce. 3.Simmer for 1 minute. Spoon sauce over the pork chops and serve with braised rapini.

Per Serving:

calories: 435 | fat: 22g | protein: 48g | carbs: 5g | net carbs: 1g | fiber: 4g

Beef Brisket with Cabbage

Prep time: 15 minutes | Cook time: 1 hour 7 minutes | Serves 8

- 3 pounds (1.4 kg) corned beef brisket
- 4 cups water
- 3 garlic cloves, minced
- 2 teaspoons yellow mustard seed
- 2 teaspoons black peppercorns
- 3 celery stalks, chopped
- ½ large white onion, chopped
- 1 green cabbage, cut into quarters

1. Add the brisket to the Instant Pot. Pour the water into the pot. Add the garlic, mustard seed, and black peppercorns. 2. Lock the lid. Select Meat/Stew mode and set cooking time for 50 minutes on High Pressure. 3. When cooking is complete, allow the pressure to release naturally for 20 minutes, then release any remaining pressure. Open the lid and transfer only the brisket to a platter. 4. Add the celery, onion, and cabbage to the pot. 5. Lock the lid. Select Soup mode and set cooking time for 12 minutes on High Pressure. 6. When cooking is complete, quick release the pressure. Open the lid, add the brisket back to the pot and let warm in the pot for 5 minutes. 7. Transfer the warmed brisket back to the platter and thinly slice. Transfer the vegetables to the platter. Serve hot.

Per Serving:

calories: 357 | fat: 26g | protein: 26g | carbs: 7g | net carbs: 5g | fiber: 2g

Lamb and Beef Kebabs

Prep time: 15 minutes | Cook time: 25 minutes | Serves 2

- Coconut oil cooking spray
- ¼ medium onion, chopped
- 8 ounces (227 g) ground beef (80/20)
- 8 ounces (227 g) ground lamb
- 1 large egg
- 1 garlic clove, minced
- ½ teaspoon pink Himalayan sea salt
- ½ teaspoon freshly ground black pepper
- ½ teaspoon ground sumac
- ¼ teaspoon ground turmeric
- 2 tablespoons butter, melted

1. Preheat the oven to 450°F (235°C). Line a large baking sheet with aluminum foil and spray with the cooking spray. 2. In a food processor, purée the onion on high speed until a smooth paste forms. You may need to scrape down the sides of the bowl. 3. Transfer the onion paste to a fine-mesh strainer over the sink and toss it around a few times to drain off any liquid. 4. In a large bowl, combine the onion paste with the beef, lamb, egg, garlic, salt, pepper, sumac, and turmeric. Using your hands, mix the meat with the seasonings until well combined. 5. Divide the mixture into 4 equal portions, then roll each into a cylinder. Slide metal skewers through the cylinders, if desired, or you can bake them as is. 6.

Transfer the kebabs to the baking sheet and bake for 15 minutes. 7. Brush the tops of the kebabs with the melted butter, then return them to the oven for an additional 5 to 10 minutes of baking. An instant-read thermometer should reach 155°F (68°C) when inserted in the center, and no pink should remain in the meat. 8. Let the kebabs cool for 5 minutes, then serve.

Per Serving:

calories: 724 | fat: 60g | protein: 46g | carbs: 2g | net carbs: 2g | fiber: 0g

Parmesan-Crusted Pork Chops

Prep time: 5 minutes | Cook time: 12 minutes | Serves 4

- 1 large egg
- ½ cup grated Parmesan cheese
- 4 (4-ounce / 113-g) boneless
- pork chops
- ½ teaspoon salt
- ¼ teaspoon ground black pepper

1. Whisk egg in a medium bowl and place Parmesan in a separate medium bowl. 2. Sprinkle pork chops on both sides with salt and pepper. Dip each pork chop into egg, then press both sides into Parmesan. 3. Place pork chops into ungreased air fryer basket. Adjust the temperature to 400°F (204°C) and air fry for 12 minutes, turning chops halfway through cooking. Pork chops will be golden and have an internal temperature of at least 145°F (63°C) when done. Serve warm.

Per Serving:

calories: 272 | fat: 15g | protein: 32g | carbs: 2g | net carbs: 2g | fiber: 0g

Herbed Lamb Shank

Prep time: 15 minutes | Cook time: 35 minutes | Serves 2

- 2 lamb shanks
- 1 rosemary spring
- 1 teaspoon coconut flour
- ¼ teaspoon onion powder
- ¼ teaspoon chili powder
- ¾ teaspoon ground ginger
- ½ cup beef broth
- ½ teaspoon avocado oil

1. Put all ingredients in the Instant Pot. Stir to mix well. 2. Close the lid. Select Manual mode and set cooking time for 35 minutes on High Pressure. 3. When timer beeps, use a natural pressure release for 15 minutes, then release any remaining pressure. Open the lid. 4. Discard the rosemary sprig and serve warm.

Per Serving:

calories: 179 | fat: 7g | protein: 25g | carbs: 2g | net carbs: 1g | fiber: 1g

Rack of Lamb in Red Bell Pepper Butter Sauce

Prep time: 10 minutes | Cook time: 30 minutes | Serves 4

- 1 pound (454 g) rack of lamb
- Salt to cure
- 3 cloves garlic, minced
- ⅓ cup olive oil
- ⅓ cup white wine
- 6 sprigs fresh rosemary
- Sauce
- 2 tablespoons olive oil
- 1 large red bell pepper, seeded, diced
- 2 cloves garlic, minced
- 1 cup chicken broth
- 2 ounces butter
- Salt and white pepper to taste

1. Fill a large bowl with water and soak in the lamb for 30 minutes. Drain the meat after and season with salt. Let the lamb sit on a rack to drain completely and then rinse it afterward. Put in a bowl. 2. Mix the olive oil with wine and garlic, and brush the mixture all over the lamb. Drop the rosemary sprigs on it, cover the bowl with plastic wrap, and place in the refrigerator to marinate the meat. 3. The next day, preheat the grill to 450°F and cook the lamb for 6 minutes on both sides. Remove after and let rest for 4 minutes. 4. Heat the olive oil in a frying pan and sauté the garlic and bell pepper for 5 minutes. Pour in the chicken broth and continue cooking the ingredients until the liquid reduces by half, about 10 minutes. Add the butter, salt, and white pepper. Stir to melt the butter and turn the heat off. 5. Use the stick blender to puree the ingredients until very smooth and strain the sauce through a fine mesh into a bowl. Slice the lamb, serve with the sauce, and your favorite red wine.

Per Serving:

calories: 432 | fat: 28g | protein: 42g | carbs: 3g | net carbs: 3g | fiber: 0g

Beef and Egg Rice Bowls

Prep time: 5 minutes | Cook time: 15 minutes | Serves 4

- 2 cups cauli rice
- 3 cups frozen mixed vegetables
- 3 tablespoons ghee
- 1 pound skirt steak
- Salt and black pepper to taste
- 4 eggs
- Hot sauce for topping

1. Mix the cauli rice and mixed vegetables in a bowl, sprinkle with a little water, and steam in the microwave for 1 minute until tender. Share into 4 serving bowls. 2. Melt the ghee in a skillet, season the beef with salt and black pepper, and brown for 5 minutes on each side. Use a perforated spoon to ladle the meat onto the vegetables. 3. Wipe out the skillet and return to medium heat, crack in an egg, season with salt and pepper and cook until the egg white has set, but the yolk is still runny 3 minutes. 4.Remove egg onto the vegetable bowl and fry the remaining 3 eggs. Add to the other bowls. Drizzle the beef bowls with hot sauce and serve.

Per Serving:

calories: 491 | fat: 32g | protein: 31g | carbs: 22g | net carbs: 15g | fiber: 7g

Grilled Lamb on Lemony Sauce

Prep time: 5 minutes | Cook time: 6 minutes | Serves 4

- 8 lamb chops
- 2 tablespoons favorite spice
- Sauce:
- ¼ cup olive oil
- 1 teaspoon red pepper flakes
- 2 tablespoons lemon juice
- 2 tablespoons fresh mint
- mix
- 2 tablespoons olive oil
- 3 garlic cloves, pressed
- 2 tablespoons lemon zest
- ¼ cup parsley
- ½ teaspoon smoked paprika

1. Rub lamb with olive oil and sprinkle with the seasoning. Preheat the grill to medium. Grill the lamb chops for about 3 minutes per side. Whisk together the sauce ingredients. Serve the lamb with sauce.

Per Serving:

calories: 479 | fat: 38g | protein: 29g | carbs: 4g | net carbs: 3g | fiber: 1g

Beef Tripe in Vegetable Sauté

Prep time: 10 minutes | Cook time: 23 minutes | Serves 6

- 1½ pounds beef tripe
- 4 cups buttermilk
- Salt to taste
- 2 teaspoons creole seasoning
- 3 tablespoons olive oil
- 2 large onions, sliced
- 3 tomatoes, diced

1. Put the tripe in a bowl and cover with buttermilk. Refrigerate for 3 hours to extract bitterness and gamey taste. Remove from buttermilk, pat dry with a paper towel, and season with salt and creole seasoning. 2. Heat 2 tablespoons of oil in a skillet over medium heat and brown the tripe on both sides for 6 minutes in total. Set aside. Add the remaining oil and sauté the onions for 3 minutes until soft. Include the tomatoes and cook for 10 minutes. Pour in a few tablespoons of water if necessary. Put the tripe in the sauce and cook for 3 minutes. Adjust taste with salt and serve with low carb rice.

Per Serving:

calories: 314 | fat: 15g | protein: 26g | carbs: 18g | net carbs: 16g | fiber: 2g

Pulled Pork with Avocado

Prep time: 10 minutes | Cook time: 2 hours | Serves 12

- 4 pounds pork shoulder
- 1 tablespoon avocado oil
- ½ cup vegetable stock
- ¼ cup jerk seasoning
- 6 avocado, sliced

1. Rub the pork shoulder with jerk seasoning, and set in a greased baking dish. Pour in the stock, and cook for 1 hour 45 minutes in your oven at 350°F covered with aluminium foil. 2. Discard the foil and cook for another 20 minutes. Leave to rest for 30 minutes, and shred it with 2 forks. Serve topped with avocado slices.

Per Serving:

calories: 389 | fat: 27g | protein: 30g | carbs: 9g | net carbs: 4g | fiber: 5g

Pepper Steak Stir-Fry

Prep time: 10 minutes | Cook time: 20 minutes | Serves 3

- 1 tablespoon extra-virgin olive oil, or more as needed
- 1 red bell pepper, cored, seeded, and cut into ½-inch-wide strips
- 1 green bell pepper, cored, seeded, and cut into ½-inch-wide strips
- ½ medium onion, thinly sliced
- 2 garlic cloves, minced
- 1 pound (454 g) flank steak, cut into ½-inch-wide strips
- Pink Himalayan sea salt
- Freshly ground black pepper
- ¼ cup coconut aminos or soy sauce
- 2 tablespoons granulated erythritol
- 1 teaspoon ground ginger
- Cauliflower rice, cooked (optional)

1. In a large sauté pan or skillet, heat 1 tablespoon of olive oil over medium heat. Add the bell peppers, onion, and garlic and cook until tender, about 5 minutes. Transfer the vegetables to a bowl. 2. Season the steak with salt and pepper and transfer it to the skillet. If there is no oil left in the pan, add about 1 teaspoon olive oil. 3. Increase the temperature to medium high and cook the steak for 5 to 7 minutes, with 5 minutes being for medium and 7 minutes being for well done. 4. In a small bowl, mix the coconut aminos, erythritol, and ginger. 5. Return the pepper mixture to the pan and drizzle with the sauce. 6. Reduce the heat to medium low and simmer for about 5 minutes, until the sauce reduces by about half, then serve with the cauliflower rice, if desired.

Per Serving:

calories: 316 | fat: 16g | protein: 35g | carbs: 8g | net carbs: 6g | fiber: 2g

Zucchini Boats with Beef and Pimiento Rojo

Prep time: 10 minutes | Cook time: 25 minutes | Serves 4

- 4 zucchinis
- 2 tablespoons olive oil
- 1½ pounds ground beef
- 1 medium red onion, chopped
- 2 tablespoons chopped
- pimiento
- Pink salt and black pepper to taste
- 1 cup grated yellow cheddar cheese

1. Preheat oven to 350°F. 2. Lay the zucchinis on a flat surface, trim off the ends and cut in half lengthwise. Scoop out the pulp from each half with a spoon to make shells. Chop the pulp. 3. Heat oil in a skillet; add the ground beef, red onion, pimiento, and zucchini pulp, and season with salt and black pepper. Cook for 6 minutes while stirring to break up lumps until beef is no longer pink. Turn the heat off. Spoon the beef into the boats and sprinkle with cheddar cheese. 4. Place on a greased baking sheet and cook to melt the cheese for 15 minutes until zucchini boats are tender. Take out, cool for 2 minutes, and serve warm with a mixed green salad.

Per Serving:

calories: 508 | fat: 38g | protein: 33g | carbs: 9g | net carbs: 7g | fiber: 2g

Lemon Pork Chops with Buttered Brussels Sprouts

Prep time: 10 minutes | Cook time: 22 minutes | Serves 6

- 3 tablespoons lemon juice
- 3 cloves garlic, pureed
- 1 tablespoon olive oil
- 6 pork loin chops
- 1 tablespoon butter
- 1 pound brussels sprouts, trimmed and halved
- 2 tablespoons white wine
- Salt and black pepper to taste

1. Preheat broiler to 400°F and mix the lemon juice, garlic, salt, black pepper, and oil in a bowl. 2. Brush the pork with the mixture, place in a baking sheet, and cook for 6 minutes on each side until browned. Share into 6 plates and make the side dish. 3. Melt butter in a small wok or pan and cook in brussels sprouts for 5 minutes until tender. Drizzle with white wine, sprinkle with salt and black pepper and cook for another 5 minutes. Ladle brussels sprouts to the side of the chops and serve with a hot sauce.

Per Serving:

calories: 300 | fat: 11g | protein: 42g | carbs: 7g | net carbs: 4g | fiber: 3g

Buttery Beef and Spinach

Prep time: 2 minutes | Cook time: 10 minutes | Serves 4

- 1 pound (454 g) 85% lean ground beef
- 1 cup water
- 4 cups fresh spinach
- ¾ teaspoon salt
- ¼ cup butter
- ¼ teaspoon pepper
- ¼ teaspoon garlic powder

1. Press the Sauté button and add ground beef to Instant Pot. Brown beef until fully cooked and spoon into 7-cup glass bowl. Drain grease and replace pot. 2. Pour water into pot and place steam rack in bottom. Place baking dish on steam rack and add fresh spinach, salt, butter, pepper, and garlic powder to ground beef. Cover with aluminum foil. Click lid closed. 3. Press the Manual button and adjust time for 2 minutes. When timer beeps, quick-release the pressure. Remove aluminum foil and stir.

Per Serving:

calories: 272 | fat: 19g | protein: 18g | carbs: 1g | net carbs: 0g | fiber: 1g

Lamb Kofte with Yogurt Sauce

Prep time: 30 minutes | Cook time: 15 minutes | Serves 4

- 1 pound (454 g) ground lamb
- ½ cup finely chopped fresh mint, plus 2 tablespoons
- ¼ cup almond or coconut flour
- ¼ cup finely chopped red onion
- ¼ cup toasted pine nuts
- 2 teaspoons ground cumin
- 1½ teaspoons salt, divided
- 1 teaspoon ground cinnamon
- 1 teaspoon ground ginger
- ½ teaspoon ground nutmeg
- ½ teaspoon freshly ground black pepper
- 1 cup plain whole-milk Greek yogurt
- 2 tablespoons extra-virgin olive oil
- Zest and juice of 1 lime

1. Heat the oven broiler to the low setting. You can also bake these at high heat (450 to 475°F/ 235 to 245°C) if you happen to have a very hot broiler. Submerge four wooden skewers in water and let soak at least 10 minutes to prevent them from burning. 2. In a large bowl, combine the lamb, ½ cup mint, almond flour, red onion, pine nuts, cumin, 1 teaspoon salt, cinnamon, ginger, nutmeg, and pepper and, using your hands, incorporate all the ingredients together well. 3. Form the mixture into 12 egg-shaped patties and let sit for 10 minutes. 4. Remove the skewers from the water, thread 3 patties onto each skewer, and place on a broiling pan or wire rack on top of a baking sheet lined with aluminum foil. Broil on the top rack until golden and cooked through, 8 to 12 minutes, flipping once halfway through cooking. 5. While the meat cooks, in a small bowl, combine the yogurt, olive oil, remaining 2 tablespoons chopped mint, remaining ½ teaspoon salt, and lime zest and juice and whisk

to combine well. Keep cool until ready to use. 6. Serve the skewers with yogurt sauce.

Per Serving:

calories: 592 | fat: 46g | protein: 28g | carbs: 12g | net carbs: 8g | fiber: 4g

Beef and Broccoli Roast

Prep time: 10 minutes | Cook time: 4 hours 30 minutes | Serves 2

- 1 pound beef chuck roast
- Pink Himalayan salt
- Freshly ground black pepper
- ½ cup beef broth, plus more if needed
- ¼ cup soy sauce (or coconut aminos)
- 1 teaspoon toasted sesame oil
- 1 (16-ounce) bag frozen broccoli

1. With the crock insert in place, preheat the slow cooker to low. 2. On a cutting board, season the chuck roast with pink Himalayan salt and pepper, and slice the roast thin. Put the sliced beef in the slow cooker. 3. In a small bowl, mix together the beef broth, soy sauce, and sesame oil. Pour over the beef. 4. Cover and cook on low for 4 hours. 5. Add the frozen broccoli, and cook for 30 minutes more. If you need more liquid, add additional beef broth. 6. Serve hot.

Per Serving:

calories: 806 | fat: 49g | protein: 74g | carbs: 18g | net carbs: 12g | fiber: 6g

Beery Boston-Style Butt

Prep time: 10 minutes | Cook time: 1 hour 1 minutes | Serves 4

- 1 tablespoon butter
- 1 pound (454 g) Boston-style butt
- ½ cup leeks, chopped
- ¼ cup beer
- ½ cup chicken stock
- Pinch of grated nutmeg
- Sea salt, to taste
- ¼ teaspoon ground black pepper
- ¼ cup water

1. Press the Sauté button to heat up the Instant Pot. Once hot, melt the butter. 2. Cook the Boston-style butt for 3 minutes on each side. Remove from the pot and reserve. 3. Sauté the leeks for 5 minutes or until fragrant. Add the remaining ingredients and stir to combine. 4. Secure the lid. Choose the Manual mode and set cooking time for 50 minutes on High pressure. 5. Once cooking is complete, use a natural pressure release for 20 minutes, then release any remaining pressure. Carefully remove the lid. 6. Serve immediately.

Per Serving:

calories: 330 | fat: 13g | protein: 48g | carbs: 2g | net carbs: 0g | fiber: 2g

Italian Beef Burgers

Prep time: 10 minutes | Cook time: 12 minutes | Serves 4

- 1 pound 75% lean ground beef
- ¼ cup ground almonds
- 2 tablespoons chopped fresh basil
- 1 teaspoon minced garlic
- ¼ teaspoon sea salt
- 1 tablespoon olive oil
- 1 tomato, cut into 4 thick slices
- ¼ sweet onion, sliced thinly

1. In a medium bowl, mix together the ground beef, ground almonds, basil, garlic, and salt until well mixed. 2. Form the beef mixture into four equal patties and flatten them to about ½ inch thick. 3. Place a large skillet on medium-high heat and add the olive oil. 4. Panfry the burgers until cooked through, flipping them once, about 12 minutes in total. 5. Pat away any excess grease with paper towels and serve the burgers with a slice of tomato and onion.

Per Serving:

calories: 441 | fat: 37g | protein: 22g | carbs: 4g | net carbs: 3g | fiber: 1g

Chipotle-Spiced Meatball Subs

Prep time: 15 minutes | Cook time: 35 minutes | Serves 15

Meatballs:
- 1⅔ pounds (750 g) ground pork
- 1 pound (455 g) ground chicken
- ½ cup (160 g) grated white onions

Sauce:
- 2½ cups (600 ml) crushed tomatoes
- ½ cup (120 ml) refined avocado oil or melted chicken fat
- ⅔ cup (80 ml) chicken bone broth
- 1 tablespoon dried oregano leaves

For Serving:
- 1 large head green cabbage
- Finely chopped fresh cilantro

- 1½ teaspoons dried oregano leaves
- 1¼ teaspoons ground cumin
- 1 teaspoon finely ground gray sea salt

- 1¼ teaspoons chipotle powder
- 1 teaspoon garlic powder
- ½ teaspoon onion powder
- ½ teaspoon smoked paprika
- ½ teaspoon finely ground gray sea salt
- ¼ teaspoon ground black pepper

(optional)

1. Preheat the oven to 350°F (177°C) and line a rimmed baking sheet with parchment paper or a silicone baking mat. 2. Place the ingredients for the meatballs in a large bowl. Mix with your hands until combined. 3. Wet your hands and pinch a 1½-tablespoon piece from the bowl, then roll it between your palms to form a ball. Place on the prepared baking sheet and repeat with the remaining meat mixture, making a total of 30 meatballs. Keeping your palms wet will help you shape the meatballs quicker. 4. Bake the meatballs for 25 to 30 minutes, until the internal temperature reaches 165°F (74°C). 5. Meanwhile, place the ingredients for the sauce in a large saucepan. Stir to combine, then cover, placing the lid slightly askew to allow steam to escape. Bring to a boil over medium-high heat, then reduce the heat to low and simmer for 20 minutes. 6. While the meatballs and sauce are cooking, remove 30 medium-sized leaves from the head of cabbage and lightly steam for 1 to 2 minutes. 7. Remove the meatballs from the oven and transfer to the saucepan with the sauce. Turn them to coat, cover, and cook on low for 5 minutes. 8. To serve, stack 2 cabbage leaves on top of one another, top with 2 meatballs, a dollop of extra sauce, and a sprinkle of cilantro, if using.

Per Serving:

calories: 253 | fat: 17g | protein: 18g | carbs: 8g | net carbs: 5g | fiber: 3g

BBQ Beef & Slaw

Prep time: 10 minutes | Cook time: 45 minutes | Serves 4

BBQ Beef:
- 1 pound (455 g) boneless beef chuck roast
- 1 cup (240 ml) beef bone broth

Slaw:
- 9 ounces (255 g) coleslaw mix

- ½ teaspoon finely ground sea salt
- ½ cup (80 g) sugar-free barbecue sauce

- ½ cup (120 ml) sugar-free poppy seed dressing

1. Place the chuck roast, broth, and salt in a pressure cooker or slow cooker. If using a pressure cooker, seal the lid and cook on high pressure for 45 minutes. When complete, allow the pressure to release naturally before removing the lid. If using a slow cooker, cook on high for 4 hours or on low for 6 hours. 2. When the meat is done, drain it almost completely, leaving ¼ cup (60 ml) of the cooking liquid in the cooker. Shred the meat with two forks, then add the barbecue sauce and toss to coat. 3. Place the coleslaw mix and dressing in a salad bowl and toss to coat. 4. Divide the BBQ beef and coleslaw among 4 dinner plates, placing the beef first and then the slaw on top, and enjoy.

Per Serving:

calories: 354 | fat: 27g | protein: 24g | carbs: 5g | net carbs: 3g | fiber: 2g

Bone Broth Brisket with Tomatoes

Prep time: 5 minutes | Cook time: 75 minutes | Serves 4 to 5

- 2 tablespoons coconut oil
- ½ teaspoon garlic salt
- ½ teaspoon crushed red pepper
- ½ teaspoon dried basil
- ½ teaspoon kosher salt
- ½ teaspoon freshly ground
- black pepper
- 1 (14-ounce / 397-g) can sugar-free or low-sugar diced tomatoes
- 1 cup grass-fed bone broth
- 1 pound (454 g) beef brisket, chopped

1. Set the Instant Pot to Sauté and melt the oil. Mix the garlic salt, red pepper, basil, kosher salt, black pepper, and tomatoes in a medium bowl. 2. Pour bone broth into the Instant Pot, then add the brisket, and top with the premixed sauce. Close the lid, set the pressure release to Sealing, and hit Cancel to stop the current program. Select Manual, set the Instant Pot to 75 minutes on High Pressure, and let cook. 3. Once cooked, carefully switch the pressure release to Venting. Open the Instant Pot, and serve. You can pour remaining sauce over brisket, if desired.

Per Serving:

calories: 240 | fat: 11g | protein: 29g | carbs: 5g | net carbs: 3g | fiber: 2g

Pork Casserole

Prep time: 15 minutes | Cook time: 30 minutes | Serves 4

- 1 pound (454 g) ground pork
- 1 large yellow squash, thinly sliced
- Salt and black pepper to taste
- 1 clove garlic, minced
- 4 green onions, chopped
- 1 cup chopped cremini mushrooms
- 1 (15 -ounce / 425-g) can diced tomatoes
- ½ cup pork rinds, crushed
- ¼ cup chopped parsley
- 1 cup cottage cheese
- 1 cup Mexican cheese blend
- 3 tablespoons olive oil
- ⅓ cup water

1. Preheat the oven to 370°F. 2. Heat the olive oil in a skillet over medium heat, add the pork, season it with salt and black pepper, and cook for 3 minutes or until no longer pink. Stir occasionally while breaking any lumps apart. 3. Add the garlic, half of the green onions, mushrooms, and 2 tablespoons of pork rinds. Cook for 3 minutes. Stir in the tomatoes, half of the parsley, and water. Cook further for 3 minutes, and then turn the heat off. 4. Mix the remaining parsley, cottage cheese, and Mexican cheese blend. Set aside. Sprinkle the bottom of a baking dish with 3 tablespoons of pork rinds; top with half of the squash and a season of salt, 2/3 of the pork mixture, and the cheese mixture. Repeat the layering

process a second time to exhaust the ingredients. 5. Cover the baking dish with foil and bake for 20 minutes. After, remove the foil and brown the top of the casserole with the broiler side of the oven for 2 minutes. Remove the dish when ready and serve warm.

Per Serving:

calories: 717 | fat: 58g | protein: 36g | carbs: 14g | net carbs: 9g | fiber: 5g

Mississippi Pork Butt Roast

Prep time: 10 minutes | Cook time: 6 hours | Serves 7

- 1 tablespoon ranch dressing mix
- 1½ pound (680 g) pork butt roast, chopped
- 1 cup butter
- 1 chili pepper, chopped
- ½ cup water

1. Put all ingredients in the instant pot. 2. Close the instant pot and cook the meal for 6 hours on Low Pressure. 3. When the time is over, shred the meat gently and transfer in the serving plate.

Per Serving:

calories: 414 | fat: 38g | protein: 17g | carbs: 0g | net carbs: 0g | fiber: 0g

Mustard Lamb Chops

Prep time: 5 minutes | Cook time: 14 minutes | Serves 4

- Oil, for spraying
- 1 tablespoon Dijon mustard
- 2 teaspoons lemon juice
- ½ teaspoon dried tarragon
- ¼ teaspoon salt
- ¼ teaspoon freshly ground black pepper
- 4 (1¼-inch-thick) loin lamb chops

1. Preheat the air fryer to 390°F (199°C). Line the air fryer basket with parchment and spray lightly with oil. 2. In a small bowl, mix together the mustard, lemon juice, tarragon, salt, and black pepper. 3. Pat dry the lamb chops with a paper towel. Brush the chops on both sides with the mustard mixture. 4. Place the chops in the prepared basket. You may need to work in batches, depending on the size of your air fryer. 5. Cook for 8 minutes, flip, and cook for another 6 minutes, or until the internal temperature reaches 125°F (52°C) for rare, 145°F (63°C) for medium-rare, or 155°F (68°C) for medium.

Per Serving:

calories: 244 | fat: 13g | protein: 27g | carbs: 1g | net carbs: 1g | fiber: 0g

Russian Beef Gratin

Prep time: 10 minutes | Cook time: 25 minutes | Serves 5

- 2 teaspoons onion flakes
- 2 pounds ground beef
- 2 garlic cloves, minced
- Salt and black pepper, to taste
- 1 cup mozzarella cheese, shredded
- 2 cups fontina cheese, shredded
- 1 cup Russian dressing
- 2 tablespoons sesame seeds, toasted
- 20 dill pickle slices
- 1 iceberg lettuce head, torn

1. Set a pan over medium heat, place in beef, garlic, salt, onion flakes, and pepper, and cook for 5 minutes. Remove to a baking dish, stir in Russian dressing, mozzarella, and spread 1 cup of the fontina cheese. 2. Lay the pickle slices on top, spread over the remaining fontina cheese and sesame seeds, place in the oven at 350ºF, and bake for 20 minutes. Arrange the lettuce on a serving platter and top with the gratin.

Per Serving:

calories: 735 | fat: 56g | protein: 53g | carbs: 6g | net carbs: 5g | fiber: 1g

---

North African Lamb

Prep time: 10 minutes | Cook time: 10 minutes | Serves 4

- 2 teaspoons paprika
- 2 garlic cloves, minced
- 2 teaspoons dried oregano
- 2 tablespoons sumac
- 12 lamb cutlets
- ¼ cup sesame oil
- 2 teaspoons cumin
- 4 carrots, sliced
- ¼ cup fresh parsley, chopped
- 2 teaspoons harissa paste
- 1 tablespoon red wine vinegar
- Salt and black pepper, to taste
- 2 tablespoons black olives, sliced
- 2 cucumbers, sliced

1. In a bowl, combine the cutlets with the paprika, oregano, black pepper, 2 tablespoons water, half of the oil, sumac, garlic, and salt, and rub well. Add the carrots in a pot, cover with water, bring to a boil over medium heat, cook for 2 minutes then drain before placing them in a salad bowl. 2. Place the cucumbers and olives to the carrots. In another bowl, combine the harissa with the rest of the oil, a splash of water, parsley, vinegar, and cumin. Place this to the carrots mixture, season with pepper and salt, and toss well to coat. 3. Preheat the grill to medium heat and arrange the lamb cutlets on it, grill each side for 3 minutes, and split among separate plates. Serve alongside the carrot salad.

Per Serving:

calories: 354 | fat: 23g | protein: 27g | carbs: 7g | net carbs: 4g | fiber: 3g

---

Cinnamon Beef with Blackberries

Prep time: 15 minutes | Cook time: 30 minutes | Serves 2

- 15 ounces (425 g) beef loin, chopped
- 1 tablespoon blackberries
- 1 cup water
- ½ teaspoon ground cinnamon
- ⅓ teaspoon ground black pepper
- ½ teaspoon salt
- 1 tablespoon butter

1. Pour water in the instant pot bowl. 2. Add chopped beef loin, blackberries, ground cinnamon, salt, and ground black pepper. Add butter. 3. Close the instant pot lid and set the Meat/Stew mode. 4. Cook the meat for 30 minutes. Then remove the meat from the instant pot. Blend the remaining blackberry mixture. 5. Pour it over the meat.

Per Serving:

calories: 372 | fat: 21g | protein: 39g | carbs: 4g | net carbs: 3g | fiber: 1g

Chapter 6

Stews and Soups

Chapter 6 Stews and Soups

Beef and Okra Stew

Prep time: 15 minutes | Cook time: 25 minutes | Serves 3

- 8 ounces (227 g) beef sirloin, chopped
- ¼ teaspoon cumin seeds
- 1 teaspoon dried basil
- 1 tablespoon avocado oil
- ¼ cup coconut cream
- 1 cup water
- 6 ounces (170 g) okra, chopped

1. Sprinkle the beef sirloin with cumin seeds and dried basil and put in the Instant Pot. 2. Add avocado oil and roast the meat on Sauté mode for 5 minutes. Flip occasionally. 3. Add coconut cream, water, and okra. 4. Close the lid and select Manual mode. Set cooking time for 25 minutes on High Pressure. 5. When timer beeps, use a natural pressure release for 10 minutes, the release any remaining pressure. Open the lid. 6. Serve warm.

Per Serving:

calories: 216 | fat: 10g | protein: 25g | carbs: 6g | net carbs: 3g | fiber: 3g

Garlicky Chicken Soup

Prep time: 5 minutes | Cook time: 20 minutes | Serves 6

- 10 roasted garlic cloves
- ½ medium onion, diced
- 4 tablespoons butter
- 4 cups chicken broth
- ½ teaspoon salt
- ¼ teaspoon pepper
- 1 teaspoon thyme
- 1 pound (454 g) boneless, skinless chicken thighs, cubed
- ½ cup heavy cream
- 2 ounces (57 g) cream cheese

1. In small bowl, mash roasted garlic into paste. Press the Sauté button and add garlic, onion, and butter to Instant Pot. Sauté for 2 to 3 minutes until onion begins to soften. Press the Cancel button. 2. Add Chicken Broth, salt, pepper, thyme, and chicken to Instant Pot. Click lid closed. Press the Manual button and adjust time for 20 minutes. 3. When timer beeps, quick-release the pressure. Stir in heavy cream and cream cheese until smooth. Serve warm.

Per Serving:

calories: 291 | fat: 21g | protein: 17g | carbs: 4g | net carbs: 3g | fiber: 1g

Beef and Eggplant Tagine

Prep time: 15 minutes | Cook time: 25 minutes | Serves 6

- 1 pound (454 g) beef fillet, chopped
- 1 eggplant, chopped
- 6 ounces (170 g) scallions, chopped
- 4 cups beef broth
- 1 teaspoon ground allspices
- 1 teaspoon erythritol
- 1 teaspoon coconut oil

1. Put all ingredients in the Instant Pot. Stir to mix well. 2. Close the lid. Select Manual mode and set cooking time for 25 minutes on High Pressure. 3. When timer beeps, use a natural pressure release for 15 minutes, then release any remaining pressure. Open the lid. 4. Serve warm.

Per Serving:

calories: 158 | fat: 5g | protein: 21g | carbs: 8g | net carbs: 5g | fiber: 4g

Sausage Zoodle Soup

Prep time: 10 minutes | Cook time: 25 minutes | Serves 8

- 1 tablespoon olive oil
- 4 cloves garlic, minced
- 1 pound (454 g) pork sausage (no sugar added)
- ½ tablespoon Italian
- seasoning
- 3 cups regular beef broth
- 3 cups beef bone broth
- 2 medium zucchini (6 ounces / 170 g each), spiralized

1. In a large soup pot, heat the oil over medium heat. Add the garlic and cook for about 1 minute, until fragrant. 2. Add the sausage, increase the heat to medium-high, and cook for about 10 minutes, stirring occasionally and breaking apart into small pieces, until browned. 3. Add the seasoning, regular broth, and bone broth, and simmer for 10 minutes. 4. Add the zucchini. Bring to a simmer again, then simmer for about 2 minutes, until the zucchini is soft. (Don't overcook or the zoodles will be mushy.)

Per Serving:

calories: 216 | fat: 17g | protein: 12g | carbs: 2g | net carbs: 2g | fiber: 0g

Chicken and Mushroom Soup

Prep time: 5 minutes | Cook time: 15 minutes | Serves 4

- 1 onion, cut into thin slices
- 3 garlic cloves, minced
- 2 cups chopped mushrooms
- 1 yellow summer squash, chopped
- 1 pound (454 g) boneless, skinless chicken breast, cut into large chunks
- 2½ cups chicken broth
- 1 teaspoon salt
- 1 teaspoon freshly ground black pepper
- 1 teaspoon Italian seasoning or poultry seasoning
- 1 cup heavy (whipping) cream

1. Put the onion, garlic, mushrooms, squash, chicken, chicken broth, salt, pepper, and Italian seasoning in the inner cooking pot of the Instant Pot. 2. Lock the lid into place. Select Manual and adjust the pressure to High. Cook for 15 minutes. When the cooking is complete, let the pressure release naturally for 10 minutes, then quick-release any remaining pressure. Unlock the lid. 3. Using tongs, transfer the chicken pieces to a bowl and set aside. 4. Tilt the pot slightly. Using an immersion blender, roughly purée the vegetables, leaving a few intact for texture and visual appeal. 5. Shred the chicken and stir it back in to the soup. 6. Add the cream and stir well. Serve.

Per Serving:

calories: 427 | fat: 28g | protein: 31g | carbs: 13g | net carbs: 11g | fiber: 2g

Chicken and Asparagus Soup

Prep time: 7 minutes | Cook time: 11 minutes | Serves 8

- 1 tablespoon unsalted butter (or coconut oil for dairy-free)
- ¼ cup finely chopped onions
- 2 cloves garlic, minced
- 1 (14-ounce / 397-g) can full-fat coconut milk
- 1 (14-ounce / 397-g) can sugar-free tomato sauce
- 1 cup chicken broth
- 1 tablespoon red curry paste
- 1 teaspoon fine sea salt
- ½ teaspoon ground black pepper
- 2 pounds (907 g) boneless, skinless chicken breasts, cut into ½-inch chunks
- 2 cups asparagus, trimmed and cut into 2-inch pieces
- Fresh cilantro leaves, for garnish
- Lime wedges, for garnish

1. Place the butter in the Instant Pot and press Sauté. Once melted, add the onions and garlic and sauté for 4 minutes, or until the onions are soft. Press Cancel to stop the Sauté. 2. Add the coconut milk, tomato sauce, broth, curry paste, salt, and pepper and whisk to combine well. Stir in the chicken and asparagus. 3. Seal the lid, press Manual, and set the timer for 7 minutes. Once finished, turn the valve to venting for a quick release. 4. Remove the lid and stir

well. Taste and adjust the seasoning to your liking. Ladle the soup into bowls and garnish with cilantro. Serve with lime wedges or a squirt of lime juice.

Per Serving:

calories: 235 | fat: 13g | protein: 24g | carbs: 8g | net carbs: 6g | fiber: 2g

Beef and Spinach Stew

Prep time: 20 minutes | Cook time: 30 minutes | Serves 4

- 1 pound (454 g) beef sirloin, chopped
- 2 cups spinach, chopped
- 3 cups chicken broth
- 1 cup coconut milk
- 1 teaspoon allspices
- 1 teaspoon coconut aminos

1. Put all ingredients in the Instant Pot. Stir to mix well. 2. Close the lid. Set the Manual mode and set cooking time for 30 minutes on High Pressure. 3. When timer beeps, use a natural pressure release for 10 minutes, then release any remaining pressure. Open the lid. 4. Blend with an immersion blender until smooth. 5. Serve warm.

Per Serving:

calories: 383 | fat: 22g | protein: 40g | carbs: 5g | net carbs: 3g | fiber: 2g

Cabbage Roll Soup

Prep time: 10 minutes | Cook time: 8 minutes | Serves 4

- ½ pound (227 g) 84% lean ground pork
- ½ pound (227 g) 85% lean ground beef
- ½ medium onion, diced
- ½ medium head cabbage, thinly sliced
- 2 tablespoons sugar-free
- tomato paste
- ½ cup diced tomatoes
- 2 cups chicken broth
- 1 teaspoon salt
- ½ teaspoon thyme
- ½ teaspoon garlic powder
- ¼ teaspoon pepper

1. Press the Sauté button and add beef and pork to Instant Pot. Brown meat until no pink remains. Add onion and continue cooking until onions are fragrant and soft. Press the Cancel button. 2. Add remaining ingredients to Instant Pot. Press the Manual button and adjust time for 8 minutes. 3. When timer beeps, allow a 15-minute natural release and then quick-release the remaining pressure. Serve warm.

Per Serving:

calories: 304 | fat: 16g | protein: 24g | carbs: 12g | net carbs: 8g | fiber: 4g

New England Clam Chowder

Prep time: 10 minutes | Cook time: 30 minutes | Serves 8

- ¼ pound uncured bacon, chopped
- 2 tablespoons grass-fed butter
- ½ onion, finely chopped
- 1 celery stalk, chopped
- 2 teaspoons minced garlic
- 2 tablespoons arrowroot
- 4 cups fish or chicken stock
- 1 teaspoon chopped fresh thyme
- 2 bay leaves
- 3 (6½-ounce) cans clams, drained
- 1½ cups heavy (whipping) cream
- Sea salt, for seasoning
- Freshly ground black pepper, for seasoning
- 2 tablespoons chopped fresh parsley

1. Cook the bacon. In a medium stockpot over medium-high heat, fry the bacon until it's crispy. Transfer the bacon with a slotted spoon to a plate and set it aside. 2. Sauté the vegetables. Melt the butter in the stockpot, add the onion, celery, and garlic and sauté them until they've softened, about 3 minutes. Whisk in the arrowroot and cook for 1 minute. Add the stock, thyme, and bay leaves and bring the soup to just before it boils. Then reduce the heat to medium-low and simmer until the soup thickens, about 10 minutes. 3. Finish the soup. Stir in the clams and cream and simmer the soup until it's heated through, about 5 minutes. Find and throw out the bay leaves. 4. Serve. Season the chowder with salt and pepper. Ladle it into bowls, garnish with the parsley, and crumbles of the bacon, then serve.

Per Serving:

calories: 384 | fat: 28g | protein: 23g | carbs: 6g | net carbs: 6g | fiber: 2g

Miso Magic

Prep time: 5 minutes | Cook time: 10 minutes | serves 8

- 8 cups water
- 6 to 7 tablespoons miso paste
- 3 sheets dried seaweed
- 2 cups thinly sliced shiitake mushrooms
- 1 cup drained and cubed sprouted tofu
- 1 cup chopped scallions
- 1 teaspoon sesame oil

1. In a large stockpot over medium heat, add the miso paste and seaweed to the water and bring to a low boil. 2. Toss in the mushrooms, tofu, scallions, and sesame oil. 3. Allow to simmer for about 5 minutes and serve.

Per Serving:

calories: 80 | fat: 2g | protein: 4g | carbs: 12g | net carbs: 10g | fiber: 2g

Vegan Pho

Prep time: 10 minutes | Cook time: 20 minutes | serves 8

- 8 cups vegetable broth
- 1-inch knob fresh ginger, peeled and chopped
- 2 tablespoons tamari
- 3 cups shredded fresh spinach
- 2 cups chopped broccoli
- 1 cup sliced mushrooms
- ½ cup chopped carrots
- ⅓ cup chopped scallions
- 1 (8-ounce) package shirataki noodles
- 2 cups shredded cabbage
- 2 cups mung bean sprouts
- Fresh Thai basil leaves, for garnish
- Fresh cilantro leaves, for garnish
- Fresh mint leaves, for garnish
- 1 lime, cut into 8 wedges, for garnish

1. In a large stockpot over medium-high heat, bring the vegetable broth to a simmer with the ginger and tamari. 2. Once the broth is hot, add the spinach, broccoli, mushrooms, carrots, and scallions, and simmer for a few minutes, just until the vegetables start to become tender. 3. Stir in the shirataki noodles, then remove the pot from the heat and divide the soup among serving bowls. 4. Top each bowl with cabbage, sprouts, basil, cilantro, mint, and a lime wedge.

Per Serving:

calories: 47 | fat: 0g | protein: 3g | carbs: 10g | net carbs: 7g | fiber: 3g

Buffalo Chicken Soup

Prep time: 7 minutes | Cook time: 10 minutes | Serves 2

- 1 ounce (28 g) celery stalk, chopped
- 4 tablespoons coconut milk
- ¾ teaspoon salt
- ¼ teaspoon white pepper
- 1 cup water
- 2 ounces (57 g) Mozzarella, shredded
- 6 ounces (170 g) cooked chicken, shredded
- 2 tablespoons keto-friendly Buffalo sauce

1. Place the chopped celery stalk, coconut milk, salt, white pepper, water, and Mozzarella in the Instant Pot. Stir to mix well. 2. Set the Manual mode and set timer for 7 minutes on High Pressure. 3. When timer beeps, use a quick pressure release and open the lid. 4. Transfer the soup on the bowls. Stir in the chicken and Buffalo sauce. Serve warm.

Per Serving:

calories: 287 | fat: 15g | protein: 33g | carbs: 4g | net carbs: 3g | fiber: 1g

Beef Chili

Prep time: 5 minutes | Cook time: 50 minutes | Serves 4

- ½ green bell pepper, cored, seeded, and chopped
- ½ medium onion, chopped
- 2 tablespoons extra-virgin olive oil
- 1 tablespoon minced garlic
- 1 pound (454 g) ground beef (80/20)
- 1 (14-ounce / 397-g) can crushed tomatoes
- 1 cup beef broth
- 1 tablespoon ground cumin
- 1 tablespoon chili powder
- 2 teaspoons paprika
- 1 teaspoon pink Himalayan sea salt
- ¼ teaspoon cayenne pepper

1. In a medium pot, combine the bell pepper, onion, and olive oil. Cook over medium heat for 8 to 10 minutes, until the onion is translucent. 2. Add the garlic and cook for 1 minute longer, until fragrant. 3. Add the ground beef and cook for 7 to 10 minutes, until browned. 4. Add the tomatoes, broth, cumin, chili powder, paprika, salt, and cayenne. Stir to combine. 5. Simmer the chili for 30 minutes, until the flavors come together, then enjoy.

Per Serving:

calories: 406 | fat: 31g | protein: 22g | carbs: 12g | net carbs: 8g | fiber: 4g

Thai Shrimp and Mushroom Soup

Prep time: 15 minutes | Cook time: 10 minutes | Serves 6

- 2 tablespoons unsalted butter, divided
- ½ pound (227 g) medium uncooked shrimp, shelled and deveined
- ½ medium yellow onion, diced
- 2 cloves garlic, minced
- 1 cup sliced fresh white mushrooms
- 1 tablespoon freshly grated ginger root
- 4 cups chicken broth
- 2 tablespoons fish sauce
- 2½ teaspoons red curry paste
- 2 tablespoons lime juice
- 1 stalk lemongrass, outer stalk removed, crushed, and finely chopped
- 2 tablespoons coconut aminos
- 1 teaspoon sea salt
- ½ teaspoon ground black pepper
- 13½ ounces (383 g) can unsweetened, full-fat coconut milk
- 3 tablespoons chopped fresh cilantro

1. Select the Instant Pot on Sauté mode. Add 1 tablespoon butter. 2. Once the butter is melted, add the shrimp and sauté for 3 minutes or until opaque. Transfer the shrimp to a medium bowl. Set aside. 3. Add the remaining butter to the pot. Once the butter is melted, add the onions and garlic and sauté for 2 minutes or until the garlic is fragrant and the onions are softened. 4. Add the mushrooms, ginger root, chicken broth, fish sauce, red curry paste, lime juice, lemongrass, coconut aminos, sea salt, and black pepper to the pot. Stir to combine. 5. Lock the lid. Select Manual mode and set cooking time for 5 minutes on High Pressure. 6. When cooking is complete, allow the pressure to release naturally for 5 minutes, then release the remaining pressure. 7. Open the lid. Stir in the cooked shrimp and coconut milk. 8. Select Sauté mode. Bring the soup to a boil and then press Keep Warm / Cancel. Let the soup rest in the pot for 2 minutes. 9. Ladle the soup into bowls and sprinkle the cilantro over top. Serve hot.

Per Serving:

calories: 237 | fat: 20g | protein: 9g | carbs: 9g | net carbs: 6g | fiber: 2g

Butternut Squash Soup with Turmeric & Ginger

Prep time: 5 minutes | Cook time: 35 minutes | serves 8

- 1 small butternut squash
- 3 tablespoons coconut oil
- 3 shallots, coarsely chopped
- 1-inch knob fresh ginger, peeled and coarsely chopped
- 1-inch knob fresh turmeric root, peeled and coarsely chopped
- 1 fresh lemongrass stalk, coarsely chopped
- ½ cup dry Marsala wine (optional)
- 8 cups miso broth
- 1 cup coconut cream
- Cold-pressed olive oil, for drizzling
- Handful toasted pumpkin seeds, for garnish (optional)

1. Preheat the oven to 365°F. 2. Puncture the squash skin with a fork several times to create air vents. Put the entire squash into a baking dish and bake for 30 minutes or until it is extremely tender. 3. While the squash is baking, heat the oil in a large stockpot over medium heat. Add the shallots, ginger, turmeric, and lemongrass to the pan and sauté until the spices become fragrant and the shallots are tender. 4. Deglaze the pot by pouring in the Marsala wine (if using), and stirring, scraping the bottom of the pot to loosen any stuck bits. Once the alcohol starts to reduce, add the miso broth and turn the heat to low. 5. Remove the squash from oven and poke it with a fork to check for tenderness. Carefully cut the squash in half lengthwise, allowing any liquid to drain out. 6. Once the squash is cool enough to handle, scoop out the seeds. With a paring knife, remove the skin. Roughly chop the squash and add it to the stockpot. 7. Pour the coconut cream into the pot, bring to a simmer, and remove from the heat. 8. Using an immersion blender, blend the soup thoroughly until smooth and velvety. Drizzle with olive oil, and top with toasted pumpkin seeds, if desired. Serve warm.

Per Serving:

calories: 149 | fat: 13g | protein: 2g | carbs: 10g | net carbs: 9g | fiber: 1g

Coconut Red Curry Soup

Prep time: 10 minutes | Cook time: 20 minutes | Serves 4

- ¼ cup (55 g) coconut oil, or ¼ cup (60 ml) avocado oil
- 2 cloves garlic, minced
- 1 (2-in/5-cm) piece fresh ginger root, peeled and minced
- 1 pound (455 g) boneless, skinless chicken thighs, cut

For Serving:
- 2 medium zucchinis, spiral sliced
- 3 green onions, sliced
- into small cubes
- 2 cups (475 ml) chicken bone broth
- 1 cup (240 ml) full-fat coconut milk
- ⅓ cup (80 g) red curry paste
- 1 teaspoon finely ground sea salt
- ¼ cup (15 g) fresh cilantro leaves, chopped

1. Heat the oil in a large saucepan over medium-low heat. Add the garlic and ginger and cook until fragrant, about 2 minutes. 2. Add the chicken thighs, broth, coconut milk, curry paste, and salt. Stir to combine, cover, and bring to a light simmer over medium-high heat. Once simmering, reduce the heat and continue to simmer for 15 minutes, until the flavors meld. 3. Divide the spiral-sliced zucchinis among 4 bowls and top with the curry soup. Sprinkle with the green onions and cilantro before serving.

Per Serving:

calories: 567 | fat: 40g | protein: 40g | carbs: 11g | net carbs: 10g | fiber: 1g

Summer Vegetable Soup

Prep time: 10 minutes | Cook time: 6 minutes | Serves 6

- 3 cups finely sliced leeks
- 6 cups chopped rainbow chard, stems and leaves separated
- 1 cup chopped celery
- 2 tablespoons minced garlic, divided
- 1 teaspoon dried oregano
- 1 teaspoon salt
- 2 teaspoons freshly ground
- black pepper
- 3 cups chicken broth, plus more as needed
- 2 cups sliced yellow summer squash, ½-inch slices
- ¼ cup chopped fresh parsley
- ¾ cup heavy (whipping) cream
- 4 to 6 tablespoons grated Parmesan cheese

1. Put the leeks, chard, celery, 1 tablespoon of garlic, oregano, salt, pepper, and broth into the inner cooking pot of the Instant Pot. 2. Lock the lid into place. Select Manual and adjust the pressure to High. Cook for 3 minutes. When the cooking is complete, quick-release the pressure. Unlock the lid. 3. Add more broth if needed. 4. Turn the pot to Sauté and adjust the heat to high. Add the yellow squash, parsley, and remaining 1 tablespoon of garlic. 5. Allow the soup to cook for 2 to 3 minutes, or until the squash is softened and cooked through. 6. Stir in the cream and ladle the soup into bowls. Sprinkle with the Parmesan cheese and serve.

Per Serving:

calories: 210 | fat: 14g | protein: 10g | carbs: 12g | net carbs: 8g | fiber: 4g

Broccoli Cheddar Soup

Prep time: 5 minutes | Cook time: 10 minutes | Serves 4

- 2 tablespoons butter
- ⅛ cup onion, diced
- ½ teaspoon garlic powder
- ½ teaspoon salt
- ¼ teaspoon pepper
- 2 cups chicken broth
- 1 cup chopped broccoli
- 1 tablespoon cream cheese, softened
- ¼ cup heavy cream
- 1 cup shredded Cheddar cheese

1. Press the Sauté button and add butter to Instant Pot. Add onion and sauté until translucent. Press the Cancel button and add garlic powder, salt, pepper, broth, and broccoli to pot. 2. Click lid closed. Press the Soup button and set time for 5 minutes. When timer beeps, stir in heavy cream, cream cheese, and Cheddar.

Per Serving:

calories: 250 | fat: 20g | protein: 9g | carbs: 4g | net carbs: 3g | fiber: 1g

Broc Obama Cheese Soup

Prep time: 25 minutes | Cook time: 25 minutes | Serves 8

- 8 cups chicken broth
- 2 large heads broccoli, chopped into bite-sized florets
- 1 clove garlic, peeled and minced
- ¼ cup heavy whipping cream
- ¼ cup shredded Cheddar cheese
- ⅛ teaspoon salt
- ⅛ teaspoon black pepper

1. In a medium pot over medium heat, add broth and bring to boil (about 5 minutes). Add broccoli and garlic. Reduce heat to low, cover pot, and simmer until vegetables are fully softened, about 15 minutes. 2. Remove from heat and blend using a hand immersion blender to desired consistency while still in pot. Leave some chunks of varying sizes for variety. 3. Return pot to medium heat and add cream and cheese. Stir 3 to 5 minutes until fully blended. Add salt and pepper. 4. Remove from heat, let cool 10 minutes, and serve.

Per Serving:

calories: 82 | fat: 4g | protein: 5g | carbs: 8g | net carbs: 5g | fiber: 3g

Chicken Poblano Pepper Soup

Prep time: 10 minutes | Cook time: 20 minutes | Serves 8

- 1 cup diced onion
- 3 poblano peppers, chopped
- 5 garlic cloves
- 2 cups diced cauliflower
- 1½ pounds (680 g) chicken breast, cut into large chunks
- ¼ cup chopped fresh cilantro
- 1 teaspoon ground coriander
- 1 teaspoon ground cumin
- 1 to 2 teaspoons salt
- 2 cups water
- 2 ounces (57 g) cream cheese, cut into small chunks
- 1 cup sour cream

1. To the inner cooking pot of the Instant Pot, add the onion, poblanos, garlic, cauliflower, chicken, cilantro, coriander, cumin, salt, and water. 2. Lock the lid into place. Select Manual and adjust the pressure to High. Cook for 15 minutes. When the cooking is complete, let the pressure release naturally for 10 minutes, then quick-release any remaining pressure. Unlock the lid. 3. Remove the chicken with tongs and place in a bowl. 4. Tilting the pot, use an immersion blender to roughly purée the vegetable mixture. It should still be slightly chunky. 5. Turn the Instant Pot to Sauté and adjust to high heat. When the broth is hot and bubbling, add the cream cheese and stir until it melts. Use a whisk to blend in the cream cheese if needed. 6. Shred the chicken and stir it back into the pot. Once it is heated through, serve, topped with sour cream, and enjoy.

Per Serving:

calories: 202 | fat: 10g | protein: 20g | carbs: 8g | net carbs: 5g | fiber: 3g

Cream of Cauliflower Gazpacho

Prep time: 15 minutes | Cook time: 25 minutes | Serves 4 to 6

- 1 cup raw almonds
- ½ teaspoon salt
- ½ cup extra-virgin olive oil, plus 1 tablespoon, divided
- 1 small white onion, minced
- 1 small head cauliflower, stalk removed and broken into florets (about 3 cups)
- 2 garlic cloves, finely minced
- 2 cups chicken or vegetable stock or broth, plus more if needed
- 1 tablespoon red wine vinegar
- ¼ teaspoon freshly ground black pepper

1. Bring a small pot of water to a boil. Add the almonds to the water and boil for 1 minute, being careful to not boil longer or the almonds will become soggy. Drain in a colander and run under cold water. Pat dry and, using your fingers, squeeze the meat of each almond out of its skin. Discard the skins. 2. In a food processor or blender, blend together the almonds and salt. With the processor running, drizzle in ½ cup extra-virgin olive oil, scraping down the sides as needed. Set the almond paste aside. 3. In a large stockpot,

heat the remaining 1 tablespoon olive oil over medium-high heat. Add the onion and sauté until golden, 3 to 4 minutes. Add the cauliflower florets and sauté for another 3 to 4 minutes. Add the garlic and sauté for 1 minute more. 4. Add 2 cups stock and bring to a boil. Cover, reduce the heat to medium-low, and simmer the vegetables until tender, 8 to 10 minutes. Remove from the heat and allow to cool slightly. 5. Add the vinegar and pepper. Using an immersion blender, blend until smooth. Alternatively, you can blend in a stand blender, but you may need to divide the mixture into two or three batches. With the blender running, add the almond paste and blend until smooth, adding extra stock if the soup is too thick. 6. Serve warm, or chill in refrigerator at least 4 to 6 hours to serve a cold gazpacho.

Per Serving:

calories: 562 | fat: 51g | protein: 13g | carbs: 19g | net carbs: 13g | fiber: 6g

Tomato-Basil Parmesan Soup

Prep time: 5 minutes | Cook time: 12 minutes | Serves 12

- 2 tablespoons unsalted butter or coconut oil
- ½ cup finely diced onions
- Cloves squeezed from 1 head roasted garlic , or 2 cloves garlic, minced
- 1 tablespoon dried basil leaves
- 1 teaspoon dried oregano leaves
- 1 (8 ounces / 227 g) package
- cream cheese, softened
- 4 cups chicken broth
- 2 (14½ ounces / 411 g) cans diced tomatoes
- 1 cup shredded Parmesan cheese, plus more for garnish
- 1 teaspoon fine sea salt
- ¼ teaspoon ground black pepper
- Fresh basil leaves, for garnish

1. Place the butter in the Instant Pot and press Sauté. Once melted, add the onions, garlic, basil, and oregano and cook, stirring often, for 4 minutes, or until the onions are soft. Press Cancel to stop the Sauté. 2. Add the cream cheese and whisk to loosen. (If you don't use a whisk to loosen the cream cheese, you will end up with clumps in your soup.) Slowly whisk in the broth. Add the tomatoes, Parmesan, salt, and pepper and stir to combine. 3. Seal the lid, press Manual, and set the timer for 8 minutes. Once finished, turn the valve to venting for a quick release. 4. Remove the lid and purée the soup with a stick blender, or transfer the soup to a regular blender or food processor and process until smooth. If using a regular blender, you may need to blend the soup in two batches; if you overfill the blender jar, the soup will not purée properly. 5. Season with salt and pepper to taste, if desired. Ladle the soup into bowls and garnish with more Parmesan and basil leaves.

Per Serving:

calories: 146 | fat: 10g | protein: 8g | carbs: 4g | net carbs: 3g | fiber: 1g

Keto Pho with Shirataki Noodles

Prep time: 20 minutes | Cook time: 10 minutes | Makes 4 bowls

- 8 ounces (227 g) sirloin, very thinly sliced
- 3 tablespoons coconut oil (or butter or ghee)
- 2 garlic cloves, minced
- 2 tablespoons liquid or coconut aminos
- 2 tablespoons fish sauce
- 1 teaspoon freshly grated or ground ginger
- 8 cups bone broth
- 4 (7-ounce / 198-g) packages shirataki noodles, drained and rinsed
- 1 cup bean sprouts
- 1 scallion, chopped
- 1 tablespoon toasted sesame seeds (optional)

1. Put the sirloin in the freezer while you prepare the broth and other ingredients (about 15 to 20 minutes). This makes it easier to slice. 2. In a large pot over medium heat, melt the coconut oil. Add the garlic and cook for 3 minutes. Then add the aminos, fish sauce, ginger, and bone broth. Bring to a boil. 3. Remove the beef from the freezer and slice it very thin. 4. Divide the noodles, beef, and bean sprouts evenly among four serving bowls. Carefully ladle 2 cups of broth into each bowl. Cover the bowls with plates and let sit for 3 to 5 minutes to cook the meat. 5. Serve garnished with the chopped scallion and sesame seeds (if using).

Per Serving:

1 bowl: calories: 385 | fat: 29g | protein: 23g | carbs: 8g | net carbs: 4g | fiber: 4g

Power Green Soup

Prep time: 10 minutes | Cook time: 15 minutes | Serves 6

- 1 broccoli head, chopped
- 1 cup spinach
- 1 onion, chopped
- 2 garlic cloves, minced
- ½ cup watercress
- 5 cups veggie stock
- 1 cup coconut milk
- 1 tablespoon ghee
- 1 bay leaf
- Salt and black pepper, to taste

1. Melt the ghee in a large pot over medium heat. Add onion and garlic, and cook for 3 minutes. Add broccoli and cook for an additional 5 minutes. Pour the stock over and add the bay leaf. Close the lid, bring to a boil, and reduce the heat. Simmer for about 3 minutes. 2. At the end, add spinach and watercress, and cook for 3 more minutes. Stir in the coconut cream, salt and black pepper. Discard the bay leaf, and blend the soup with a hand blender.

Per Serving:

calories: 392 | fat: 38g | protein: 5g | carbs: 7g | net carbs: 6g | fiber: 1g

Curried Chicken Soup

Prep time: 10 minutes | Cook time: 10 minutes | Serves 6

- 1 pound (454 g) boneless, skinless chicken thighs
- 1½ cups unsweetened coconut milk
- ½ onion, finely diced
- 3 or 4 garlic cloves, crushed
- 1 (2-inch) piece ginger, finely chopped
- 1 cup sliced mushrooms, such
- as cremini and shiitake
- 4 ounces (113 g) baby spinach
- 1 teaspoon salt
- ½ teaspoon ground turmeric
- ½ teaspoon cayenne
- 1 teaspoon garam masala
- ¼ cup chopped fresh cilantro

1. In the inner cooking pot of your Instant Pot, add the chicken, coconut milk, onion, garlic, ginger, mushrooms, spinach, salt, turmeric, cayenne, garam masala, and cilantro. 2. Lock the lid into place. Select Manual and adjust the pressure to High. Cook for 10 minutes. When the cooking is complete, let the pressure release naturally. Unlock the lid. 3. Use tongs to transfer the chicken to a bowl. Shred the chicken, then stir it back into the soup. 4. Eat and rejoice.

Per Serving:

calories: 378 | fat: 26g | protein: 26g | carbs: 6g | net carbs: 2g | fiber: 4g

Lamb and Broccoli Soup

Prep time: 10 minutes | Cook time: 25 minutes | Serves 4

- 7 ounces (198 g) lamb fillet, chopped
- 1 tablespoon avocado oil
- ½ cup broccoli, roughly chopped
- ¼ daikon, chopped
- 2 bell peppers, chopped
- ¼ teaspoon ground cumin
- 5 cups beef broth

1. Sauté the lamb fillet with avocado oil in the Instant Pot for 5 minutes. 2. Add the broccoli, daikon, bell peppers, ground cumin, and beef broth. 3. Close the lid. Select Manual mode and set cooking time for 20 minutes on High Pressure. 4. When timer beeps, use a natural pressure release for 10 minutes, then release any remaining pressure. Open the lid. 5. Serve warm.

Per Serving:

calories: 169 | fat: 6g | protein: 21g | carbs: 7g | net carbs: 6g | fiber: 1g

Chicken and Zoodles Soup

Prep time: 25 minutes | Cook time: 15 minutes | Serves 2

- 2 cups water
- 6 ounces (170 g) chicken fillet, chopped
- 1 teaspoon salt
- 2 ounces (57 g) zucchini, spiralized
- 1 tablespoon coconut aminos

1. Pour water in the Instant Pot. Add chopped chicken fillet and salt. Close the lid. 2. Select Manual mode and set cooking time for 15 minutes on High Pressure. 3. When cooking is complete, perform a natural pressure release for 10 minutes, then release any remaining pressure. Open the lid. 4. Fold in the zoodles and coconut aminos. 5. Leave the soup for 10 minutes to rest. Serve warm.

Per Serving:

calories: 175 | fat: 6g | protein: 25g | carbs: 5g | net carbs: 2g | fiber: 3g

Coconut and Cauliflower Curry Shrimp Soup

Prep time: 5 minutes | Cook time: 2 hours 15 minutes | Serves 4

- 8 ounces water
- 1 (13½ounces) can unsweetened full-fat coconut milk
- 2 cups riced/shredded cauliflower (I buy it pre-riced at Trader Joe's)
- 2 tablespoons red curry paste
- 2 tablespoons chopped fresh cilantro leaves, divided
- Pink Himalayan salt
- Freshly ground black pepper
- 1 cup shrimp (I use defrosted Trader Joe's Frozen Medium Cooked Shrimp, which are peeled and deveined, with tail off)

1. With the crock insert in place, preheat the slow cooker to high. 2. Add the water, coconut milk, riced cauliflower, red curry paste, and 1 tablespoon of chopped cilantro, and season with pink Himalayan salt and pepper. Stir to combine. 3. Cover and cook on high for 2 hours. 4. Season the shrimp with pink Himalayan salt and pepper, add them to the slow cooker, and stir. Cook for an additional 15 minutes. 5. Ladle the soup into four bowls, top each with half of the remaining 1 tablespoon of chopped cilantro, and serve.

Per Serving:

calories: 269 | fat: 21g | protein: 16g | carbs: 8g | net carbs: 5g | fiber: 3g

Chapter **7**

Vegetarian Mains

Chapter 7 Vegetarian Mains

Cheesy Broccoli Casserole

Prep time: 10 minutes | Cook time: 35 minutes | Serves 4

- 2 tablespoons butter
- ¼ white onion, diced
- 1 garlic clove, minced
- 1 pound (454 g) broccoli florets, roughly chopped
- Salt, to taste
- Freshly ground black pepper, to taste
- 4 ounces (113 g) cream cheese, at room temperature
- 1 cup shredded Cheddar cheese, divided
- ½ cup heavy (whipping) cream
- 2 eggs

1. Preheat the oven to 350ºF (180ºC). 2. In a large skillet over medium heat, melt the butter. 3. Add the onion and garlic. Sauté for 5 to 7 minutes until the onion is softened and translucent. 4. Add the broccoli. Season with salt and pepper. Cook for 4 to 5 minutes until just softened. Transfer to a 7-by-11-inch baking dish. 5. In a medium bowl, stir together the cream cheese, ½ cup of Cheddar, the cream, and eggs. Pour over the broccoli. Season with more salt and pepper, and top with the remaining ½ cup of Cheddar. Bake for 20 minutes. Refrigerate leftovers in an airtight container for up to 1 week.

Per Serving:

calories: 440 | fat: 39g | protein: 16g | carbs: 11g | net carbs: 8g | fiber: 3g

Broccoli-Cheese Fritters

Prep time: 5 minutes | Cook time: 20 to 25 minutes | Serves 4

- 1 cup broccoli florets
- 1 cup shredded Mozzarella cheese
- ¾ cup almond flour
- ½ cup flaxseed meal, divided
- 2 teaspoons baking powder
- 1 teaspoon garlic powder
- Salt and freshly ground black pepper, to taste
- 2 eggs, lightly beaten
- ½ cup ranch dressing

1. Preheat the air fryer to 400ºF (204ºC). 2. In a food processor fitted with a metal blade, pulse the broccoli until very finely chopped. 3. Transfer the broccoli to a large bowl and add the Mozzarella, almond flour, ¼ cup of the flaxseed meal, baking powder, and garlic powder. Stir until thoroughly combined. Season to taste with salt and black pepper. Add the eggs and stir again to form a sticky dough. Shape the dough into 1¼-inch fritters. 4. Place the remaining ¼ cup flaxseed meal in a shallow bowl and roll the fritters in the meal to form an even coating. 5. Working in batches if necessary, arrange the fritters in a single layer in the basket of the air fryer and spray generously with olive oil. Pausing halfway through the cooking time to shake the basket, air fry for 20 to 25 minutes until the fritters are golden brown and crispy. Serve with the ranch dressing for dipping.

Per Serving:

calories: 638 | fat: 54g | protein: 28g | carbs: 16g | net carbs: 9g | fiber: 7g

Spinach-Artichoke Stuffed Mushrooms

Prep time: 10 minutes | Cook time: 10 to 14 minutes | Serves 4

- 2 tablespoons olive oil
- 4 large portobello mushrooms, stems removed and gills scraped out
- ½ teaspoon salt
- ¼ teaspoon freshly ground pepper
- 4 ounces (113 g) goat cheese, crumbled
- ½ cup chopped marinated artichoke hearts
- 1 cup frozen spinach, thawed and squeezed dry
- ½ cup grated Parmesan cheese
- 2 tablespoons chopped fresh parsley

1. Preheat the air fryer to 400ºF (204ºC). 2. Rub the olive oil over the portobello mushrooms until thoroughly coated. Sprinkle both sides with the salt and black pepper. Place top-side down on a clean work surface. 3. In a small bowl, combine the goat cheese, artichoke hearts, and spinach. Mash with the back of a fork until thoroughly combined. Divide the cheese mixture among the mushrooms and sprinkle with the Parmesan cheese. 4. Air fry for 10 to 14 minutes until the mushrooms are tender and the cheese has begun to brown. Top with the fresh parsley just before serving.

Per Serving:

calories: 255 | fat: 20g | protein: 13g | carbs: 7g | net carbs: 4g | fiber: 3g

Green Vegetable Stir-Fry with Tofu

Prep time: 15 minutes | Cook time: 15 minutes | Serves 2

- 3 tablespoons avocado oil, divided
- 1 cup Brussels sprouts, halved
- ½ onion, diced
- ½ leek, white and light green parts diced
- ½ head green cabbage, diced
- ¼ cup water, plus more if needed
- ½ cup kale, coarsely chopped
- 1 cup spinach, coarsely chopped
- 8 ounces (227 g) tofu, diced
- 2 teaspoons garlic powder
- Salt and freshly ground black pepper, to taste
- ½ avocado, pitted, peeled, and diced
- MCT oil (optional)

1. In a large skillet with a lid (or a wok if you have one), heat 2 tablespoons of avocado oil over medium-high heat. Add the Brussels sprouts, onion, leek, and cabbage and stir together. Add the water, cover, lower the heat to medium, and cook for about 5 minutes. 2. Toss in the kale and spinach and cook for 3 minutes, stirring constantly, until the onion, leek, and cabbage are caramelized. 3. Add the tofu to the stir-fry, then season with the garlic, salt, pepper, and the remaining tablespoon of avocado oil. 4. Turn the heat back up to medium-high and cook for about 10 minutes, stirring constantly, until the tofu is nice and caramelized on all sides. If you experience any burning, turn down the heat and add 2 to 3 tablespoons of water. 5. Divide the stir-fry between two plates and sprinkle with diced avocado. Feel free to drizzle algae oil or MCT oil over the top for a little extra fat.

Per Serving:

calories: 473 | fat: 33g | protein: 17g | carbs: 27g | net carbs: 15g | fiber: 12g

Buffalo Cauliflower Bites with Blue Cheese

Prep time: 10 minutes | Cook time: 8 to 10 minutes | Serves 4

- 1 large head cauliflower, chopped into florets
- 1 tablespoon olive oil
- Salt and freshly ground black
Garlic Blue Cheese Dip:
- ½ cup mayonnaise
- ¼ cup sour cream
- 2 tablespoons heavy cream
- 1 tablespoon fresh lemon juice
- pepper, to taste
- ¼ cup unsalted butter, melted
- ¼ cup hot sauce

- 1 clove garlic, minced
- ¼ cup crumbled blue cheese
- Salt and freshly ground black pepper, to taste

1. Preheat the air fryer to 400°F (204°C). 2. In a large bowl, combine the cauliflower and olive oil. Season to taste with salt and black pepper. Toss until the vegetables are thoroughly coated. 3. Working in batches, place half of the cauliflower in the air fryer basket. Pausing halfway through the cooking time to shake the basket, air fry for 8 to 10 minutes until the cauliflower is evenly browned. Transfer to a large bowl and repeat with the remaining cauliflower. 4. In a small bowl, whisk together the melted butter and hot sauce. 5. To make the dip: In a small bowl, combine the mayonnaise, sour cream, heavy cream, lemon juice, garlic, and blue cheese. Season to taste with salt and freshly ground black pepper. 6. Just before serving, pour the butter mixture over the cauliflower and toss gently until thoroughly coated. Serve with the dip on the side.

Per Serving:

calories: 420 | fat: 39g | protein: 9g | carbs: 14g | net carbs: 11g | fiber: 3g

Stuffed Eggplant

Prep time: 20 minutes | Cook time: 1 hour | Serves 2 to 4

- 1 small eggplant, halved lengthwise
- 3 tablespoons olive, avocado, or macadamia nut oil
- 1 onion, diced
- 12 asparagus spears or green beans, diced
- 1 red bell pepper, diced
- 1 large tomato, chopped
- 2 garlic cloves, minced
- ½ block (8 ounces / 227 g)
- extra-firm tofu (optional)
- 3 tablespoons chopped fresh basil leaves
- Salt and freshly ground black pepper, to taste
- ¼ cup water
- 2 eggs
- Chopped fresh parsley, for garnish (optional)
- Shredded cheese, for garnish (optional)

1. Preheat the oven to 350°F (180°C). 2. Scoop out the flesh from the halved eggplant and chop it into cubes. Reserve the eggplant skin. 3. In a sauté pan with a lid, heat the oil over medium-high heat. Add the eggplant, onion, asparagus, bell pepper, tomato, garlic, and tofu (if using) and stir. Stir in the basil, season with salt and pepper, and cook for about 5 minutes. 4. Add the water, cover the pan, reduce the heat to medium, and cook for about 15 minutes longer. 5. Put the eggplant "boats" (the reserved skin) on a baking sheet. Scoop some of the cooked eggplant mixture into each boat (you may have some filling left over, which is fine—you can roast it alongside the eggplant). 6. Crack an egg into each eggplant boat, on top of the filling, then bake for about 40 minutes, or until desired doneness. 7. Remove the eggplant from the oven and, if desired, sprinkle parsley and cheese over the top. Let the cheese melt and cool for about 5 minutes, then serve them up!

Per Serving:

calories: 380 | fat: 26g | protein: 12g | carbs: 25g | net carbs: 15g | fiber: 10g

Cauliflower Steak with Gremolata

Prep time: 15 minutes | Cook time: 25 minutes | Serves 4

- 2 tablespoons olive oil
- 1 tablespoon Italian seasoning
- 1 large head cauliflower, outer leaves removed and sliced lengthwise through
- the core into thick "steaks"
- Salt and freshly ground black pepper, to taste
- ¼ cup Parmesan cheese

Gremolata:

- 1 bunch Italian parsley (about 1 cup packed)
- 2 cloves garlic
- Zest of 1 small lemon, plus 1
- to 2 teaspoons lemon juice
- ½ cup olive oil
- Salt and pepper, to taste

1. Preheat the air fryer to 400ºF (204ºC). 2. In a small bowl, combine the olive oil and Italian seasoning. Brush both sides of each cauliflower "steak" generously with the oil. Season to taste with salt and black pepper. 3. Working in batches if necessary, arrange the cauliflower in a single layer in the air fryer basket. Pausing halfway through the cooking time to turn the "steaks," air fry for 15 to 20 minutes until the cauliflower is tender and the edges begin to brown. Sprinkle with the Parmesan and air fry for 5 minutes longer. 4. To make the gremolata: In a food processor fitted with a metal blade, combine the parsley, garlic, and lemon zest and juice. With the motor running, add the olive oil in a steady stream until the mixture forms a bright green sauce. Season to taste with salt and black pepper. Serve the cauliflower steaks with the gremolata spooned over the top.

Per Serving:

calories: 257 | fat: 23g | protein: 6g | carbs: 9g | net carbs: 7g | fiber: 4g

Broccoli Crust Pizza

Prep time: 15 minutes | Cook time: 12 minutes | Serves 4

- 3 cups riced broccoli, steamed and drained well
- 1 large egg
- ½ cup grated vegetarian Parmesan cheese
- 3 tablespoons low-carb Alfredo sauce
- ½ cup shredded Mozzarella cheese

1. In a large bowl, mix broccoli, egg, and Parmesan. 2. Cut a piece of parchment to fit your air fryer basket. Press out the pizza mixture to fit on the parchment, working in two batches if necessary. Place into the air fryer basket. 3. Adjust the temperature to 370ºF (188ºC) and air fry for 5 minutes. 4. The crust should be firm enough to flip. If not, add 2 additional minutes. Flip crust. 5. Top with Alfredo sauce and Mozzarella. Return to the air fryer basket and cook an additional 7 minutes or until cheese is golden and bubbling. Serve warm.

Per Serving:

calories: 178 | fat: 11g | protein: 15g | carbs: 10g | net carbs: 4g | fiber: 6g

Cheese Stuffed Peppers

Prep time: 20 minutes | Cook time: 15 minutes | Serves 2

- 1 red bell pepper, top and seeds removed
- 1 yellow bell pepper, top and seeds removed
- Salt and pepper, to taste
- 1 cup Cottage cheese
- 4 tablespoons mayonnaise
- 2 pickles, chopped

1. Arrange the peppers in the lightly greased air fryer basket. Cook in the preheated air fryer at 400ºF (204ºC) for 15 minutes, turning them over halfway through the cooking time. 2. Season with salt and pepper. Then, in a mixing bowl, combine the cream cheese with the mayonnaise and chopped pickles. Stuff the pepper with the cream cheese mixture and serve. Enjoy!

Per Serving:

calories: 250 | fat: 20g | protein: 11g | carbs: 8g | net carbs: 6g | fiber: 2g

Vegetable Burgers

Prep time: 10 minutes | Cook time: 12 minutes | Serves 4

- 8 ounces (227 g) cremini mushrooms
- 2 large egg yolks
- ½ medium zucchini, trimmed and chopped
- ¼ cup peeled and chopped
- yellow onion
- 1 clove garlic, peeled and finely minced
- ½ teaspoon salt
- ¼ teaspoon ground black pepper

1. Place all ingredients into a food processor and pulse twenty times until finely chopped and combined. 2. Separate mixture into four equal sections and press each into a burger shape. Place burgers into ungreased air fryer basket. Adjust the temperature to 375ºF (191ºC) and air fry for 12 minutes, turning burgers halfway through cooking. Burgers will be browned and firm when done. 3. Place burgers on a large plate and let cool 5 minutes before serving.

Per Serving:

calories: 62 | fat: 3g | protein: 3g | carbs: 6g | net carbs: 4g | fiber: 2g

Vegetable Vodka Sauce Bake

Prep time: 10 minutes | Cook time: 30 minutes | Serves 4

- 3 tablespoons melted grass-fed butter, divided
- 4 cups mushrooms, halved
- 4 cups cooked cauliflower florets
- 1½ cups purchased vodka sauce
- ¾ cup heavy (whipping) cream
- ½ cup grated Asiago cheese
- Sea salt, for seasoning
- Freshly ground black pepper, for seasoning
- 1 cup shredded provolone cheese
- 2 tablespoons chopped fresh oregano

1. Preheat the oven. Set the oven temperature to 350°F and use 1 tablespoon of the melted butter to grease a 9-by-13-inch baking dish. 2. Mix the vegetables. In a large bowl, combine the mushrooms, cauliflower, vodka sauce, cream, Asiago, and the remaining 2 tablespoons of butter. Season the vegetables with salt and pepper. 3. Bake. Transfer the vegetable mixture to the baking dish and top it with the provolone cheese. Bake for 30 to 35 minutes until it's bubbly and heated through. 4. Serve. Divide the mixture between four plates and top with the oregano.

Per Serving:

calories: 537 | fat: 45g | protein: 19g | carbs: 14g | net carbs: 8g | fiber: 19g

Greek Vegetable Briam

Prep time: 10 minutes | Cook time: 30 minutes | Serves 4

- ⅓ cup good-quality olive oil, divided
- 1 onion, thinly sliced
- 1 tablespoon minced garlic
- ¾ small eggplant, diced
- 2 zucchini, diced
- 2 cups chopped cauliflower
- 1 red bell pepper, diced
- 2 cups diced tomatoes
- 2 tablespoons chopped fresh parsley
- 2 tablespoons chopped fresh oregano
- Sea salt, for seasoning
- Freshly ground black pepper, for seasoning
- 1½ cups crumbled feta cheese
- ¼ cup pumpkin seeds

1. Preheat the oven. Set the oven to broil and lightly grease a 9-by-13-inch casserole dish with olive oil. 2. Sauté the aromatics. In a medium stockpot over medium heat, warm 3 tablespoons of the olive oil. Add the onion and garlic and sauté until they've softened, about 3 minutes. 3. Sauté the vegetables. Stir in the eggplant and cook for 5 minutes, stirring occasionally. Add the zucchini, cauliflower, and red bell pepper and cook for 5 minutes. Stir in the tomatoes, parsley, and oregano and cook, giving it a stir from time to time, until the vegetables are tender, about 10 minutes. Season it with salt and pepper. 4. Broil. Transfer the vegetable mixture to the casserole dish and top with the crumbled feta. Broil for about 4 minutes until the cheese is golden. 5. Serve. Divide the casserole between four plates and top it with the pumpkin seeds. Drizzle with the remaining olive oil.

Per Serving:

calories: 356 | fat: 28g | protein: 11g | carbs: 18g | net carbs: 11g | fiber: 7g

Spinach Cheese Casserole

Prep time: 15 minutes | Cook time: 15 minutes | Serves 4

- 1 tablespoon salted butter, melted
- ¼ cup diced yellow onion
- 8 ounces (227 g) full-fat cream cheese, softened
- ⅓ cup full-fat mayonnaise
- ⅓ cup full-fat sour cream
- ¼ cup chopped pickled jalapeños
- 2 cups fresh spinach, chopped
- 2 cups cauliflower florets, chopped
- 1 cup artichoke hearts, chopped

1. In a large bowl, mix butter, onion, cream cheese, mayonnaise, and sour cream. Fold in jalapeños, spinach, cauliflower, and artichokes. 2. Pour the mixture into a round baking dish. Cover with foil and place into the air fryer basket. 3. Adjust the temperature to 370ºF (188ºC) and set the timer for 15 minutes. In the last 2 minutes of cooking, remove the foil to brown the top. Serve warm.

Per Serving:

calories: 490 | fat: 46g | protein: 9g | carbs: 12g | net carbs: 8g | fiber: 4g

Cauliflower Rice-Stuffed Peppers

Prep time: 10 minutes | Cook time: 15 minutes | Serves 4

- 2 cups uncooked cauliflower rice
- ¾ cup drained canned petite diced tomatoes
- 2 tablespoons olive oil
- 1 cup shredded Mozzarella
- cheese
- ¼ teaspoon salt
- ¼ teaspoon ground black pepper
- 4 medium green bell peppers, tops removed, seeded

1. In a large bowl, mix all ingredients except bell peppers. Scoop mixture evenly into peppers. 2. Place peppers into ungreased air fryer basket. Adjust the temperature to 350ºF (177ºC) and air fry for 15 minutes. Peppers will be tender and cheese will be melted when done. Serve warm.

Per Serving:

\calories: 309 | fat: 23g | protein: 16g | carbs: 11g | net carbs: 7g | fiber: 4g

Cheese Stuffed Zucchini

Prep time: 20 minutes | Cook time: 8 minutes | Serves 4

- 1 large zucchini, cut into four pieces
- 2 tablespoons olive oil
- 1 cup Ricotta cheese, room temperature
- 2 tablespoons scallions, chopped
- 1 heaping tablespoon fresh parsley, roughly chopped
- 1 heaping tablespoon coriander, minced
- 2 ounces (57 g) Cheddar cheese, preferably freshly grated
- 1 teaspoon celery seeds
- ½ teaspoon salt
- ½ teaspoon garlic pepper

1. Cook your zucchini in the air fryer basket for approximately 10 minutes at 350ºF (177ºC). Check for doneness and cook for 2-3 minutes longer if needed. 2. Meanwhile, make the stuffing by mixing the other items. 3. When your zucchini is thoroughly cooked, open them up. Divide the stuffing among all zucchini pieces and bake an additional 5 minutes.

Per Serving:

calories: 360 | fat: 27g | protein: 18g | carbs: 11g | net carbs: 8g | fiber: 3g

Almond-Cauliflower Gnocchi

Prep time: 5 minutes | Cook time: 25 to 30 minutes | Serves 4

- 5 cups cauliflower florets
- ⅔ cup almond flour
- ½ teaspoon salt
- ¼ cup unsalted butter, melted
- ¼ cup grated Parmesan cheese

1. In a food processor fitted with a metal blade, pulse the cauliflower until finely chopped. Transfer the cauliflower to a large microwave-safe bowl and cover it with a paper towel. Microwave for 5 minutes. Spread the cauliflower on a towel to cool. 2. When cool enough to handle, draw up the sides of the towel and squeeze tightly over a sink to remove the excess moisture. Return the cauliflower to the food processor and whirl until creamy. Sprinkle in the flour and salt and pulse until a sticky dough comes together. 3. Transfer the dough to a workspace lightly floured with almond flour. Shape the dough into a ball and divide into 4 equal sections. Roll each section into a rope 1 inch thick. Slice the dough into squares with a sharp knife. 4. Preheat the air fryer to 400ºF (204ºC). 5. Working in batches if necessary, place the gnocchi in a single layer in the basket of the air fryer and spray generously with olive oil. Pausing halfway through the cooking time to turn the gnocchi, air fry for 25 to 30 minutes until golden brown and crispy on the edges. Transfer to a large bowl and toss with the melted butter and Parmesan cheese.

Per Serving:

calories: 220 | fat: 20g | protein: 7g | carbs: 8g | net carbs: 5g | fiber: 3g

Roasted Spaghetti Squash

Prep time: 10 minutes | Cook time: 45 minutes | Serves 6

- 1 (4 pounds / 1.8 kg) spaghetti squash, halved and seeded
- 2 tablespoons coconut oil
- 4 tablespoons salted butter, melted
- 1 teaspoon garlic powder
- 2 teaspoons dried parsley

1. Brush shell of spaghetti squash with coconut oil. Brush inside with butter. Sprinkle inside with garlic powder and parsley. 2. Place squash skin side down into ungreased air fryer basket, working in batches if needed. Adjust the temperature to 350ºF (177ºC) and set the timer for 30 minutes. When the timer beeps, flip squash and cook an additional 15 minutes until fork-tender. 3. Use a fork to remove spaghetti strands from shell and serve warm.

Per Serving:

calories: 210 | fat: 19g | protein: 2g | carbs: 11g | net carbs: 8g | fiber: 3g

Herbed Ricotta–Stuffed Mushrooms

Prep time: 10 minutes | Cook time: 30 minutes | Serves 4

- 6 tablespoons extra-virgin olive oil, divided
- 4 portobello mushroom caps, cleaned and gills removed
- 1 cup whole-milk ricotta cheese
- ⅓ cup chopped fresh herbs
- (such as basil, parsley, rosemary, oregano, or thyme)
- 2 garlic cloves, finely minced
- ½ teaspoon salt
- ¼ teaspoon freshly ground black pepper

1. Preheat the oven to 400ºF (205ºC). 2. Line a baking sheet with parchment or foil and drizzle with 2 tablespoons olive oil, spreading evenly. Place the mushroom caps on the baking sheet, gill-side up. 3. In a medium bowl, mix together the ricotta, herbs, 2 tablespoons olive oil, garlic, salt, and pepper. Stuff each mushroom cap with one-quarter of the cheese mixture, pressing down if needed. Drizzle with remaining 2 tablespoons olive oil and bake until golden brown and the mushrooms are soft, 30 to 35 minutes, depending on the size of the mushrooms.

Per Serving:

calories: 400 | fat: 36g | protein: 12g | carbs: 7g | net carbs: 6g | fiber: 1g

Cheesy Garden Veggie Crustless Quiche

Prep time: 5 minutes | Cook time: 25 minutes | Serves 4

- 1 tablespoon grass-fed butter, divided
- 6 eggs
- ¾ cup heavy (whipping) cream
- 3 ounces goat cheese, divided
- ½ cup sliced mushrooms, chopped
- 1 scallion, white and green parts, chopped
- 1 cup shredded fresh spinach
- 10 cherry tomatoes, cut in half

1. Preheat the oven. Set the oven temperature to 350°F. Grease a 9-inch pie plate with ½ teaspoon of the butter and set it aside. 2. Mix the quiche base. In a medium bowl, whisk the eggs, cream, and 2 ounces of the cheese until it's all well blended. Set it aside. 3. Sauté the vegetables. In a small skillet over medium-high heat, melt the remaining butter. Add the mushrooms and scallion and sauté them until they've softened, about 2 minutes. Add the spinach and sauté until it's wilted, about 2 minutes. 4. Assemble and bake. Spread the vegetable mixture in the bottom of the pie plate and pour the egg-and-cream mixture over the vegetables. Scatter the cherry tomatoes and the remaining 1 ounce of goat cheese on top. Bake for 20 to 25 minutes until the quiche is cooked through, puffed, and lightly browned. 5. Serve. Cut the quiche into wedges and divide it between four plates. Serve it warm or cold.

Per Serving:

calories: 355 | fat: 30g | protein: 18g | carbs: 5g | net carbs: 4g | fiber: 1g

Asparagus and Fennel Frittata

Prep time: 10 minutes | Cook time: 30 minutes | Serves 4

- 1 teaspoon coconut or regular butter, plus more for greasing
- 8 asparagus spears, diced
- ½ cup diced fennel
- ½ cup mushrooms, sliced (optional)
- 8 eggs
- ½ cup full-fat regular milk or coconut milk
- 1 tomato, sliced
- 1 teaspoon salt
- ½ teaspoon freshly ground black pepper
- Grated cheese (optional)

1. Preheat the oven to 350ºF (180ºC). Grease a pie dish with butter. 2. Melt 1 teaspoon of butter in a shallow skillet over medium-high heat and sauté the asparagus, fennel, and mushrooms (if using) for about 5 minutes, or until fork-tender. 3. Transfer the vegetables to the prepared pie dish. 4. Crack the eggs into a mixing bowl and pour in the milk. Whisk together until fully combined. 5. Pour the egg mixture over the vegetables in the pie dish, season with salt and pepper, and carefully and lightly mix everything together. Lay the tomato slices on top. 6. Bake the frittata for about 30 minutes. 7. Remove from the oven and let cool for 5 to 10 minutes. Slice into wedges and sprinkle with grated cheese, if desired.

Per Serving:

calories: 188 | fat: 12g | protein: 14g | carbs: 6g | net carbs: 4g | fiber: 2g

Quiche-Stuffed Peppers

Prep time: 5 minutes | Cook time: 15 minutes | Serves 2

- 2 medium green bell peppers
- 3 large eggs
- ¼ cup full-fat ricotta cheese
- ¼ cup diced yellow onion
- ½ cup chopped broccoli
- ½ cup shredded medium Cheddar cheese

1. Cut the tops off of the peppers and remove the seeds and white membranes with a small knife. 2. In a medium bowl, whisk eggs and ricotta. 3. Add onion and broccoli. Pour the egg and vegetable mixture evenly into each pepper. Top with Cheddar. Place peppers into a 4-cup round baking dish and place into the air fryer basket. 4. Adjust the temperature to 350ºF (177ºC) and bake for 15 minutes. 5. Eggs will be mostly firm and peppers tender when fully cooked. Serve immediately.

Per Serving:

calories: 382 | fat: 27g | protein: 24g | carbs: 11g | net carbs: 7g | fiber: 4g

Sweet Pepper Nachos

Prep time: 10 minutes | Cook time: 5 minutes | Serves 2

- 6 mini sweet peppers, seeded and sliced in half
- ¾ cup shredded Colby jack cheese
- ¼ cup sliced pickled
- jalapeños
- ½ medium avocado, peeled, pitted, and diced
- 2 tablespoons sour cream

1. Place peppers into an ungreased round nonstick baking dish. Sprinkle with Colby and top with jalapeños. 2. Place dish into air fryer basket. Adjust the temperature to 350ºF (177ºC) and bake for 5 minutes. Cheese will be melted and bubbly when done. 3. Remove dish from air fryer and top with avocado. Drizzle with sour cream. Serve warm.

Per Serving:

calories: 255 | fat: 21g | protein: 11g | carbs: 9g | net carbs: 5g | fiber: 4g

Crustless Spanakopita

Prep time: 15 minutes | Cook time: 45 minutes | Serves 6

- 12 tablespoons extra-virgin olive oil, divided
- 1 small yellow onion, diced
- 1 (32-ounce / 907-g) bag frozen chopped spinach, thawed, fully drained, and patted dry (about 4 cups)
- 4 garlic cloves, minced
- ½ teaspoon salt
- ½ teaspoon freshly ground black pepper
- 1 cup whole-milk ricotta cheese
- 4 large eggs
- ¾ cup crumbled traditional feta cheese
- ¼ cup pine nuts

1. Preheat the oven to 375°F (190°C). 2. In a large skillet, heat 4 tablespoons olive oil over medium-high heat. Add the onion and sauté until softened, 6 to 8 minutes. 3. Add the spinach, garlic, salt, and pepper and sauté another 5 minutes. Remove from the heat and allow to cool slightly. 4. In a medium bowl, whisk together the ricotta and eggs. Add to the cooled spinach and stir to combine. 5. Pour 4 tablespoons olive oil in the bottom of a 9-by-13-inch glass baking dish and swirl to coat the bottom and sides. Add the spinach-ricotta mixture and spread into an even layer. 6. Bake for 20 minutes or until the mixture begins to set. Remove from the oven and crumble the feta evenly across the top of the spinach. Add the pine nuts and drizzle with the remaining 4 tablespoons olive oil. Return to the oven and bake for an additional 15 to 20 minutes, or until the spinach is fully set and the top is starting to turn golden brown. Allow to cool slightly before cutting to serve.

Per Serving:

calories: 440 | fat: 38g | protein: 17g | carbs: 9g | net carbs: 8g | fiber: 1g

Mediterranean Filling Stuffed Portobello Mushrooms

Prep time: 10 minutes | Cook time: 35 minutes | Serves 4

- 4 large portobello mushroom caps
- 3 tablespoons good-quality olive oil, divided
- 1 cup chopped fresh spinach
- 1 red bell pepper, chopped
- 1 celery stalk, chopped
- ½ cup chopped sun-dried tomato
- ¼ onion, chopped
- 2 teaspoons minced garlic
- 1 teaspoon chopped fresh oregano
- 2 cups chopped pecans
- ¼ cup balsamic vinaigrette
- Sea salt, for seasoning
- Freshly ground black pepper, for seasoning

1. Preheat the oven. Set the oven temperature to 350°F. Line a baking sheet with parchment paper. 2. Prepare the mushrooms. Use a spoon to scoop the black gills out of the mushrooms. Massage 2 tablespoons of the olive oil all over the mushroom caps and place the mushrooms on the prepared baking sheet. Set them aside. 3. Prepare the filling. In a large skillet over medium-high heat, warm the remaining 1 tablespoon of olive oil. Add the spinach, red bell pepper, celery, sun-dried tomato, onion, garlic, and oregano and sauté until the vegetables are tender, about 10 minutes. Stir in the

pecans and balsamic vinaigrette and season the mixture with salt and pepper. 4. Assemble and bake. Stuff the mushroom caps with the filling and bake for 20 to 25 minutes until they're tender and golden. 5. Serve. Place one stuffed mushroom on each of four plates and serve them hot.

Per Serving:

calories: 595 | fat: 56g | protein: 10g | carbs: 18g | net carbs: 9g | fiber: 9g

Crispy Tofu

Prep time: 30 minutes | Cook time: 15 to 20 minutes | Serves 4

- 1 (16-ounce / 454-g) block extra-firm tofu
- 2 tablespoons coconut aminos
- 1 tablespoon toasted sesame oil
- 1 tablespoon olive oil
- 1 tablespoon chili-garlic sauce
- 1½ teaspoons black sesame seeds
- 1 scallion, thinly sliced

1. Press the tofu for at least 15 minutes by wrapping it in paper towels and setting a heavy pan on top so that the moisture drains. 2. Slice the tofu into bite-size cubes and transfer to a bowl. Drizzle with the coconut aminos, sesame oil, olive oil, and chili-garlic sauce. Cover and refrigerate for 1 hour or up to overnight. 3. Preheat the air fryer to 400°F (204°C). 4. Arrange the tofu in a single layer in the air fryer basket. Pausing to shake the pan halfway through the cooking time, air fry for 15 to 20 minutes until crisp. Serve with any juices that accumulate in the bottom of the air fryer, sprinkled with the sesame seeds and sliced scallion.

Per Serving:

calories: 186 | fat: 14g | protein: 12g | carbs: 4g | net carbs: 3g | fiber: 1g

Cheesy Cauliflower Pizza Crust

Prep time: 15 minutes | Cook time: 11 minutes | Serves 2

- 1 (12 ounces / 340 g) steamer bag cauliflower
- ½ cup shredded sharp Cheddar cheese
- 1 large egg
- 2 tablespoons blanched finely ground almond flour
- 1 teaspoon Italian blend seasoning

1. Cook cauliflower according to package instructions. Remove from bag and place into cheesecloth or paper towel to remove excess water. Place cauliflower into a large bowl. 2. Add cheese, egg, almond flour, and Italian seasoning to the bowl and mix well. 3. Cut a piece of parchment to fit your air fryer basket. Press cauliflower into 6-inch round circle. Place into the air fryer basket. 4. Adjust the temperature to 360°F (182°C) and air fry for 11 minutes. 5. After 7 minutes, flip the pizza crust. 6. Add preferred toppings to pizza. Place back into air fryer basket and cook an additional 4 minutes or until fully cooked and golden. Serve immediately.

Per Serving:

calories: 248 | fat: 18g | protein: 16g | carbs: 8g | net carbs: 4g | fiber: 4g

Zucchini Pasta with Spinach, Olives, and Asiago

Prep time: 10 minutes | Cook time: 10 minutes | Serves 4

- 3 tablespoons good-quality olive oil
- 1 tablespoon grass-fed butter
- 1½ tablespoons minced garlic
- 1 cup packed fresh spinach
- ½ cup sliced black olives
- ½ cup halved cherry tomatoes
- 2 tablespoons chopped fresh

- basil
- 3 zucchini, spiralized
- Sea salt, for seasoning
- Freshly ground black pepper, for seasoning
- ½ cup shredded Asiago cheese

1. Sauté the vegetables. In a large skillet over medium-high heat, warm the olive oil and butter. Add the garlic and sauté until it's tender, about 2 minutes. Stir in the spinach, olives, tomatoes, and basil and sauté until the spinach is wilted, about 4 minutes. Stir in the zucchini noodles, toss to combine them with the sauce, and cook until the zucchini is tender, about 2 minutes. 2. Serve. Season with salt and pepper. Divide the mixture between four bowls and serve topped with the Asiago.

Per Serving:

calories: 199 | fat: 18g | protein: 6g | carbs: 4g | net carbs: 3g | fiber: 1g

Zucchini-Ricotta Tart

Prep time: 15 minutes | Cook time: 60 minutes | Serves 6

- ½ cup grated Parmesan cheese, divided
- 1½ cups almond flour
- 1 tablespoon coconut flour
- ½ teaspoon garlic powder
- ¾ teaspoon salt, divided
- ¼ cup unsalted butter, melted

- 1 zucchini, thinly sliced (about 2 cups)
- 1 cup ricotta cheese
- 3 eggs
- 2 tablespoons heavy cream
- 2 cloves garlic, minced
- ½ teaspoon dried tarragon

1. Preheat the air fryer to 330ºF (166ºC). Coat a round pan with olive oil and set aside. 2. In a large bowl, whisk ¼ cup of the Parmesan with the almond flour, coconut flour, garlic powder, and ¼ teaspoon of the salt. Stir in the melted butter until the dough resembles coarse crumbs. Press the dough firmly into the bottom and up the sides of the prepared pan. Air fry for 12 to 15 minutes until the crust begins to brown. Let cool to room temperature. 3. Meanwhile, place the zucchini in a colander and sprinkle with the remaining ½ teaspoon salt. Toss gently to distribute the salt and let sit for 30 minutes. Use paper towels to pat the zucchini dry. 4. In a large bowl, whisk together the ricotta, eggs, heavy cream, garlic, and tarragon. Gently stir in the zucchini slices. Pour the cheese mixture into the cooled crust and sprinkle with the remaining ¼ cup Parmesan. 5. Increase the air fryer to 350ºF (177ºC). Place the pan in the air fryer basket and air fry for 45 to 50 minutes, or until set and a tester inserted into the center of the tart comes out clean. Serve warm or at room temperature.

Per Serving:

calories: 530 | fat: 43g | protein: 24g | carbs: 11g | net carbs: 5g | fiber: 6g

Pesto Spinach Flatbread

Prep time: 10 minutes | Cook time: 8 minutes | Serves 4

- 1 cup blanched finely ground almond flour
- 2 ounces (57 g) cream cheese
- 2 cups shredded Mozzarella

- cheese
- 1 cup chopped fresh spinach leaves
- 2 tablespoons basil pesto

1. Place flour, cream cheese, and Mozzarella in a large microwave-safe bowl and microwave on high 45 seconds, then stir. 2. Fold in spinach and microwave an additional 15 seconds. Stir until a soft dough ball forms. 3. Cut two pieces of parchment paper to fit air fryer basket. Separate dough into two sections and press each out on ungreased parchment to create 6-inch rounds. 4. Spread 1 tablespoon pesto over each flatbread and place rounds on parchment into ungreased air fryer basket. Adjust the temperature to 350ºF (177ºC) and air fry for 8 minutes, turning crusts halfway through cooking. Flatbread will be golden when done. 5. Let cool 5 minutes before slicing and serving.

Per Serving:

calories: 506 | fat: 43g | protein: 27g | carbs: 9g | net carbs: 5g | fiber: 4g

White Cheddar and Mushroom Soufflés

Prep time: 15 minutes | Cook time: 12 minutes | Serves 4

- 3 large eggs, whites and yolks separated
- ½ cup sharp white Cheddar cheese
- 3 ounces (85 g) cream cheese, softened

- ¼ teaspoon cream of tartar
- ¼ teaspoon salt
- ¼ teaspoon ground black pepper
- ½ cup cremini mushrooms, sliced

1. In a large bowl, whip egg whites until stiff peaks form, about 2 minutes. In a separate large bowl, beat Cheddar, egg yolks, cream cheese, cream of tartar, salt, and pepper together until combined. 2. Fold egg whites into cheese mixture, being careful not to stir. Fold in mushrooms, then pour mixture evenly into four ungreased ramekins. Place ramekins into air fryer basket. Adjust the temperature to 350ºF (177ºC) and bake for 12 minutes. Eggs will be browned on the top and firm in the center when done. Serve warm.

Per Serving:

calories: 228 | fat: 19g | protein: 13g | carbs: 2g | net carbs: 2g | fiber: 0g

Chapter 8

Snacks and Appetizers

Chapter 8 Snacks and Appetizers

Buffalo Chicken Meatballs

Prep time: 5 minutes | Cook time: 10 minutes | Serves 4

- 1 pound (454 g) ground chicken
- ½ cup almond flour
- 2 tablespoons cream cheese
- 1 packet dry ranch dressing mix
- ½ teaspoon salt
- ¼ teaspoon pepper
- ¼ teaspoon garlic powder
- 1 cup water
- 2 tablespoons butter, melted
- ⅓ cup hot sauce
- ¼ cup crumbled feta cheese
- ¼ cup sliced green onion

1. In large bowl, mix ground chicken, almond flour, cream cheese, ranch, salt, pepper, and garlic powder. Roll mixture into 16 balls. 2. Place meatballs on steam rack and add 1 cup water to Instant Pot. Click lid closed. Press the Meat/Stew button and set time for 10 minutes. 3. Combine butter and hot sauce. When timer beeps, remove meatballs and place in clean large bowl. Toss in hot sauce mixture. Top with sprinkled feta and green onions to serve.

Per Serving:

calories: 367 | fat: 25g | protein: 25g | carbs: 9g | net carbs: 7g | fiber: 2g

Goat Cheese-Stuffed Jalapeño Poppers

Prep time: 15 minutes | Cook time: 20 minutes | Serves 8

- 1 (5-ounce / 142-g) package goat cheese, at room temperature
- ¼ cup shredded white Cheddar cheese
- 1 teaspoon paprika
- ½ teaspoon garlic powder
- ½ teaspoon onion powder
- ½ teaspoon sea salt
- ½ teaspoon freshly ground black pepper
- 8 jalapeño peppers
- 8 bacon slices

1. Preheat the oven to 400ºF (205ºC) and line a baking sheet with aluminum foil. Put a baking rack on the sheet. 2. In a medium bowl, mix together the goat cheese, Cheddar, paprika, garlic powder, onion powder, salt, and pepper. 3. Cut the jalapeños in half lengthwise and scoop out the seeds. Fill each half generously with the cheese mixture. 4. Cut the bacon slices in half to make 16 individual pieces. Wrap each jalapeño half with one piece of bacon

and place on the baking rack. 5. Cook for 15 to 20 minutes until the bacon begins to crisp. 6. Broil for an additional 2 to 3 minutes until the cheese is bubbly and slightly browned.

Per Serving:

2 poppers: calories: 121 | fat: 9g | protein: 8g | carbs: 2g | net carbs: 1g | fiber: 1g

Taco Beef Bites

Prep time: 10 minutes | Cook time: 15 minutes | Serves 6

- 10 ounces (283 g) ground beef
- 3 eggs, beaten
- ⅓ cup shredded Mozzarella
- cheese
- 1 teaspoon taco seasoning
- 1 teaspoon sesame oil

1. In the mixing bowl mix up ground beef, eggs, Mozzarella, and taco seasoning. 2. Then make the small meat bites from the mixture. 3. Heat up sesame oil in the instant pot. 4. Put the meat bites in the hot oil and cook them for 5 minutes from each side on Sauté mode.

Per Serving:

calories: 132 | fat: 6g | protein: 17g | carbs: 1g | net carbs: 1g | fiber: 0g

Broccoli Cheese Dip

Prep time: 5 minutes | Cook time: 10 minutes | Serves 6

- 4 tablespoons butter
- ½ medium onion, diced
- 1½ cups chopped broccoli
- 8 ounces (227 g) cream cheese
- ½ cup mayonnaise
- ½ cup chicken broth
- 1 cup shredded Cheddar cheese

1. Press the Sauté button and then press the Adjust button to set heat to Less. Add butter to Instant Pot. Add onion and sauté until softened, about 5 minutes. Press the Cancel button. 2. Add broccoli, cream cheese, mayo, and broth to pot. Press the Manual button and adjust time for 4 minutes. 3. When timer beeps, quick-release the pressure and stir in Cheddar. Serve warm.

Per Serving:

calories: 411 | fat: 37g | protein: 8g | carbs: 4g | net carbs: 3g | fiber: 1g

Curried Broccoli Skewers

Prep time: 15 minutes | Cook time: 1 minute | Serves 2

- 1 cup broccoli florets
- ½ teaspoon curry paste
- 2 tablespoons coconut cream
- 1 cup water, for cooking

1. In the shallow bowl mix up curry paste and coconut cream. 2. Then sprinkle the broccoli florets with curry paste mixture and string on the skewers. 3. Pour water and insert the steamer rack in the instant pot. 4. Place the broccoli skewers on the rack. Close and seal the lid. 5. Cook the meal on Manual mode (High Pressure) for 1 minute. 6. Make a quick pressure release.

Per Serving:

calories: 58 | fat: 4g | protein: 2g | carbs: 4g | net carbs: 2g | fiber: 2g

Everything Bagel Cream Cheese Dip

Prep time: 10 minutes | Cook time: 0 minutes | Serves 4

- 1 (8-ounce / 227-g) package cream cheese, at room temperature
- ½ cup sour cream
- 1 tablespoon garlic powder
- 1 tablespoon dried onion, or onion powder
- 1 tablespoon sesame seeds
- 1 tablespoon kosher salt

1. In a small bowl, combine the cream cheese, sour cream, garlic powder, dried onion, sesame seeds, and salt. Stir well to incorporate everything together. Serve immediately or cover and refrigerate for up to 6 days.

Per Serving:

calories: 291 | fat: 27g | protein: 6g | carbs: 6g | net carbs: 5g | fiber: 1g

Sesame Mushrooms

Prep time: 2 minutes | Cook time: 10 minutes | Serves 6

- 3 tablespoons sesame oil
- ¾ pound (340 g) small button mushrooms
- 1 teaspoon minced garlic
- ½ teaspoon smoked paprika
- ½ teaspoon cayenne pepper
- Salt and ground black pepper, to taste

1. Set your Instant Pot to Sauté and heat the sesame oil. 2. Add the mushrooms and sauté for 4 minutes until just tender, stirring occasionally. 3. Add the remaining ingredients to the Instant Pot and stir to mix well. 4. Lock the lid. Select the Manual mode and

set the cooking time for 5 minutes at High Pressure. 5. When the timer beeps, perform a quick pressure release. Carefully remove the lid. 6. Serve warm.

Per Serving:

calories: 77 | fat: 8g | protein: 2g | carbs: 2g | net carbs: 1g | fiber: 1g

Cucumber Salmon Coins

Prep time: 5 minutes | Cook time: 0 minutes | Serves 2

- ¼ cup (52 g) mayonnaise
- Grated zest of ½ lemon
- 1 tablespoon plus 1 teaspoon lemon juice
- 1 teaspoon Dijon mustard
- 1 clove garlic, minced
- ¼ teaspoon finely ground sea salt
- ⅛ teaspoon ground black
- pepper
- 1 English cucumber (about 12 in/30.5 cm long), sliced crosswise into coins
- 8 ounces (225 g) smoked salmon, separated into small pieces
- 2 fresh chives, sliced

1. Place the mayonnaise, lemon zest, lemon juice, mustard, garlic, salt, and pepper in a small bowl and whisk to combine. 2. Divide the cucumber coins between 2 plates. Top each coin with a piece of smoked salmon, then drizzle with the mayonnaise mixture and sprinkle with sliced chives. 3. Serve right away or store in the fridge for up to 1 day.

Per Serving:

calories: 337 | fat: 25g | protein: 22g | carbs: 5g | net carbs: 4g | fiber: 2g

Jumbo Pickle Cuban Sandwich

Prep time: 5 minutes | Cook time: 5 minutes | Serves 2

- 2 deli ham slices
- 2 deli pork tenderloin slices
- 4 Swiss cheese slices
- 2 jumbo dill pickles, halved lengthwise
- 1 tablespoon yellow mustard

1. In a small sauté pan or skillet, heat the ham and tenderloin slices over medium heat until warm. 2. Using a spatula, roll the deli meats into loose rolls. Top with the Swiss cheese slices and allow the cheese to begin to melt. 3. Transfer the rolls to 2 pickle halves. 4. Top the cheese with some mustard, then close the sandwiches by topping them with the matching pickle halves. 5. Secure with toothpicks and slice in half crosswise, then serve.

Per Serving:

calories: 256 | fat: 16g | protein: 23g | carbs: 5g | net carbs: 1g | fiber: 4g

Devilish Eggs

Prep time: 10 minutes | Cook time: 9 minutes | Serves 6

- 6 large eggs
- 3 tablespoons full-fat mayonnaise
- 1 teaspoon plain white vinegar
- 1 teaspoon spicy mustard
- ⅛ teaspoon salt
- ⅛ teaspoon black pepper
- ⅛ teaspoon ground cayenne
- ⅛ teaspoon paprika

1. Preferred Method: Hard-boil eggs using a steamer basket in the Instant Pot® on high pressure for 9 minutes. Release pressure and remove eggs. 2. Alternate Method: Place eggs in a large pot. Cover with water by 1". Cover with a lid and place the pot over high heat until it reaches a boil. Turn off heat, leave covered, and let it sit for 13 minutes. Then, remove the eggs from the pan, place them in an ice water bath, and let them cool 5 minutes. 3. When cooled, peel eggs and slice in half lengthwise. Place yolks in a medium bowl. 4. Mash and mix yolks with mayonnaise, vinegar, mustard, salt, and black pepper. 5. Scrape mixture into a sandwich-sized plastic bag and snip off one corner, making a hole about the width of a pencil. Use makeshift pastry bag to fill egg white halves with yolk mixture. 6. Garnish Devilish Eggs with cayenne and paprika (mostly for color) and serve.

Per Serving:

calories: 125| fat: 9g | protein: 6g | carbs: 1g | net carbs: 1g | fiber: 0g

Cheesy Spinach Puffs

Prep time: 10 minutes | Cook time: 10 minutes | Serves 8

- 16 ounces (454 g) frozen spinach, thawed, drained, and squeezed of as much excess liquid as possible
- 1 cup almond flour
- 4 tablespoons butter, melted, plus more for the baking sheet
- 2 eggs
- ¼ cup grated Parmesan cheese
- ¼ cup cream cheese
- 3 tablespoons heavy (whipping) cream
- 1 tablespoon onion powder
- 1 teaspoon garlic powder
- Salt and freshly ground black pepper, to taste

1. In a food processor, combine the spinach, almond flour, butter, eggs, Parmesan, cream cheese, cream, onion powder, and garlic powder. Season with salt and pepper. Blend until smooth. Transfer to the refrigerator and chill for 10 to 15 minutes. 2. Preheat the oven to 350ºF (180ºC). 3. Grease a baking sheet with butter. 4. Scoop the spinach mixture in heaping tablespoons and roll into balls. Place on the prepared baking sheet and bake for about 10 minutes until set. When tapped with your finger, they should not still be soft. Enjoy warm (best!) or cold. Refrigerate in an airtight container for up to 4 days.

Per Serving:

calories: 159 | fat: 14g | protein: 6g | carbs: 3g | net carbs: 1g | fiber: 2g

Pimento Cheese

Prep time: 20 minutes | Cook time: 0 minutes | serves 8

- 1 (8-ounce) block sharp cheddar cheese
- 1 (8-ounce) block mild cheddar cheese
- 1 cup mayonnaise
- 1 (4-ounce) jar diced pimentos, drained
- 3 ounces cream cheese (6 tablespoons), softened
- 1 tablespoon finely chopped
- onions
- 1 tablespoon dill relish
- ½ teaspoon onion powder
- ¼ teaspoon garlic powder
- ¼ teaspoon ground black pepper
- Serving Suggestions:
- Sliced bell peppers or celery
- Pork rinds

1. Using the large holes on the side of a box grater, shred the cheeses into a large bowl. 2. Add the rest of the ingredients to the bowl with the shredded cheese and mix with a spoon until well combined. Refrigerate for at least 1 hour before serving. Leftovers can be stored in an airtight container in the refrigerator for up to a week.

Per Serving:

calories: 464 | fat: 46g | protein: 14g | carbs: 3g | net carbs: 3g | fiber: 0g

Avocado Salsa

Prep time: 10 minutes | Cook time: 0 minutes | Serves 4

- 2 or 3 avocados, peeled, pitted, and diced
- ¼ red onion, diced
- 1 garlic clove, minced
- Zest of ½ lime
- Juice of 1 lime
- ¼ cup olive oil
- Salt and freshly ground black pepper, to taste
- ¼ cup chopped fresh cilantro

1. In a large bowl, gently toss together the diced avocados, onion, garlic, lime zest and juice, and olive oil. Season with salt and pepper. Cover and refrigerate in an airtight container for up to 4 days. Top with the cilantro before serving.

Per Serving:

calories: 450 | fat: 42g | protein: 3g | carbs: 15g | net carbs: 5g | fiber: 10g

English Cucumber Tea Sandwiches

Prep time: 10 minutes | Cook time: 0 minutes | Makes 12 snacks

- 1 large cucumber, peeled (approximately 10 ounces / 283 g)
- 4 ounces (113 g) cream cheese, softened
- 2 tablespoons finely chopped fresh dill
- Freshly ground black pepper, to taste

1. Slice the cucumbers into 24 rounds approximately ¼ inch (6 mm) thick. Place in a single layer between two kitchen towels. Put a cutting board on top. Allow to sit about 5 minutes. 2. Mix the cream cheese and dill. 3. Spread 2 teaspoons cream cheese on half the cucumber slices. Grind black pepper over the cheese. Place another slice of cucumber on top of each and secure with a toothpick, if desired.

Per Serving:

calories: 96 | fat: 8g | protein: 3g | carbs: 3g | net carbs: 1g | fiber: 2g

EL Presidente Guac

Prep time: 10 minutes | Cook time: 0 minutes | Serves 4

- 2 large avocados, peeled and pitted
- 1 tablespoon garlic powder
- 1 tablespoon onion powder
- ⅛ teaspoon salt
- ⅛ teaspoon chili powder
- 4 tablespoons finely chopped cilantro
- 1 Roma tomato, finely chopped
- 4 teaspoons lime juice

1. In a medium bowl, mash avocados and combine with dry spices. 2. Add cilantro, tomato, and lime juice and mix again. Serve.

Per Serving:

calories: 131| fat: 9g | protein: 2g | carbs: 10g | net carbs: 5g | fiber: 5g

Sweet Pepper Poppers

Prep time: 10 minutes | Cook time: 20 minutes | serves 4

- 12 mini sweet peppers
- 1 (8 ounces) package cream cheese, softened
- 5 slices bacon, cooked and
- crumbled
- 1 green onion, thinly sliced
- ¼ teaspoon ground black pepper

1. Preheat the oven to 400°F. Line a sheet pan with parchment paper. 2. Cut each sweet pepper in half lengthwise, then remove and discard the seeds; set the peppers aside. 3. In a small bowl, mix together the cream cheese, bacon, green onion (reserve some of the slices for garnish, if desired), and black pepper. Spoon the mixture into the sweet pepper halves. 4. Place the stuffed peppers on the lined sheet pan and bake for 20 minutes, until the peppers are tender and the tops are starting to brown. Garnish with the reserved green onion slices, if desired.

Per Serving:

calories: 163 | fat: 12g | protein: 7g | carbs: 5g | net carbs: 4g | fiber: 1g

Avocado Feta Dip

Prep time: 15 minutes | Cook time: 0 minutes | Serves 8

- 2 avocados, diced
- 2 Roma tomatoes, chopped
- ¼ medium red onion, finely chopped (about ½ cup)
- 2 garlic cloves, minced
- 2 tablespoons chopped fresh parsley (or cilantro)
- 2 tablespoons olive oil or avocado oil
- 2 tablespoons red wine vinegar
- 1 tablespoon freshly squeezed lemon or lime juice
- ½ teaspoon sea salt
- ¼ teaspoon freshly ground black pepper
- 8 ounces (227 g) feta cheese, crumbled

1. In a large bowl, gently stir together the avocados, tomatoes, onion, garlic, and parsley. 2. In a small bowl, whisk together the oil, vinegar, lemon juice, salt, and pepper. Pour the mixture over the avocado mixture. Fold in the cheese. 3. Cover and let chill in the refrigerator for 1 to 2 hours before serving.

Per Serving:

½ cup: calories: 190 | fat: 16g | protein: 6g | carbs: 6g | net carbs: 3g | fiber: 3g

Parmesan Crisps

Prep time: 5 minutes | Cook time: 5 minutes | Makes about 25 crisps

- 2 cups grated Parmesan cheese

1. Heat the oven to 400ºF (205ºC). Line a baking sheet with a silicone mat or parchment paper. Scoop a generous tablespoon of the cheese onto the sheet and flatten it slightly. Repeat with the rest of the cheese, leaving about 1 inch (2.5 cm) space in between them. 2. Bake for 3 to 5 minutes, until crisp.

Per Serving:

calories: 169 | fat: 11g | protein: 11g | carbs: 6g | net carbs: 6g | fiber: 0g

Sweet Pepper Nacho Bites

Prep time: 5 minutes | Cook time: 5 minutes | Makes 24 bites

- 12 mini sweet peppers (approximately 8 ounces / 227 g)
- ½ cup shredded Monterey

Jack cheese
- ½ cup guacamole
- Juice of 1 lime

1. Preheat the oven to 400°F (205°C). 2. Carefully cut each pepper in half lengthwise and remove the seeds. Place them cut side up on a rimmed baking sheet so they aren't touching. Place 1 teaspoon of shredded cheese inside each. Bake 3 to 5 minutes, until the cheese starts to melt. 3. Remove from the oven and top each with 1 teaspoon of guacamole. Squeeze the lime juice over top. Serve immediately.

Per Serving:

calories: 137 | fat: 12g | protein: 4g | carbs: 5g | net carbs: 3g | fiber: 2g

Fathead Crackers

Prep time: 10 minutes | Cook time: 10 minutes | Serves 8

- 1½ cups shredded mozzarella cheese (about 6 ounces)
- 2 ounces cream cheese (¼ cup)
- 1 cup blanched almond flour
- 1 large egg
- ½ teaspoon dried parsley
- ½ teaspoon pink Himalayan salt

1. Preheat the oven to 425°F and line a baking sheet with parchment paper. 2. Put the mozzarella and cream cheese in a large microwave-safe mixing bowl and microwave for 30 seconds. Combine using a rubber spatula. Microwave for another 30 seconds, until the cheese has melted, then stir once more. 3. Add the almond flour, egg, parsley, and salt and, using a fork, combine everything thoroughly until you have a soft, sticky, and pliable dough. 4. Once the dough comes together, transfer it to the lined baking sheet and place another piece of parchment paper on top. Roll out into a thin rectangle, about ¼ inch thick. Using a pizza cutter or knife, cut the flattened dough into 20 to 25 small crackers, about 1 inch. 5. Discard any extra dough and spread out the crackers so they are not touching one another. Bake for 7 to 10 minutes, until the crackers have puffed up and browned. Allow to cool on the baking sheet for 10 minutes prior to eating. 6. These are best eaten the same day they are baked, but leftovers can be stored in a sealed container in the refrigerator for up to 5 days. To recrisp, place in a preheated 250°F oven for 5 minutes; however, they will not get as crispy as when freshly baked.

Per Serving:

calories: 174 | fat: 15g | protein: 9g | carbs: 4g | net carbs: 2g | fiber: 2g

Pecan Ranch Cheese Ball

Prep time: 15 minutes | Cook time: 0 minutes | serves 8

- 2 (8 ounces) packages cream cheese, softened
- 1 cup shredded sharp cheddar cheese
- 2 tablespoons ranch seasoning
- 1 cup chopped raw pecans
- Serving Suggestions:
- Celery sticks
- Mini sweet peppers
- Pork rinds

1. Put the cream cheese, cheddar cheese, and ranch seasoning in a medium-sized bowl. Using a spoon, mix the ingredients together until well blended. 2. Shape the mixture into a ball or disc shape and roll it in the pecans. Wrap and refrigerate overnight before serving. 3. Serve with the scoopers of your choice. Leftovers can be stored in an airtight container in the refrigerator for up to 5 days.

Per Serving:

calories: 303 | fat: 27g | protein: 9g | carbs: 11g | net carbs: 5g | fiber: 2g

Haystack Cookies

Prep time: 10 minutes | Cook time: 5 minutes | Makes 20 cookies

- ½ cup (95 g) erythritol
- ¼ cup (60 ml) full-fat coconut milk
- 3 tablespoons coconut oil, ghee, or cacao butter
- ¼ cup (20 g) cocoa powder
- ⅓ cup (30 g) unflavored MCT oil powder (optional)
- 2 cups (200 g) unsweetened shredded coconut

1. Line a rimmed baking sheet or large plate with parchment paper or a silicone baking mat. 2. Place the erythritol, coconut milk, and oil in a large frying pan. Slowly bring to a simmer over medium-low heat, whisking periodically to prevent burning; this should take about 5 minutes. 3. When the mixture reaches a simmer, remove from the heat and stir in the cocoa powder. Once fully combined, stir in the MCT oil powder, if using, and then the shredded coconut. 4. Using a 1-tablespoon measuring spoon, carefully scoop out a portion of the mixture and press it into the spoon. Place the haystack on the lined baking sheet and repeat, making a total of 20 cookies. 5. Refrigerate for 30 to 45 minutes before enjoying.

Per Serving:

calories: 122 | fat: 11g | protein: 1g | carbs: 4g | net carbs: 2g | fiber: 2g

Smoky "Hummus" and Veggies

Prep time: 15 minutes | Cook time: 20 minutes | serves 6

- Nonstick coconut oil cooking spray
- 1 cauliflower head, cut into florets
- ¼ cup tahini
- ¼ cup cold-pressed olive oil, plus extra for drizzling
- Juice of 1 lemon
- 1 tablespoon ground paprika
- 1 teaspoon sea salt
- ¼ cup chopped fresh parsley, for garnish
- 2 tablespoons pine nuts (optional)
- Flax crackers, for serving
- Sliced cucumbers, for serving
- Celery pieces, for serving

1. Preheat the oven to 400°F and grease a baking sheet with cooking spray. 2. Spread the cauliflower florets out on the prepared baking sheet and bake for 20 minutes. 3. Remove the cauliflower from the oven and allow it to cool for 10 minutes. 4. In a food processor or high-powered blender, combine the cauliflower with the tahini, olive oil, lemon juice, paprika, and salt. Blend on high until a fluffy, creamy texture is achieved. If the mixture seems too thick, slowly add a few tablespoons of water until smooth. 5. Scoop the "hummus" into an airtight container and chill in the refrigerator for about 20 minutes. 6. Transfer the "hummus" to a serving bowl and drizzle with olive oil. Garnish with the parsley and pine nuts (if using). 7. Serve with your favorite flax crackers and sliced cucumbers and celery.

Per Serving:

calories: 169 | fat: 15g | protein: 4g | carbs: 9g | net carbs: 5g | fiber: 4g

Vanilla Toasted Coconut Chips

Prep time: 5 minutes | Cook time: 10 minutes | Serves 8

- 1 tablespoon coconut oil, melted
- 2 tablespoons powdered erythritol
- ½ teaspoon vanilla extract
- Pinch of sea salt
- 2 cups unsweetened coconut chips (no other ingredients added)

1. Preheat the oven to 325°F (163°C). Line a baking sheet with parchment paper. 2. In a medium bowl, whisk together the melted coconut oil, powdered erythritol, vanilla, and sea salt. It may clump, which is okay. Add the coconut chips and toss to coat. 3. Arrange the coconut chips in a single layer on the baking sheet. Bake for about 5 minutes, or until some pieces are starting to turn golden. Stir, then bake for another 3 to 5 minutes, until more golden. 4. Cool completely to crisp up; they will not be crisp right out of the oven.

Per Serving:

calories: 155 | fat: 15g | protein: 1g | carbs: 7g | net carbs: 2g | fiber: 5g

Pesto-Stuffed Mushrooms

Prep time: 20 minutes | Cook time: 20 minutes | Makes 1 dozen mushrooms

- 1 dozen baby bella mushroom caps, cleaned
- 8 ounces (227 g) fresh Mozzarella
- ½ cup pesto
- Sea salt and ground black pepper, to taste

1. Preheat the oven to 350°F (180°C). 2. Place the mushrooms on a rimmed baking sheet cup side down and bake for 10 minutes, or until some of the moisture is released. 3. While the mushrooms are baking, slice the Mozzarella into small pieces, approximately the size of the mushrooms. 4. Turn the mushrooms cup side up and fill each one with a spoonful of pesto and 1 or 2 pieces of Mozzarella. Return the mushrooms to the oven and bake for about 10 minutes, until golden brown on top. 5. Sprinkle with salt and pepper before serving.

Per Serving:

calories: 132 | fat: 11g | protein: 4g | carbs: 5g | net carbs: 4g | fiber: 1g

Goat Cheese–Mackerel Pâté

Prep time: 10 minutes | Cook time: 0 minutes | Serves 4

- 4 ounces (113 g) olive oil-packed wild-caught mackerel
- 2 ounces (57 g) goat cheese
- Zest and juice of 1 lemon
- 2 tablespoons chopped fresh parsley
- 2 tablespoons chopped fresh arugula
- 1 tablespoon extra-virgin olive oil
- 2 teaspoons chopped capers
- 1 to 2 teaspoons fresh horseradish (optional)
- Crackers, cucumber rounds, endive spears, or celery, for serving (optional)

1. In a food processor, blender, or large bowl with immersion blender, combine the mackerel, goat cheese, lemon zest and juice, parsley, arugula, olive oil, capers, and horseradish (if using). Process or blend until smooth and creamy. 2. Serve with crackers, cucumber rounds, endive spears, or celery. 3. Store covered in the refrigerator for up to 1 week.

Per Serving:

calories: 190 | fat: 15g | protein: 11g | carbs: 3g | net carbs: 2g | fiber: 1g

Bacon-Pepper Fat Bombs

Prep time: 10 minutes | Cook time: 0 minutes | Makes 12 fat bombs

- 2 ounces goat cheese, at room temperature
- 2 ounces cream cheese, at room temperature
- ¼ cup butter, at room temperature
- 8 bacon slices, cooked and chopped
- Pinch freshly ground black pepper

1. Line a small baking sheet with parchment paper and set aside. 2. In a medium bowl, stir together the goat cheese, cream cheese, butter, bacon, and pepper until well combined. 3. Use a tablespoon to drop mounds of the bomb mixture on the baking sheet and place the sheet in the freezer until the fat bombs are very firm but not frozen, about 1 hour. 4. Store the fat bombs in a sealed container in the refrigerator for up to 2 weeks.

Per Serving:

1 fat bomb: calories: 89 | fat: 8g | protein: 3g | carbs: 0g | net carbs: 0g | fiber: 0g

Mac Fatties

Prep time: 10 minutes | Cook time: 0 minutes | Makes 20 fat cups

- 1¾ cups (280 g) roasted and salted macadamia nuts

Rosemary Lemon Flavor:
- 1 teaspoon finely chopped fresh rosemary

Spicy Cumin Flavor:
- ½ teaspoon ground cumin

Turmeric Flavor:
- ½ teaspoon turmeric powder

Garlic Herb Flavor:
- 1¼ teaspoons dried oregano leaves
- ⅓ cup (70 g) coconut oil

- ¼ teaspoon lemon juice

- ¼ teaspoon cayenne pepper

- ¼ teaspoon ginger powder

- ½ teaspoon paprika
- ½ teaspoon garlic powder

1. Place the macadamia nuts and oil in a blender or food processor. Blend until smooth, or as close to smooth as you can get it with the equipment you're using. 2. Divide the mixture among 4 small bowls, placing ¼ cup (87 g) in each bowl. 3. To the first bowl, add the rosemary and lemon juice and stir to combine. 4. To the second bowl, add the cumin and cayenne and stir to combine. 5. To the third bowl, add the turmeric and ginger and stir to combine. 6. To the fourth bowl, add the oregano, paprika, and garlic powder and stir to combine. 7. Set a 24-well silicone or metal mini muffin pan on the counter. If using a metal pan, line 20 of the wells with mini foil liners. (Do not use paper; it would soak up all the fat.) Spoon the mixtures into the wells, using about 1 tablespoon per well. 8.

Place in the freezer for 1 hour, or until firm. Enjoy directly from the freezer.

Per Serving:

calories: 139 | fat: 14g | protein: 1g | carbs: 2g | net carbs: 1g | fiber: 1g

Hot Chard Artichoke Dip

Prep time: 10 minutes | Cook time: 20 minutes | Serves 4

- 4 ounces cream cheese, at room temperature
- ½ cup coconut milk
- ½ cup grated Asiago cheese
- ½ cup shredded Cheddar cheese
- 1 teaspoon minced garlic
- Dash hot sauce (optional)
- 2 cups chopped Swiss chard
- ½ cup roughly chopped artichoke hearts (packed in brine, not oil)

1. Preheat the oven. Set the oven temperature to 450°F. 2. Mix the ingredients. In a large bowl, stir together the cream cheese, coconut milk, Asiago, Cheddar, garlic, and hot sauce (if using), until everything is well mixed. Stir in the chard and the artichoke hearts and mix until they're well incorporated. Note: You've got to use artichokes packed in brine rather than oil because the extra oil will come out of the dip when you heat it, which will mess up the texture. 3. Bake. Spoon the mixture into a 1-quart baking dish, and bake it for 15 to 20 minutes until it's bubbly and lightly golden. 4. Serve. Cut up low-carb veggies to serve with this creamy, rich dip.

Per Serving:

calories: 280 | fat: 25g | protein: 11g | carbs: 5g | net carbs: 4g | fiber: 1g

Cheddar Chips

Prep time: 10 minutes | Cook time: 5 minutes | Serves 4

- 1 cup shredded Cheddar cheese
- 1 tablespoon almond flour

1. Mix up Cheddar cheese and almond flour. 2. Then preheat the instant pot on Sauté mode. 3. Line the instant pot bowl with baking paper. 4. After this, make the small rounds from the cheese in the instant pot (on the baking paper) and close the lid. 5. Cook them for 5 minutes on Sauté mode or until the cheese is melted. 6. Then switch off the instant pot and remove the baking paper with cheese rounds from it. 7. Cool the chips well and remove them from the baking paper.

Per Serving:

calories: 154 | fat: 13g | protein: 9g | carbs: 2g | net carbs: 1g | fiber: 1g

Smoked Salmon Fat Bombs

Prep time: 10 minutes | Cook time: 0 minutes | Makes 12 fat bombs

- ½ cup goat cheese, at room temperature
- ½ cup butter, at room temperature
- 2 ounces smoked salmon
- 2 teaspoons freshly squeezed lemon juice
- Pinch freshly ground black pepper

1. Line a baking sheet with parchment paper and set aside. 2. In a medium bowl, stir together the goat cheese, butter, smoked salmon, lemon juice, and pepper until very well blended. 3. Use a tablespoon to scoop the salmon mixture onto the baking sheet until you have 12 even mounds. 4. Place the baking sheet in the refrigerator until the fat bombs are firm, 2 to 3 hours. 5. Store the fat bombs in a sealed container in the refrigerator for up to 1 week.

Per Serving:

2 fat bomb: calories: 193 | fat: 18g | protein: 8g | carbs: 0g | net carbs: 0g | fiber: 0g

Manchego Crackers

Prep time: 15 minutes | Cook time: 15 minutes | Makes 40 crackers

- 4 tablespoons butter, at room temperature
- 1 cup finely shredded Manchego cheese
- 1 cup almond flour
- 1 teaspoon salt, divided
- ¼ teaspoon freshly ground black pepper
- 1 large egg

1. Using an electric mixer, cream together the butter and shredded cheese until well combined and smooth. 2. In a small bowl, combine the almond flour with ½ teaspoon salt and pepper. Slowly add the almond flour mixture to the cheese, mixing constantly until the dough just comes together to form a ball. 3. Transfer to a piece of parchment or plastic wrap and roll into a cylinder log about 1½ inches thick. Wrap tightly and refrigerate for at least 1 hour. 4. Preheat the oven to 350°F(180°C). Line two baking sheets with parchment paper or silicone baking mats. 5. To make the egg wash, in a small bowl, whisk together the egg and remaining ½ teaspoon salt. 6. Slice the refrigerated dough into small rounds, about ¼ inch thick, and place on the lined baking sheets. 7. Brush the tops of the crackers with egg wash and bake until the crackers are golden and crispy, 12 to 15 minutes. Remove from the oven and allow to cool on a wire rack. 8. Serve warm or, once fully cooled, store in an airtight container in the refrigerator for up to 1 week.

Per Serving:

2 crackers: calories: 100 | fat: 9g | protein: 3g | carbs: 2g | net carbs: 1g | fiber: 1g

Bacon-Studded Pimento Cheese

Prep time: 10 minutes | Cook time: 5 minutes | Serves 6

- 2 ounces (57 g) bacon (about 4 thick slices)
- 4 ounces (113 g) cream cheese, room temperature
- ¼ cup mayonnaise
- ¼ teaspoon onion powder
- ¼ teaspoon cayenne pepper (optional)
- 1 cup thick-shredded extra-sharp Cheddar cheese
- 2 ounces (57 g) jarred diced pimentos, drained

1. Chop the raw bacon into ½-inch-thick pieces. Cook in a small skillet over medium heat until crispy, 3 to 4 minutes. Use a slotted spoon to transfer the bacon onto a layer of paper towels. Reserve the rendered fat. 2. In a large bowl, combine the cream cheese, mayonnaise, onion powder, and cayenne (if using), and beat with an electric mixer or by hand until smooth and creamy. 3. Add the rendered bacon fat, Cheddar cheese, and pimentos and mix until well combined. 4. Refrigerate for at least 30 minutes before serving to allow flavors to blend. Serve cold with raw veggies.

Per Serving:

calories: 216 | fat: 20g | protein: 8g | carbs: 2g | net carbs: 0g | fiber: 2

Pancetta Pizza Dip

Prep time: 10 minutes | Cook time: 4 minutes | Serves 10

- 10 ounces (283 g) Pepper Jack cheese
- 10 ounces (283 g) cream cheese
- 10 ounces (283 g) pancetta, chopped
- 1 pound (454 g) tomatoes, puréed
- 1 cup green olives, pitted and halved
- 1 teaspoon dried oregano
- ½ teaspoon garlic powder
- 1 cup chicken broth
- 4 ounces (113 g) Mozzarella cheese, thinly sliced

1. Mix together the Pepper Jack cheese, cream cheese, pancetta, tomatoes, olives, oregano, and garlic powder in the Instant Pot. Pour in the chicken broth. 2. Lock the lid. Select the Manual mode and set the cooking time for 4 minutes at High Pressure. 3. When the timer beeps, perform a quick pressure release. Carefully remove the lid. 4. Scatter the Mozzarella cheese on top. Cover and allow to sit in the residual heat. Serve warm.

Per Serving:

calories: 287 | fat: 21g | protein: 21g | carbs: 3g | net carbs: 2g | fiber: 1g

Sausage Balls

Prep time: 5 minutes | Cook time: 25 minutes | Makes 2 dozen

- 1 pound (454 g) bulk Italian sausage (not sweet)
- 1 cup almond flour
- 1½ cups finely shredded Cheddar cheese
- 1 large egg
- 2 teaspoons baking powder
- 1 teaspoon onion powder
- 1 teaspoon fennel seed (optional)
- ½ teaspoon cayenne pepper (optional)

1. Preheat the oven to 350ºF (180ºC) and line a rimmed baking sheet with aluminum foil. 2. In a large bowl, combine all the ingredients. Use a fork to mix until well blended. 3. Form the sausage mixture into 1½-inch balls and place 1 inch apart on the prepared baking sheet. 4. Bake for 20 to 25 minutes, or until browned and cooked through.

Per Serving:

calories: 241 | fat: 21g | protein: 11g | carbs: 3g | net carbs: 2g | fiber: 1g

Cauliflower Popcorn

Prep time: 5 minutes | Cook time: 40 minutes | Serves 2 to 3

- Nonstick avocado oil cooking spray, for greasing
- 1 small to medium head cauliflower, florets with stems chopped into bite-size pieces
- ½ cup avocado oil
- ½ cup neutral-flavored grass-
- fed collagen protein powder (optional)
- Popcorn seasonings of choice: salt, freshly ground black pepper, garlic powder, onion powder, dried oregano, dried sage, and/or nutritional yeast

1. Preheat the oven to 400ºF (205ºC). Coat a broiling pan with nonstick avocado oil spray. (If you have an air fryer, you can make your Cauliflower Popcorn in there instead; just coat the fryer basket with nonstick spray.) 2. Put the cauliflower in a mixing bowl. Pour the avocado oil over the top and sprinkle in the protein powder. Add the seasonings of your choice to the bowl. Stir all together to evenly coat the cauliflower. 3. Spread the cauliflower in an even layer on the prepared pan and place in the oven (or pour into your air fryer). Cook for roughly 40 minutes, checking periodically and stirring every 10 minutes or so (same goes for the air fryer, if using). 4. Remove from the oven (or air fryer) and serve.

Per Serving:

calories: 389 | fat: 37g | protein: 4g | carbs: 10g | net carbs: 5g | fiber: 5g

Chocolate Soft-Serve Ice Cream

Prep time: 10 minutes | Cook time: 0 minutes | Serves 4

- 1 (13½ ounces/400 ml) can full-fat coconut milk
- ¼ cup (40 g) collagen peptides or protein powder (optional)
- ¼ cup (25 g) unflavored MCT oil powder (optional)
- 2 tablespoons smooth unsweetened almond butter
- 2 tablespoons cocoa powder
- 3 drops liquid stevia, or 1 tablespoon erythritol
- 1 teaspoon vanilla extract

1. Place all the ingredients in a blender or food processor. Blend until smooth and fully incorporated. 2. Divide the mixture among 4 freezer-safe serving bowls and place in the freezer for 30 minutes. At the 30 minutes mark, remove from the freezer and mash with a fork until the ice cream is smooth. If it's still too runny and doesn't develop the consistency of soft-serve as you mash it, freeze for another 15 minutes, then mash with a fork again. 3. Enjoy immediately.

Per Serving:

calories: 478 | fat: 47g | protein: 6g | carbs: 9g | net carbs: 4g | fiber: 5g

Cheese Stuffed Bell Peppers

Prep time: 10 minutes | Cook time: 5 minutes | Serves 5

- 1 cup water
- 10 baby bell peppers, seeded and sliced lengthwise
- 4 ounces (113 g) Monterey Jack cheese, shredded
- 4 ounces (113 g) cream cheese
- 2 tablespoons chopped scallions
- 1 tablespoon olive oil
- 1 teaspoon minced garlic
- ½ teaspoon cayenne pepper
- ¼ teaspoon ground black pepper, or more to taste

1. Pour the water into the Instant Pot and insert a steamer basket. 2. Stir together the remaining ingredients except the bell peppers in a mixing bowl until combined. Stuff the peppers evenly with the mixture. Arrange the stuffed peppers in the basket. 3. Lock the lid. Select the Manual mode and set the cooking time for 5 minutes at High Pressure. 4. When the timer beeps, perform a quick pressure release. Carefully remove the lid. 5. Cool for 5 minutes and serve.

Per Serving:

calories: 226 | fat: 18g | protein: 9g | carbs: 9g | net carbs: 7g | fiber: 2g

Spicy Baked Feta in Foil

Prep time: 10 minutes | Cook time: 6 minutes | Serves 6

- 12 ounces (340 g) feta cheese
- ½ tomato, sliced
- 1 ounce (28 g) bell pepper, sliced
- 1 teaspoon ground paprika
- 1 tablespoon olive oil
- 1 cup water, for cooking

1. Sprinkle the cheese with olive oil and ground paprika and place it on the foil. 2. Then top feta cheese with sliced tomato and bell pepper. Wrap it in the foil well. 3. After this, pour water and insert the steamer rack in the instant pot. 4. Put the wrapped cheese on the rack. Close and seal the lid. 5. Cook the cheese on Manual mode (High Pressure) for 6 minutes. Then make a quick pressure release. 6. Discard the foil and transfer the cheese on the serving plates.

Per Serving:

calories: 178 | fat: 14g | protein: 8g | carbs: 4g | net carbs: 3g | fiber: 1g

Jelly Cups

Prep time: 10 minutes | Cook time: 10 minutes | Makes 16 jelly cups

Butter Base:
- ⅔ cup (170 g) coconut butter or smooth unsweetened nut or seed butter
- ⅔ cup (145 g) coconut oil, ghee, or cacao butter, melted
- 2 teaspoons vanilla extract
- 7 drops liquid stevia, or 2 teaspoons confectioners'-style erythritol

Jelly Filling:
- ½ cup (70 g) fresh raspberries
- ¼ cup (60 ml) water
- 3 drops liquid stevia, or 1 teaspoon confectioners'-style erythritol
- 1½ teaspoons unflavored gelatin

Special Equipment:
- 16 mini muffin cup liners, or 1 silicone mini muffin pan

1. Set 16 mini muffin cup liners on a tray or have on hand a silicone mini muffin pan. 2. Make the base: Place the coconut butter, melted oil, vanilla, and sweetener in a medium-sized bowl and stir to combine. 3. Take half of the base mixture and divide it equally among the 16 mini muffin cup liners or 16 wells of the mini muffin pan, filling each about one-quarter full. Place the muffin cup liners (or muffin pan) in the fridge. Set the remaining half of the base mixture aside. 4. Make the jelly filling: Place the raspberries, water, and sweetener in a small saucepan and bring to a simmer over medium heat. Simmer for 5 minutes, then sprinkle with the gelatin and mash with a fork. Transfer to the fridge to set for 15 minutes. 5. Pull the muffin cup liners and jelly filling out of the fridge. Using a ½-teaspoon measuring spoon, scoop out a portion of the jelly and roll it into a ball between your palms, then flatten it into a disc about 1 inch (2.5 cm) in diameter (or in a diameter to fit the size of the liners you're using). Press into a chilled butter base cup. Repeat with the remaining jelly filling and cups. Then spoon the remaining butter base mixture over the tops. 6. Place in the fridge for another 15 minutes before serving.

Per Serving:

calories: 151 | fat: 15g | protein: 1g | carbs: 3g | net carbs: 1g | fiber: 2g

90-Second Bread

Prep time: 5 minutes | Cook time: 90 seconds | Serves 1

- 1 heaping tablespoon coconut flour
- ½ teaspoon baking powder
- 1 large egg
- 1½ tablespoons butter, melted
- Pinch salt

1. In a small, 3- to 4-inch diameter, microwave-safe bowl, combine the coconut flour, baking powder, egg, butter, and salt, and mix until well combined. 2. Place the bowl in the microwave and cook on high for 90 seconds. 3. Dump the bread from the bowl and allow to cool for a couple of minutes. 4. With a serrated knife, cut the bread in half horizontally to make two halves, if desired.

Per Serving:

calories: 204 | fat: 17g | protein: 8g | carbs: 5g | net carbs: 2g | fiber: 3g

Marinated Feta and Artichokes

Prep time: 10 minutes | Cook time: 0 minutes | Makes 1½ cups

- 4 ounces (113 g) traditional Greek feta, cut into ½-inch cubes
- 4 ounces (113 g) drained artichoke hearts, quartered lengthwise
- ⅓ cup extra-virgin olive oil
- Zest and juice of 1 lemon
- 2 tablespoons roughly chopped fresh rosemary
- 2 tablespoons roughly chopped fresh parsley
- ½ teaspoon black peppercorns

1. In a glass bowl or large glass jar, combine the feta and artichoke hearts. Add the olive oil, lemon zest and juice, rosemary, parsley, and peppercorns and toss gently to coat, being sure not to crumble the feta. 2. Cover and refrigerate for at least 4 hours, or up to 4 days. Pull out of the refrigerator 30 minutes before serving.

Per Serving:

calories: 108 | fat: 9g | protein: 3g | carbs: 5g | net carbs: 4g | fiber: 1g

Dragon Tail Jalapeño Poppahs

Prep time: 15 minutes | Cook time: 19 minutes | Serves 8

- 8 (2") jalapeños, halved, seeded, and deveined
- 4 ounces full-fat cream cheese, softened
- ¼ cup full-fat mayonnaise
- 1 (1-ounce) package ranch powder seasoning mix
- ½ cup shredded Cheddar cheese

1. Preheat oven to 375°F. Line a baking sheet with parchment paper. 2. In a medium microwave-safe bowl, microwave peppers with ¼ cup water for 3 minutes to soften. Drain and let cool. 3. Line up peppers on baking sheet, cut-side up. 4. In a separate medium microwave-safe bowl, add cream cheese, mayonnaise, ranch powder, and shredded cheese. Microwave for 30 seconds and stir. Microwave another 15 seconds and stir. 5. Carefully scoop mixture into sandwich-sized bag. Snip off one corner to make a hole (the width of a pencil). 6. Using makeshift pastry bag, fill jalapeño halves evenly with mixture. 7. Bake 15 minutes until peppers are fully softened and cheese is golden brown.

Per Serving:

calories: 137| fat: 11g | protein: 3g | carbs: 4g | net carbs: 4g | fiber: 0g

Cheesecake Balls

Prep time: 15 minutes | Cook time: 0 minutes | Makes 12 balls

Almond Flour Center:
- ½ cup (55 g) blanched almond flour
- 2 tablespoons coconut oil or

Cream Cheese Layer:
- 1 (8 ounces/225 g) package cream cheese (dairy-free or regular)
- 3 tablespoons coconut oil or ghee
- ¼ cup plus 2 tablespoons (60 g) confectioners'-style

- ghee
- 1 tablespoon confectioners'-style erythritol

- erythritol
- 2 teaspoons ground cinnamon
- Cinnamon Sugar Topping:
- ¼ cup (48 g) granulated erythritol
- 2 teaspoons ground cinnamon

1. Line a rimmed baking sheet or tray that will fit into your freezer with parchment paper. 2. Make the almond flour center: Place the almond flour, oil, and erythritol in a small bowl. Knead with your hands until incorporated. Separate the mixture into 12 pieces and roll into balls. Place the balls on the lined baking sheet and place in the freezer. 3. Make the cream cheese layer: Place the cream cheese, oil, and erythritol in a small bowl and combine with a fork or handheld mixer. Divide the mixture evenly between 2 bowls. To one bowl, add the cinnamon and mix until incorporated. Place both bowls in the freezer until the cream cheese has hardened but is still workable and not completely frozen through, about 1 hour. 4. Place the ingredients for the cinnamon sugar topping in a small bowl and whisk with a fork to combine. Set aside. 5. Once the cream cheese mixtures have chilled sufficiently, scoop a teaspoon each of the cinnamon cream cheese mixture and the plain cream cheese mixture and place them side by side on the lined baking sheet. Take the almond flour balls out of the freezer and place one ball between a pair of cream cheese pieces. Pick up the pile and roll between your palms until the almond flour ball is in the middle and the cream cheese surrounds it. Roll the ball in the cinnamon sugar mixture until coated. Place the coated ball back on the lined baking sheet and place in the freezer. 6. Repeat with the remaining almond flour balls, cream cheese mixtures, and cinnamon sugar topping, placing the coated balls on the baking sheet in the freezer as you complete them. 7. Place the coated balls in the freezer to chill for 20 minutes before enjoying.

Per Serving:

calories: 126 | fat: 13g | protein: 1g | carbs: 2g | net carbs: 1g | fiber: 1g

Lemon-Pepper Chicken Drumsticks

Prep time: 30 minutes | Cook time: 30 minutes | Serves 2

- 2 teaspoons freshly ground coarse black pepper
- 1 teaspoon baking powder
- ½ teaspoon garlic powder
- 4 chicken drumsticks (4 ounces / 113 g each)
- Kosher salt, to taste
- 1 lemon

1. In a small bowl, stir together the pepper, baking powder, and garlic powder. Place the drumsticks on a plate and sprinkle evenly with the baking powder mixture, turning the drumsticks so they're well coated. Let the drumsticks stand in the refrigerator for at least 1 hour or up to overnight. 2. Sprinkle the drumsticks with salt, then transfer them to the air fryer, standing them bone-end up and leaning against the wall of the air fryer basket. Air fry at 375°F (191°C) until cooked through and crisp on the outside, about 30 minutes. 3. Transfer the drumsticks to a serving platter and finely grate the zest of the lemon over them while they're hot. Cut the lemon into wedges and serve with the warm drumsticks.

Per Serving:

calories: 200 | fat: 9g | protein: 28g | carbs: 5g | net carbs: 4g | fiber: 1g

Baked Brie with Pecans

Prep time: 5 minutes | Cook time: 10 minutes | Serves 6

- 1 (¾ pound / 340 g) wheel Brie cheese
- 3 ounces (85 g) pecans, chopped
- 2 garlic cloves, minced
- 2 tablespoons minced fresh rosemary leaves
- 1½ tablespoons olive oil
- Salt and freshly ground black pepper, to taste

1. Preheat the oven to 400ºF (205ºC). 2. Line a baking sheet with parchment paper and place the Brie on it. 3. In a small bowl, stir together the pecans, garlic, rosemary, and olive oil. Season with salt and pepper. Spoon the mixture in an even layer over the Brie. Bake for about 10 minutes until the cheese is warm and the nuts are lightly browned. 4. Remove and let it cool for 1 to 2 minutes before serving.

Per Serving:

calories: 318 | fat: 29g | protein: 13g | carbs: 3g | net carbs: 2g | fiber: 1g

---

Lemon-Cheese Cauliflower Bites

Prep time: 5 minutes | Cook time: 8 minutes | Serves 6

- 1 cup water
- 1 pound (454 g) cauliflower, broken into florets
- Sea salt and ground black pepper, to taste
- 2 tablespoons extra-virgin olive oil
- 2 tablespoons lemon juice
- 1 cup grated Cheddar cheese

1. Pour the water into the Instant Pot and insert a steamer basket. Place the cauliflower florets in the basket. 2. Lock the lid. Select the Manual mode and set the cooking time for 3 minutes at Low Pressure. 3. When the timer beeps, perform a quick pressure release. Carefully remove the lid. 4. Season the cauliflower with salt and pepper. Drizzle with olive oil and lemon juice. Sprinkle the grated cheese all over the cauliflower. 5. Press the Sauté button to heat the Instant Pot. Allow to cook for about 5 minutes, or until the cheese melts. Serve warm.

Per Serving:

calories: 136 | fat: 10g | protein: 7g | carbs: 5g | net carbs: 3g | fiber: 2g

---

Cheese and Charcuterie Board

Prep time: 15 minutes | Cook time: 0 minutes | Serves 7

- 4 ounces prosciutto, sliced
- 4 ounces Calabrese salami, sliced
- 4 ounces capicola, sliced
- 7 ounces Parrano Gouda cheese
- 7 ounces aged Manchego cheese
- 7 ounces Brie cheese
- ½ cup roasted almonds
- ½ cup mixed olives
- 12 cornichons (small, tart pickles)

1. Sprig fresh rosemary or other herbs of choice, for garnish Arrange the meats, cheeses, and almonds on a large wooden cutting board. 2. Place the olives and pickles in separate bowls and set them on or alongside the cutting board. Garnish with a spring of rosemary or other fresh herbs of your choice.

Per Serving:

calories: 445 | fat: 35g | protein: 31g | carbs: 3g | net carbs: 2g | fiber: 1g

Chapter 9

Desserts

Chapter 9 Desserts

Vanilla-Almond Ice Pops

Prep time: 10 minutes | Cook time: 5 minutes | Makes 8 ice pops

- 2 cups almond milk
- 1 cup heavy (whipping) cream
- 1 vanilla bean, halved
- lengthwise
- 1 cup shredded unsweetened coconut

1. Place a medium saucepan over medium heat and add the almond milk, heavy cream, and vanilla bean. 2. Bring the liquid to a simmer and reduce the heat to low. Continue to simmer for 5 minutes. 3. Remove the saucepan from the heat and let the liquid cool. 4. Take the vanilla bean out of the liquid and use a knife to scrape the seeds out of the bean into the liquid. 5. Stir in the coconut and divide the liquid between the ice pop molds. 6. Freeze until solid, about 4 hours, and enjoy.

Per Serving:

1 ice pop: calories: 166 | fat: 15g | protein: 3g | carbs: 4g | net carbs: 2g | fiber: 2g

Pecan Butter Cookies

Prep time: 5 minutes | Cook time: 24 minutes | Makes 12 cookies

- 1 cup chopped pecans
- ½ cup salted butter, melted
- ½ cup coconut flour
- ¾ cup erythritol, divided
- 1 teaspoon vanilla extract

1. In a food processor, blend together pecans, butter, flour, ½ cup erythritol, and vanilla 1 minute until a dough forms. 2. Form dough into twelve individual cookie balls, about 1 tablespoon each. 3. Cut three pieces of parchment to fit air fryer basket. Place four cookies on each ungreased parchment and place one piece parchment with cookies into air fryer basket. Adjust air fryer temperature to 325°F (163°C) and set the timer for 8 minutes. Repeat cooking with remaining batches. 4. When the timer goes off, allow cookies to cool 5 minutes on a large serving plate until cool enough to handle. While still warm, dust cookies with remaining erythritol. Allow to cool completely, about 15 minutes, before serving.

Per Serving:

calories: 121 | fat: 13g | protein: 1g | carbs: 2g | net carbs: 1g | fiber: 1g

Glazed Coconut Bundt Cake

Prep time: 30 minutes | Cook time: 55 minutes | serves 10

Cake:
- 2 cups finely ground blanched almond flour
- ¼ cup coconut flour
- ¾ cup granular erythritol
- 2 teaspoons baking powder
- ½ teaspoon salt
- 5 large eggs
- ½ cup (1 stick) salted butter, softened
- ¼ cup coconut oil, softened
- 2 teaspoons vanilla extract
- 1 cup unsweetened coconut flakes

Garnish:
½ cup unsweetened coconut flakes

Glaze:
- ½ cup confectioners'-style erythritol
- ¼ cup heavy whipping cream
- ¼ teaspoon vanilla extract

1. Preheat the oven to 350°F. Grease a 12-cup Bundt pan with butter. 2. In a medium-sized bowl, whisk the almond flour, coconut flour, granular erythritol, baking powder, and salt. In a large mixing bowl, use a hand mixer on low speed to blend the eggs, butter, coconut oil, and vanilla extract. With the mixer on low speed, slowly blend in the flour mixture. Use a spoon to stir in the coconut flakes. 3. Spoon the batter into the prepared pan, then smooth the top. Bake for 45 minutes, until a toothpick or tester inserted into the middle comes out clean. Place the pan on a wire rack to cool completely. Lower the oven temperature to 325°F for toasting the coconut. 4. Make the toasted coconut garnish: Line a sheet pan with parchment paper. Spread the coconut in a thin layer on the prepared pan. Bake for 5 minutes, stir the coconut, then return to the oven and bake until golden brown. It shouldn't take more than another 5 minutes; keep a close eye on it, as coconut can burn quickly. Remove the coconut from the pan and allow to cool. 5. Make the glaze: Put the confectioners'-style erythritol, cream, and vanilla extract in a small bowl and stir until smooth. 6. To serve, gently loosen the sides of the cooled cake from the pan with a knife and turn it onto a cake plate. Pour the glaze evenly over the cake. Garnish the cake with the toasted coconut. The cake can be kept covered on the counter for a day. Leftovers can be stored in an airtight container in the refrigerator for up to a week.

Per Serving:

calories: 361 | fat: 31g | protein: 10g | carbs: 7g | net carbs: 3g | fiber: 4g

Salted Chocolate-Macadamia Nut Fat Bombs

Prep time: 10 minutes | Cook time: 10 minutes | Serves 5

- ½ cup coconut oil
- ½ cup almond butter
- ¼ cup unsweetened cocoa powder
- 1 to 2 tablespoons butter
- (optional)
- Pinch salt
- ¼ cup chopped macadamia nuts

1. In a small saucepan over low heat, melt the coconut oil. 2. Whisk in the almond butter until well combined. 3. Add the cocoa powder and butter (if using). Continue to whisk until combined. 4. Add the salt, remove the pan from the heat, and give it one more stir. Cool slightly before pouring the mixture into a mold—use silicone cupcake liners, a cocktail ice-cube tray, or even muffin tins with paper or silicone liners. Top with the macadamia nuts. 5. Freeze for 15 to 20 minutes or until they've hardened enough to handle. Refrigerate leftovers in an airtight container for up to 2 weeks.

Per Serving:

1 bomb: calories: 443 | fat: 47g | protein: 5g | carbs: 9g | net carbs: 6g | fiber: 3g

Five-Minute Keto Cookie Dough

Prep time: 5 minutes | Cook time: 0 minutes | Makes 20 dough balls

- 8 ounces (227 g) cream cheese, at room temperature
- 6 tablespoons butter or ghee, at room temperature
- ½ cup peanut butter (or almond butter)
- ¼ cup granulated sweetener (such as erythritol)
- ½ teaspoon vanilla extract
- ½ to 1 teaspoon monk fruit or stevia, or more (optional)
- ¼ teaspoon sea salt
- ¼ cup stevia-sweetened chocolate chips (or >90% dark chocolate chunks)

1. In a large bowl, mix together the cream cheese and butter using an electric hand mixer. 2. Add the peanut butter, granulated sweetener, vanilla, monk fruit, and salt and mix again until well combined. Taste and adjust the sweetness to your liking. 3. Fold in the chocolate chips and then use a tablespoon or small scoop to form 20 dough balls. Arrange the dough balls on a plate or baking sheet. 4. Let chill in the refrigerator for 1 hour and store in an airtight container for up to 3 weeks.

Per Serving:

1 dough ball: calories: 123 | fat: 11g | protein: 2g | carbs: 4g | net carbs: 3g | fiber: 1g

Coconut Whipped Cream

Prep time: 5 minutes | Cook time: 0 minutes | Serves 7

- 1 (13½-ounce/400-ml) can coconut cream, chilled, or cream from 2 (13½-ounce/400-ml) cans full-fat coconut milk, chilled for at least 12 hours (see Tip
- below)
- Optional Additions:
- 1 tablespoon confectioners'-style erythritol
- 1 teaspoon vanilla extract
- 2 tablespoons cacao powder

1. Place the coconut cream in a blender or the bowl of a stand mixer fitted with the whisk attachment. If using a blender, cover, turn the speed to low, and slowly increase the speed until you reach medium. Stay at medium speed until the coconut milk has thickened to the consistency of whipped cream, about 30 seconds if using a high-powered blender. If using a stand mixer, whisk for 30 seconds, or until fluffy. Stop here if you want your whipped cream plain and unsweetened. Continue to Step 2 for a sweetened and flavored option. 2. To make sweetened, vanilla-flavored whipped cream, add the erythritol and vanilla. To make sweetened, chocolate-flavored whipped cream, add the erythritol, vanilla, and cacao powder. Cover and blend for another 10 seconds, until the ingredients are thoroughly combined.

Per Serving:

calories: 116 | fat: 12g | protein: 1g | carbs: 2g | net carbs: 2g | fiber: 0g

Pumpkin Spice Fat Bombs

Prep time: 10 minutes | Cook time: 0 minutes | Makes 16 fat bombs

- ½ cup butter, at room temperature
- ½ cup cream cheese, at room temperature
- ⅓ cup pure pumpkin purée
- 3 tablespoons chopped almonds
- 4 drops liquid stevia
- ½ teaspoon ground cinnamon
- ¼ teaspoon ground nutmeg

1. Line an 8-by-8-inch pan with parchment paper and set aside. 2. In a small bowl, whisk together the butter and cream cheese until very smooth. 3. Add the pumpkin purée and whisk until blended. 4. Stir in the almonds, stevia, cinnamon, and nutmeg. 5. Spoon the pumpkin mixture into the pan. Use a spatula or the back of a spoon to spread it evenly in the pan, then place it in the freezer for about 1 hour. 6. Cut into 16 pieces and store the fat bombs in a tightly sealed container in the freezer until ready to serve.

Per Serving:

calories: 87 | fat: 9g | protein: 1g | carbs: 1g | net carbs: 1g | fiber: 0g

Birthday Mug Cakes

Prep time: 5 minutes | Cook time: 2 minutes | Serves 2

Frosting:
- 2 ounces (57 g) full-fat cream cheese, at room temperature
- 1 tablespoon butter, at room temperature
- 2 teaspoons granulated erythritol
- ¼ teaspoon vanilla extract

Cake:
- ⅓ cup almond flour
- 2 tablespoons granulated erythritol
- ½ teaspoon baking powder
- 1 large egg
- ¼ teaspoon vanilla extract

1. To make the frosting: In a small bowl, combine the cream cheese, butter, erythritol, and vanilla. Whisk well, then place in the refrigerator to chill. 2. To make the cake: In a 12-ounce (340-g) coffee mug, combine the almond flour, erythritol, and baking powder. Using a fork, break up any clumps and mix the ingredients well. 3. Add the egg and vanilla, then beat well. Make sure you scrape the bottom edges for any unmixed flour. 4. Microwave on high power for 70 seconds. 5. Let the cake cool for 5 to 10 minutes. 6. Flip the mug onto a plate, then tap a few times. (Alternately, you can skip this step and eat it directly from the mug.). Cut the cake in half crosswise, for 2 cupcakes. 7. Frost the cupcakes before serving.

Per Serving:

calories: 279 | fat: 26g | protein: 8g | carbs: 5g | net carbs: 3g | fiber: 2g

Fruit Pizza

Prep time: 15 minutes | Cook time: 14 minutes | serves 8

Crust:
- 1¼ cups finely ground blanched almond flour
- ⅓ cup granular erythritol
- 1 teaspoon baking powder
- 1 large egg
- 5 tablespoons salted butter, softened
- 1 teaspoon vanilla extract

Toppings:
- 5 ounces cream cheese (1/2 cup plus 2 tablespoons), softened
- 2 tablespoons granular erythritol
- 1 tablespoon heavy whipping cream
- ½ cup sliced fresh strawberries or whole raspberries
- ½ cup fresh blueberries

1. Preheat the oven to 350°F and grease the bottom of a 9-inch springform pan. 2. Make the crust: In a small bowl, whisk together the almond flour, erythritol, and baking powder. In a medium-sized bowl, whisk the egg, then stir in the butter and vanilla extract. Stir in the flour mixture, a little at a time, until well combined. 3. Spread the crust mixture evenly in the prepared pan and bake for 12 to 14 minutes, until lightly browned on top and around the edges. Allow the crust to cool completely before releasing it from the pan. 4. While the crust is cooling, prepare the toppings: In a small bowl, use a spoon to beat the cream cheese, erythritol, and cream until completely combined. Spread evenly over the cooled crust. Garnish with fresh berries. 5. Cover and refrigerate the pizza for at least 2 hours before serving. Leftovers can be stored in an airtight container in the refrigerator for up to 2 days.

Per Serving:

calories: 230 | fat: 20g | protein: 6g | carbs: 5g | net carbs: 3g | fiber: 2g

Sweetened Condensed Coconut Milk

Prep time: 10 minutes | Cook time: 35 minutes | Serves 12

- 1 (13½ ounces/400 ml) can full-fat coconut milk
- 2 tablespoons confectioners'-style erythritol

1. Place all the ingredients in a small saucepan and bring to a rapid boil over medium-high heat. Reduce the heat and simmer lightly for 32 to 35 minutes, until the milk has thickened and reduced by about half. Use immediately in a recipe that calls for it, or let it cool and store in the fridge for later use.

Per Serving:

calories: 68 | fat: 7g | protein: 1g | carbs: 1g | net carbs: 1g | fiber: 0g

Coconut Muffins

Prep time: 5 minutes | Cook time: 25 minutes | Serves 5

- ½ cup coconut flour
- 2 tablespoons cocoa powder
- 3 tablespoons erythritol
- 1 teaspoon baking powder
- 2 tablespoons coconut oil
- 2 eggs, beaten
- ½ cup coconut shred

1. In the mixing bowl, mix all ingredients. 2. Then pour the mixture into the molds of the muffin and transfer in the air fryer basket. 3. Cook the muffins at 350°F (177°C) for 25 minutes.

Per Serving:

calories: 182 | fat: 14g | protein: 6g | carbs: 12g | net carbs: 5g | fiber: 7g

Vanilla Cream Pie

Prep time: 20 minutes | Cook time: 35 minutes | Serves 12

- 1 cup heavy cream
- 3 eggs, beaten
- 1 teaspoon vanilla extract
- ¼ cup erythritol
- 1 cup coconut flour
- 1 tablespoon butter, melted
- 1 cup water, for cooking

1. In the mixing bowl, mix up coconut flour, erythritol, vanilla extract, eggs, and heavy cream. 2. Grease the baking pan with melted butter. 3. Pour the coconut mixture in the baking pan. 4. Pour water and insert the steamer rack in the instant pot. 5. Place the pie on the rack. Close and seal the lid. 6. Cook the pie on Manual mode (High Pressure) for 35 minutes. 7. Allow the natural pressure release for 10 minutes.

Per Serving:

calories: 100 | fat: 7g | protein: 3g | carbs: 12g | net carbs: 8g | fiber: 4g

Stu Can't Stop Bark

Prep time: 5 minutes | Cook time: 5 minutes | Makes 24 pieces

- 5 bars good dark chocolate, at least 80% cacao content
- 3 tablespoons coconut oil
- 2 cups macadamia nuts, or a mixture of assorted other nuts, ground into small pieces
- 3 tablespoons raw almond
- butter
- ¼ to ½ cup finely shredded coconut flakes (optional)
- 2 tablespoons coconut butter (optional)
- Sea salt or Himalayan pink salt, to sprinkle on top

1. Break the chocolate by hand into small pieces. Melt half the chocolate in a double boiler or glass bowl fitted over a small pan of boiling water. Add the coconut oil as the chocolate is melting and stir occasionally. 2. In a big mixing bowl, combine the nuts and the remaining dark chocolate pieces. Pour the melted chocolate mixture into the bowl and stir very well. 3. In a large glass pan, spread half the mixture thinly across the bottom. Drizzle a thin layer of almond butter over the chocolate, spreading carefully so there are no thick areas. (If your almond butter is too thick to drizzle, you can microwave it for 20 seconds.) 4. Spread the rest of the chocolate evenly over the almond butter. Sprinkle on the coconut or coconut butter, if using. Sprinkle the salt lightly over the top. 5. Freeze for 1 to 2 hours or refrigerate for longer, the mixture must become rock-hard. Remove from chilling, let sit for 5 minutes, then cut into squares. (You'll need a baker's blade or dough scraper or a very large chef's knife to cut successfully; be careful because it will be hard to cut into.) 6. Store the bark in an airtight container in the fridge or freezer and serve cold (but not frozen). When serving, consume immediately because the bark will melt quickly at room temperature.

Per Serving:

calories: 236 | fat: 22g | protein: 3g | carbs: 9g | net carbs: 7g | fiber: 2g

Lemon Drops

Prep time: 5 minutes | Cook time: 0 minutes | Serves 4

- ¼ cup (60 ml) melted (but not hot) cacao butter
- ¼ cup (60 ml) melted (but not hot) coconut oil
- 1½ teaspoons confectioners'-style erythritol
- 2 teaspoons lemon-flavored
- magnesium powder (optional)
- 1 teaspoon lemon extract
- Special Equipment:
- Silicone mold(s) with 20 (½-ounce/15-ml) round cavities

1. Set the silicone mold(s) on a baking sheet. 2. Place the cacao butter, coconut oil, and erythritol in a small bowl. Whisk until the erythritol has dissolved. 3. If using magnesium powder, add it to the bowl along with the lemon extract. Whisk to combine. 4. Pour the mixture into the silicone mold(s), filling to the top. Transfer the baking sheet to the fridge to harden for 1 hour. 5. Once hardened, remove the lemon drops from the molds and enjoy! Serve directly from the fridge.

Per Serving:

calories: 258 | fat: 29g | protein: 0g | carbs: 0g | net carbs: 0g | fiber: 0g

Homemade Mint Pie

Prep time: 15 minutes | Cook time: 25 minutes | Serves 2

- 1 tablespoon instant coffee
- 2 tablespoons almond butter, softened
- 2 tablespoons erythritol
- 1 teaspoon dried mint
- 3 eggs, beaten
- 1 teaspoon spearmint, dried
- 4 teaspoons coconut flour
- Cooking spray

1. Spray the air fryer basket with cooking spray. 2. Then mix all ingredients in the mixer bowl. 3. When you get a smooth mixture, transfer it in the air fryer basket. Flatten it gently. 4. Cook the pie at 365ºF (185ºC) for 25 minutes.

Per Serving:

calories: 240 | fat: 16g | protein: 12g | carbs: 11g | net carbs: 7g | fiber: 4g

Crustless Cheesecake Bites

Prep time: 10 minutes | Cook time: 30 minutes | Serves 4

- 4 ounces cream cheese, at room temperature
- ¼ cup sour cream
- 2 large eggs
- ⅓ cup Swerve natural sweetener
- ¼ teaspoon vanilla extract

1. Preheat the oven to 350°F. 2. In a medium mixing bowl, use a hand mixer to beat the cream cheese, sour cream, eggs, sweetener, and vanilla until well mixed. 3. Place silicone liners (or cupcake paper liners) in the cups of a muffin tin. 4. Pour the cheesecake batter into the liners, and bake for 30 minutes. 5. Refrigerate until completely cooled before serving, about 3 hours. Store extra cheesecake bites in a zip-top bag in the freezer for up to 3 months.

Per Serving:

calories: 169 | fat: 15g | protein: 5g | carbs: 18g | net carbs: 2g | fiber: 0g

Caramelized Pumpkin Cheesecake

Prep time: 15 minutes | Cook time: 45 minutes | Serves 8

Crust:
- 1½ cups almond flour
- 4 tablespoons butter, melted
- 1 tablespoon Swerve
- 1 tablespoon granulated

Filling:
- 16 ounces (454 g) cream cheese, softened
- ½ cup granulated erythritol
- 2 eggs
- ¼ cup pumpkin purée

- erythritol
- ½ teaspoon ground cinnamon
- Cooking spray

- 3 tablespoons Swerve
- 1 teaspoon vanilla extract
- ¼ teaspoon pumpkin pie spice
- 1½ cups water

1. To make the crust: In a medium bowl, combine the almond flour, butter, Swerve, erythritol, and cinnamon. Use a fork to press it all together. 2. Spray the pan with cooking spray and line the bottom with parchment paper. 3. Press the crust evenly into the pan. Work the crust up the sides of the pan, about halfway from the top, and make sure there are no bare spots on the bottom. 4. Place the crust in the freezer for 20 minutes while you make the filling. 5. To make the filling: In a large bowl using a hand mixer on medium speed, combine the cream cheese and erythritol. Beat until the cream cheese is light and fluffy, 2 to 3 minutes. 6. Add the eggs, pumpkin purée, Swerve, vanilla, and pumpkin pie spice. Beat until well combined. 7. Remove the crust from the freezer and pour in the filling. Cover the pan with aluminum foil and place it on the trivet. 8. Add the water to the pot and carefully lower the trivet into the pot. 9. Set the lid in place. Select the Manual mode and set the cooking

time for 45 minutes on High Pressure. When the timer goes off, do a quick pressure release. Carefully open the lid. 10. Remove the trivet and cheesecake from the pot. Remove the foil from the pan. The center of the cheesecake should still be slightly jiggly. 11. Let the cheesecake cool for 30 minutes on the counter before placing it in the refrigerator to set. Leave the cheesecake in the refrigerator for at least 6 hours before removing the sides and serving.

Per Serving:

calories: 407 | fat: 36g | protein: 10g | carbs: 7g | net carbs: 4g | fiber: 3g

Lime Muffins

Prep time: 10 minutes | Cook time: 15 minutes | Serves 6

- 1 teaspoon lime zest
- 1 tablespoon lemon juice
- 1 teaspoon baking powder
- 1 cup almond flour

- 2 eggs, beaten
- 1 tablespoon Swerve
- ¼ cup heavy cream
- 1 cup water, for cooking

1. In the mixing bowl, mix up lemon juice, baking powder, almond flour, eggs, Swerve, and heavy cream. 2. When the muffin batter is smooth, add lime zest and mix it up. 3. Fill the muffin molds with batter. 4. Then pour water and insert the rack in the instant pot. 5. Place the muffins on the rack. Close and seal the lid. 6. Cook the muffins on Manual (High Pressure) for 15 minutes. 7. Then allow the natural pressure release.

Per Serving:

calories: 153 | fat: 12g | protein: 6g | carbs: 5g | net carbs: 3g | fiber: 2g

Chocolate Pecan Clusters

Prep time: 5 minutes | Cook time: 5 minutes | Makes 8 clusters

- 3 tablespoons butter
- ¼ cup heavy cream
- 1 teaspoon vanilla extract

- 1 cup chopped pecans
- ¼ cup low-carb chocolate chips

1. Press the Sauté button and add butter to Instant Pot. Allow butter to melt and begin to turn golden brown. Once it begins to brown, immediately add heavy cream. Press the Cancel button. 2. Add vanilla and chopped pecans to Instant Pot. Allow to cool for 10 minutes, stirring occasionally. Spoon mixture onto parchment-lined baking sheet to form eight clusters, and scatter chocolate chips over clusters. Place in fridge to cool.

Per Serving:

calories: 194 | fat: 18g | protein: 2g | carbs: 7g | net carbs: 6g | fiber: 1g

Vanilla Crème Brûlée

Prep time: 7 minutes | Cook time: 9 minutes | Serves 4

- 1 cup heavy cream (or full-fat coconut milk for dairy-free)
- 2 large egg yolks
- 2 tablespoons Swerve, or more to taste
- Seeds scraped from ½ vanilla bean (about 8 inches long), or 1 teaspoon vanilla extract
- 1 cup cold water
- 4 teaspoons Swerve, for topping

1. Heat the cream in a pan over medium-high heat until hot, about 2 minutes. 2. Place the egg yolks, Swerve, and vanilla seeds in a blender and blend until smooth. 3. While the blender is running, slowly pour in the hot cream. Taste and adjust the sweetness to your liking. 4. Scoop the mixture into four ramekins with a spatula. Cover the ramekins with aluminum foil. 5. Add the water to the Instant Pot and insert a trivet. Place the ramekins on the trivet. 6. Lock the lid. Select the Manual mode and set the cooking time for 7 minutes at High Pressure. 7. When the timer beeps, perform a quick pressure release. Carefully remove the lid. 8. Keep the ramekins covered with the foil and place in the refrigerator for about 2 hours until completely chilled. 9. Sprinkle 1 teaspoon of Swerve on top of each crème brûlée. Use the oven broiler to melt the sweetener. 10. Allow the topping to cool in the fridge for 5 minutes before serving.

Per Serving:

calories: 138 | fat: 13g | protein: 2g | carbs: 2g | net carbs: 2g | fiber: 0g

Lemon Bars with Cashew Crust

Prep time: 5 minutes | Cook time: 35 minutes | Makes 12 bars

- 2 tablespoons butter, melted, plus 2 tablespoons, at room temperature, plus more for the baking dish
- 1 cup finely crushed cashews
- 1 cup almond flour
- ½ cup Swerve
- Zest of 2 lemons
- ½ cup freshly squeezed lemon juice
- 6 egg yolks
- 2 tablespoons gelatin

1. Preheat the oven to 375ºF (190ºC). 2. Grease an 8- or 9-inch square baking dish with butter. 3. In a large bowl, stir together the cashews and almond flour. Pour the melted butter over them and stir until the nut mixture becomes wet and crumbly. Scrape the crust into the prepared dish, pressing down firmly with your fingers. Bake for about 15 minutes or until the crust begins to brown. Remove from the oven and let it cool completely. 4. Reduce the oven temperature to 350ºF (180ºC). 5. In a small saucepan over low heat, melt the 2 tablespoons of room-temperature butter. 6. Stir in the Swerve, lemon zest, and lemon juice. 7. Slowly add the egg yolks one at a time, whisking to incorporate as the filling thickens. Cook for 2 to 3 minutes, whisking. 8. Remove from the heat and whisk in the gelatin until the mixture is smooth. Pour the

lemon filling over the crust and spread it evenly. Bake for 10 to 12 minutes. Remove it from the oven and let it cool. Cut into 12 squares and serve. Refrigerate, covered, for up to 1 week.

Per Serving:

1 bar: calories: 144 | fat: 13g | protein: 4g | carbs: 4g | net carbs: 4g | fiber: 0g

Almond Butter Fat Bombs

Prep time: 5 minutes | Cook time: 0 minutes | Serves 4

- ½ cup almond butter
- ½ cup coconut oil
- 4 tablespoons unsweetened
- cocoa powder
- ½ cup erythritol

1. Melt butter and coconut oil in the microwave for 45 seconds, stirring twice until properly melted and mixed. Mix in cocoa powder and erythritol until completely combined. Pour into muffin moulds and refrigerate for 3 hours to harden.

Per Serving:

calories: 247 | fat: 23g | protein: 6g | carbs: 4g | net carbs: 2g | fiber: 2g

Pecan Clusters

Prep time: 10 minutes | Cook time: 8 minutes | Serves 8

- 3 ounces (85 g) whole shelled pecans
- 1 tablespoon salted butter, melted
- 2 teaspoons confectioners'
- erythritol
- ½ teaspoon ground cinnamon
- ½ cup low-carb chocolate chips

1. In a medium bowl, toss pecans with butter, then sprinkle with erythritol and cinnamon. 2. Place pecans into ungreased air fryer basket. Adjust the temperature to 350ºF (177ºC) and air fry for 8 minutes, shaking the basket two times during cooking. They will feel soft initially but get crunchy as they cool. 3. Line a large baking sheet with parchment paper. 4. Place chocolate in a medium microwave-safe bowl. Microwave on high, heating in 20-second increments and stirring until melted. Place 1 teaspoon chocolate in a rounded mound on ungreased parchment-lined baking sheet, then press 1 pecan into top, repeating with remaining chocolate and pecans. 5. Place baking sheet into refrigerator to cool at least 30 minutes. Once cooled, store clusters in a large sealed container in refrigerator up to 5 days.

Per Serving:

calories: 104 | fat: 10g | protein: 1g | carbs: 3g | net carbs: 2g | fiber: 1g

Coconut Flour Cake

Prep time: 10 minutes | Cook time: 25 minutes | Serves 6

- 2 tablespoons salted butter, melted
- ⅓ cup coconut flour
- 2 large eggs, whisked
- ½ cup granular erythritol
- 1 teaspoon baking powder
- 1 teaspoon vanilla extract
- ½ cup sour cream

1. Mix all ingredients in a large bowl. Pour batter into an ungreased round nonstick baking dish. 2. Place baking dish into air fryer basket. Adjust the temperature to 300°F (149°C) and bake for 25 minutes. The cake will be dark golden on top, and a toothpick inserted in the center should come out clean when done. 3. Let cool in dish 15 minutes before slicing and serving.

Per Serving:

calories: 142 | fat: 10g | protein: 4g | carbs: 8g | net carbs: 4g | fiber: 4g

Lemon Vanilla Cheesecake

Prep time: 15 minutes | Cook time: 20 minutes | Serves 6

- 2 teaspoons freshly squeezed lemon juice
- 2 teaspoons vanilla extract or almond extract
- ½ cup sour cream, divided, at room temperature
- ½ cup plus 2 teaspoons Swerve
- 8 ounces (227 g) cream cheese, at room temperature
- 2 eggs, at room temperature

1. Pour 2 cups of water into the inner cooking pot of the Instant Pot, then place a trivet (preferably with handles) in the pot. Line the sides of a 6-inch springform pan with parchment paper. 2. In a food processor, put the lemon juice, vanilla, ¼ cup of sour cream, ½ cup of Swerve, and the cream cheese. 3. Gently but thoroughly blend all the ingredients, scraping down the sides of the bowl as needed. 4. Add the eggs and blend only as long as you need to in order to get them well incorporated, 20 to 30 seconds. Your mixture will be pourable by now. 5. Pour the mixture into the prepared pan. Cover the pan with aluminum foil and place on the trivet. (If your trivet doesn't have handles, you may wish to use a foil sling to make removing the pan easier.) 6. Lock the lid into place. Select Manual and adjust the pressure to High. Cook for 20 minutes. When the cooking is complete, let the pressure release naturally. Unlock the lid. 7. Meanwhile, in a small bowl, mix together the remaining ¼ cup of sour cream and 2 teaspoons of Swerve for the topping. 8. Take out the cheesecake and remove the foil. Spread the topping over the top. Doing this while the cheesecake is still hot helps melt the topping into the cheesecake. 9. Put the cheesecake in the refrigerator and leave it alone. Seriously. Leave it alone and let it chill for at least 6 to 8 hours. It won't taste right hot. 10. When you're ready to serve, open the sides of the pan and peel off the parchment paper. Slice and serve.

Per Serving:

calories: 207 | fat: 19g | protein: 5g | carbs: 4g | net carbs: 4g | fiber: 0g

Chocolate Cheesecake with Toasted Almond Crust

Prep time: 15 minutes | Cook time: 1 hour 20 minutes | Serves 10

For The Crust
- 1½ cups almond flour
- 4 tablespoons monk fruit sweetener, granulated form
- 1 tablespoon cocoa powder
- ⅓ cup melted grass-fed butter

For The Filling
- 1½ pounds cream cheese, softened
- ¾ cup monk fruit sweetener, granulated form
- 3 eggs, beaten
- 1 teaspoon vanilla extract
- ½ teaspoon almond extract
- (optional)
- 5 ounces keto-friendly chocolate chips like Lily's Dark Chocolate Chips, melted and cooled
- 1 cup sour cream

Make The Crust: 1. Preheat the oven. Set the oven temperature to 350°F. 2. Mix the crust ingredients. In a medium bowl, stir together the almond flour, sweetener, cocoa powder, and melted butter until the ingredients hold together when pressed. Press the crumbs into the bottom of a 10-inch springform pan and 1 inch up the sides. 3. Chill and bake. Chill the crust in the freezer for 10 minutes. Transfer it to the oven and bake it for 10 minutes. Cool the crust completely before filling. Make The Filling: 1. Change the oven temperature. Reduce the oven temperature to 275°F. 2. Mix the cheesecake base. In a large bowl, beat the cream cheese until very light and fluffy, scraping down the sides with a spatula at least once. Beat in the sweetener until the mixture is smooth, scraping down the sides of the bowl. 3. Add the eggs. Beat in the eggs one at a time, scraping down the sides of the bowl occasionally and then beat in the vanilla extract and almond extract (if using). 4. Add the remaining ingredients. Beat in the melted chocolate and sour cream until the filling is well blended, scraping down the sides of the bowl. 5. Bake. Pour the filling into the prebaked crust and bake it for 1 hour and 10 minutes. Turn off the oven and cool the cheesecake in the closed oven until it reaches room temperature. 6. Chill. Chill the cheesecake in the refrigerator for at least 4 to 6 hours. 7. Serve. Cut the cheesecake into 10 slices and serve.

Per Serving:

calories: 408 | fat: 40g | protein: 8g | carbs: 4g | net carbs: 4g | fiber: 0g

Lemon and Ricotta Torte

Prep time: 15 minutes | Cook time: 35 minutes | Serves 12

- ◆ Cooking spray

Torte:
- ◆ 1⅓ cups Swerve
- ◆ ½ cup (1 stick) unsalted butter, softened
- ◆ 2 teaspoons lemon or vanilla extract
- ◆ 5 large eggs, separated

Lemon Glaze:
- ◆ ½ cup (1 stick) unsalted butter
- ◆ ¼ cup Swerve
- ◆ 2 tablespoons lemon juice

- ◆ 2½ cups blanched almond flour
- ◆ 1¼ (10-ounce / 284-g) cups whole-milk ricotta cheese
- ◆ ¼ cup lemon juice
- ◆ 1 cup cold water

- ◆ 2 ounces (57 g) cream cheese (¼ cup)
- ◆ Grated lemon zest and lemon slices, for garnish

1. Line a baking pan with parchment paper and spray with cooking spray. Set aside. 2. Make the torte: In the bowl of a stand mixer, place the Swerve, butter, and extract and blend for 8 to 10 minutes until well combined. Scrape down the sides of the bowl as needed. 3. Add the egg yolks and continue to blend until fully combined. Add the almond flour and mix until smooth, then stir in the ricotta and lemon juice. 4. Whisk the egg whites in a separate medium bowl until stiff peaks form. Add the whites to the batter and stir well. Pour the batter into the prepared pan and smooth the top. 5. Place a trivet in the bottom of your Instant Pot and pour in the water. Use a foil sling to lower the baking pan onto the trivet. Tuck in the sides of the sling. 6. Seal the lid, press Pressure Cook or Manual, and set the timer for 30 minutes. Once finished, let the pressure release naturally. 7. Lock the lid. Select the Manual mode and set the cooking time for 30 minutes at High Pressure. 8. When the timer beeps, perform a natural pressure release for 10 minutes. Carefully remove the lid. 9. Use the foil sling to lift the pan out of the Instant Pot. Place the torte in the fridge for 40 minutes to chill before glazing. 10. Meanwhile, make the glaze: Place the butter in a large pan over high heat and cook for about 5 minutes until brown, stirring occasionally. Remove from the heat. While stirring the browned butter, add the Swerve. 11. Carefully add the lemon juice and cream cheese to the butter mixture. Allow the glaze to cool for a few minutes, or until it starts to thicken. 12. Transfer the chilled torte to a serving plate. Pour the glaze over the torte and return it to the fridge to chill for an additional 30 minutes. 13. Scatter the lemon zest on top of the torte and arrange the lemon slices on the plate around the torte. 14. Serve.

Per Serving:

calories: 367 | fat: 33g | protein: 12g | carbs: 10g | net carbs: 7g | fiber: 3g

Lemon Curd Pavlova

Prep time: 10 minutes | Cook time: 1 hour | Serves 4

Shell:
- ◆ 3 large egg whites
- ◆ ¼ teaspoon cream of tartar
- ◆ ¾ cup Swerve confectioners'-style sweetener or

Lemon Curd:
- ◆ 1 cup Swerve confectioners'-style sweetener or equivalent amount of liquid or powdered sweetener

For Garnish (optional):
- ◆ Blueberries
- ◆ Swerve confectioners'-style sweetener or equivalent

- equivalent amount of powdered sweetener
- ◆ 1 teaspoon grated lemon zest
- ◆ 1 teaspoon lemon extract

- ◆ ½ cup lemon juice
- ◆ 4 large eggs
- ◆ ½ cup coconut oil

- amount of powdered sweetener

1. Preheat the air fryer to 275°F (135°C). Thoroughly grease a pie pan with butter or coconut oil. 2. Make the shell: In a small bowl, use a hand mixer to beat the egg whites and cream of tartar until soft peaks form. With the mixer on low, slowly sprinkle in the sweetener and mix until it's completely incorporated. 3. Add the lemon zest and lemon extract and continue to beat with the hand mixer until stiff peaks form. 4. Spoon the mixture into the greased pie pan, then smooth it across the bottom, up the sides, and onto the rim to form a shell. Bake for 1 hour, then turn off the air fryer and let the shell stand in the air fryer for 20 minutes. (The shell can be made up to 3 days ahead and stored in an airtight container in the refrigerator, if desired.) 5. While the shell bakes, make the lemon curd: In a medium-sized heavy-bottomed saucepan, whisk together the sweetener, lemon juice, and eggs. Add the coconut oil and place the pan on the stovetop over medium heat. Once the oil is melted, whisk constantly until the mixture thickens and thickly coats the back of a spoon, about 10 minutes. Do not allow the mixture to come to a boil. 6. Pour the lemon curd mixture through a fine-mesh strainer into a medium-sized bowl. Place the bowl inside a larger bowl filled with ice water and whisk occasionally until the curd is completely cool, about 15 minutes. 7. Place the lemon curd on top of the shell and garnish with blueberries and powdered sweetener, if desired. Store leftovers in the refrigerator for up to 4 days.

Per Serving:

calories: 524 | fat: 50g | protein: 7g | carbs: 12g | net carbs: 5g | fiber: 2g

Appendix 1:

MEASUREMENT CONVERSION CHART

VOLUME EQUIVALENTS(DRY)

US STANDARD	METRIC (APPROXIMATE)
1/8 teaspoon	0.5 mL
1/4 teaspoon	1 mL
1/2 teaspoon	2 mL
3/4 teaspoon	4 mL
1 teaspoon	5 mL
1 tablespoon	15 mL
1/4 cup	59 mL
1/2 cup	118 mL
3/4 cup	177 mL
1 cup	235 mL
2 cups	475 mL
3 cups	700 mL
4 cups	1 L

WEIGHT EQUIVALENTS

US STANDARD	METRIC (APPROXIMATE)
1 ounce	28 g
2 ounces	57 g
5 ounces	142 g
10 ounces	284 g
15 ounces	425 g
16 ounces (1 pound)	455 g
1.5 pounds	680 g
2 pounds	907 g

VOLUME EQUIVALENTS(LIQUID)

US STANDARD	US STANDARD (OUNCES)	METRIC (APPROXIMATE)
2 tablespoons	1 fl.oz.	30 mL
1/4 cup	2 fl.oz.	60 mL
1/2 cup	4 fl.oz.	120 mL
1 cup	8 fl.oz.	240 mL
1 1/2 cup	12 fl.oz.	355 mL
2 cups or 1 pint	16 fl.oz.	475 mL
4 cups or 1 quart	32 fl.oz.	1 L
1 gallon	128 fl.oz.	4 L

TEMPERATURES EQUIVALENTS

FAHRENHEIT(F)	CELSIUS(C) (APPROXIMATE)
225 °F	107 °C
250 °F	120 °C
275 °F	135 °C
300 °F	150 °C
325 °F	160 °C
350 °F	180 °C
375 °F	190 °C
400 °F	205 °C
425 °F	220 °C
450 °F	235 °C
475 °F	245 °C
500 °F	260 °C

The Dirty Dozen and Clean Fifteen

The Environmental Working Group (EWG) is a nonprofit, nonpartisan organization dedicated to protecting human health and the environment Its mission is to empower people to live healthier lives in a healthier environment. This organization publishes an annual list of the twelve kinds of produce, in sequence, that have the highest amount of pesticide residue-the Dirty Dozen-as well as a list of the fifteen kinds ofproduce that have the least amount of pesticide residue-the Clean Fifteen.

THE DIRTY DOZEN

- The 2016 Dirty Dozen includes the following produce. These are considered among the year's most important produce to buy organic:

Strawberries	Spinach
Apples	Tomatoes
Nectarines	Bell peppers
Peaches	Cherry tomatoes
Celery	Cucumbers
Grapes	Kale/collard greens
Cherries	Hot peppers

- *The Dirty Dozen list contains two additional itemskale/collard greens and hot peppers-because they tend to contain trace levels of highly hazardous pesticides.*

THE CLEAN FIFTEEN

- The least critical to buy organically are the Clean Fifteen list. The following are on the 2016 list:

Avocados	Papayas
Corn	Kiw
Pineapples	Eggplant
Cabbage	Honeydew
Sweet peas	Grapefruit
Onions	Cantaloupe
Asparagus	Cauliflower
Mangos	

- *Some of the sweet corn sold in the United States are made from genetically engineered (GE) seedstock. Buy organic varieties of these crops to avoid GE produce.*

Appendix3 : Recipes Index

Made in the USA
Columbia, SC
28 September 2024